Praise for *Slaying the Dragon*

"A compelling adventure in itself."

—*The Washington Post*

"Riggs weaves a tale of corporate intrigue, personal ego, and failed saving throws that will fascinate any fan of *D&D*. Whether you're a grognard, still clutching your Red Box rules and grumbling about THAC0, or a recent convert to the greatest game the world has ever played, you're going to love *Slaying the Dragon*!"

—Tim Akers, author of *Knight Watch*

"Through in-depth interviews with the creators themselves, Ben has put together a deeply personal account of so many of the behind-the-scenes going-ons, the good and the bad, at TSR."

—Gerald Brom, former TSR artist

"When I was thirteen and sitting on the other side of the DM screen, using all my latent psionic talent to roll a 20 on that bugbear, I never thought I would ever want to read a book about the economic history of *D&D* . . . yet here we are. Riggs has written a fascinating and dishy account of the business hits and whistling misses of a band of dreamers, writers, artists, and geeks, and the real-life, sometimes terrifying adventures that eventually destroyed the company behind arguably the most imaginative American game ever created, though it was never just that. A must-read for fighters, magic-users, and even bards—and everyone else, too."

—Brad Ricca, Edgar Award–nominated author of *Mrs. Sherlock Holmes* and *True Raiders*

"Far from a fluff piece on a beloved hobby, this book goes behind the GM's screen to take a hard-nosed look at the people and circumstances that first gave rise to *D&D*, then nearly killed it—twice. Riggs takes you on a roller coaster from boom to near bankruptcy, but never loses sight of the individuals involved, the good, the bad, and the geeky."

—Marie B[illegible]thor of [illegible] series

"A fascinating and colorful page-turner that explores the rich history of *Dungeons & Dragons* and its role in the development of role-playing games. Ben Riggs's engrossing *Slaying the Dragon* takes us into the basements of Wisconsin and boardrooms of Los Angeles, where the popular role-playing genre evolved—against impossible odds—from board games to virtual reality. And he does so by speaking with the geeks who inherited this earth, putting their wild stories to paper for the first time. . . . Nine hundred XP to Riggs for his achievement!"

—Sean O'Connell, managing editor of CinemaBlend and author of *Release the Snyder Cut* and *With Great Power*

"With a trove of research and candid interviews, Riggs investigates the many missteps that would ultimately sour 'years of stunning success' for the tabletop gaming giant. . . . A compelling corporate saga mired in mythmaking."

—*Kirkus Reviews*

"So here's the thing. I've never played a game of *Dungeons & Dragons* in my life. And I've also already read *Of Dice and Men*, the *D&D* history that is the jumping-off point for this work, which promises to uncover some of the less-known dealings of Lake Geneva–based TSR's downfall. And yet I found *Slaying the Dragon* thoroughly enjoyable, partly because of the near-local setting, and partly because Riggs is a good storyteller who also highlights the corporate missteps in a way that I think will appeal to folks who read business narratives. And to think, Milwaukee finally has enough hotel rooms to keep Gen Con, only nineteen years too late."

—Daniel Goldin, Boswell Book Company, Milwaukee, WI

"Meticulously researched and passionately written, Ben Riggs's book *Slaying the Dragon* is essential reading for anyone intrigued by the absurdities of the gaming industry. This chronicle of errors answers long-standing questions about the rise and fall of role-playing's most famous game and provides an entertaining step-by-step guide for how *not* to run a corporation. Absolutely recommended!"

—Satyros Phil Brucato, designer and core author of *Mage: The Ascension; Powerchords: Music, Magic & Urban Fantasy; Mage: The Sorcerers Crusade;* the Mage 20 series; and more

LAST DRAGON
FIRST WIZARD

SLAYING the DRAGON

A Secret History of *Dungeons & Dragons*

BEN RIGGS

ST. MARTIN'S GRIFFIN
NEW YORK

Published in the United States by St. Martin's Griffin,
an imprint of St. Martin's Publishing Group

Printed in the United States of America. For information, address
St. Martin's Publishing Group, 120 Broadway, New York, NY 10271.

www.stmartins.com

Designed by Jonathan Bennett
Frontispiece by Tinnel Lovitt

The Library of Congress has cataloged the hardcover edition as follows:

Names: Riggs, Ben, 1978– author.
Title: Slaying the dragon : a secret history of Dungeons and Dragons / Ben Riggs.
Description: First edition. | New York : St. Martin's Press, [2022] | Includes bibliographical references and index.
Identifiers: LCCN 2022005283 | ISBN 9781250278043 (hardcover) | ISBN 9781250278050 (ebook)
Subjects: LCSH: Fantasy games—History. | Video games industry—History. | Dungeons and Dragons (Game)—History. | Tactical Studies Rules (Firm)
Classification: LCC GV1469.6 .R54 2022 | DDC 793.93—dc23
LC record available at https://lccn.loc.gov/2022005283

ISBN 978-1-250-81947-5 (trade paperback)

First St. Martin's Griffin Edition: 2023

10 9 8 7 6 5 4 3 2 1

To Tara and Simon

CONTENTS

Part I

◆

THE RISE AND FALL OF GARY GYGAX

THE WARDEN'S TALE

Lately, I have been reading notes from Wizards of the Coast people about why TSR died away. I have to admit some of their notes are right on. I also want to say that not everything they claimed is true. Truth doesn't matter if you are the winners in the end.

—JAMES M. WARD

JIM WARD QUIT TSR in 1996 after decades with the company. At the time, he was vice president of production, and he resigned because he'd been ordered to fire over twenty employees, among them artists, writers, and game designers. In short, the women and men who made up the company's sinews, muscles, and bones. Those firings would have taken an axe to the company he loved, and rather than do that, he quit.

That's just the kind of guy he was.

TSR was the grand old dragon of role-playing game companies. It founded the industry and published the game that dominated the field, *Dungeons & Dragons.* At its height, it had gross sales of over $40 million. It ran the largest role-playing game convention in North America, Gen Con. At its offices in Lake Geneva, Wisconsin, dozens and dozens of genius geeks gathered to create games, novels, and art that flooded game stores and malls across the world. To fans, the company was a fixed piece of geography, a mountain where the dawn rose every morning and where you could watch the stars come out every night. It had always been there, and it always would be.

Yet from such heights, it fell so low that Jim Ward was ordered to fire all of those employees. How had it come to this pitiful state? What cataclysms befell it?

Jim Ward had a story.

WARD WAS NOT looking to change his life or find a new career when he went to the Lake Geneva News Agency in 1974. He just wanted to buy some books.

While browsing the fantasy and science fiction section, he picked seven books off the shelves before he noticed a bearded and bespectacled gentleman beside him, likewise carrying seven books.

The exact same seven books.

The bespectacled man asked, "Do you really enjoy reading books like that?"

Ward replied, "Why, yes, I do!" and then turned to escape the strange fellow so closely eyeing his book selection.

But the bespectacled man was undeterred. He said, "We play games that are more enjoyable than sword-and-sorcery novels; why not stop by some time and try them out?" In this game, you could play Conan the Barbarian and fight abominable serpentine gods. It was a fantasy novel done one better. Instead of merely seeing these wondrous worlds through the eyes of Frodo or Fafhrd, you could live in them.

Had Ward come to the bookstore an hour later or chosen a few different novels that day in 1974, the next four decades of his life may have been totally different. Because the man whose book selection matched his was Gary Gygax, cocreator of *Dungeons & Dragons* and cofounder of TSR, the company he'd created to publish the game.

A few weeks later, Ward went over to Gygax's house and played. Gygax believed Ward waited a few weeks because, "during the interim he was checking up to find out if we were merely eccentric or actually dangerous lunatics."

What Ward played there was a revelation, unlike anything else at the time. In most war games, you controlled an army or a unit of soldiers. But in this game, you controlled just one person. Only one! And you could choose whether they were a fighter, a wizard, or a thief, or if they took on an even more outrageous role. Since it was a fantasy world, you could be an elf or a dwarf if you wanted. And you had total control over this one person, called a character. If a band of evil knights stood in your way, your character could try sneaking past, fighting them, or talking the knights into letting you go. It was up to you. If you wanted your character to sing "Love Potion No. 9" to distract a cyclops, you could do that too. Now you could fail, and your character could die. After all, if the cyclops didn't like music, it might try to make toothpicks out of your femurs. But the existence of failure just made every choice more vitally important. This was a burst of total freedom bounded only by the imagination.

Gygax told Ward it was called *Dungeons & Dragons.*

As the years rolled on, Ward became a regular TSR freelancer, and Gygax's trusted confidant. Ward read and commented on his work. He designed *Metamorphosis Alpha,* the first science fiction role-playing game. Modestly, he named the ship in the game after himself, calling it the *Warden.* In 1980, he was finally hired on at the company full-time.

Though fired in 1984, he was hired back again within eighteen months. The person hired to replace him quit within three months because the workload was so heavy, and Ward's freelancing duties for the company were so extensive despite not being on the payroll that it was determined it would be cheaper to hire him back. He survived the ouster of Gary Gygax as CEO of the company in 1985 and rose to the position of vice president.

TSR was, for most of its existence, the indispensable gaming company. It had created the entire genre of role-playing and had sales in the millions of dollars supporting a staff of over a hundred people. By the early 1990s, it seemed as central and eternal as the sun.

Meanwhile, in Washington State, a small game company was created called Wizards of the Coast. Like TSR, its first offices were in its owner's basement. After a few years producing role-playing games and their supplements, Wizards of the Coast published the game that would define their company and, like *D&D,* create an entire new genre of game: *Magic: The Gathering.* In *Magic,* players take on the role of dueling wizards. They gain power, or "mana," from lands they control and use them to power spells against their opponent.

The game was a stunning success, a virtual license to print money for Wizards of the Coast. What made it one of the most profitable games of all time was its all-new collectible aspect. When you bought the game, you didn't get all the cards for it. To get all the cards, you had to buy booster packs. And every time you bought a booster pack, you had no idea what cards you were going to get. Furthermore, some cards were rarer than others. Whole boxes might have to be purchased to find some of the rarest cards in the line. Better yet, having these incredibly rare cards did not just net bragging rights. You could actually use the cards in the game, making you a better player. The fusion of collectability and gameplay built *Magic* into a nigh-addictive phenomenon. Gamers spent and spent and spent on decks, packs, and cards, sending a river of money surging into the coffers of Wizards. The company burst out of its basement offices to become a titan of the gaming industry. It was even bigger than TSR!

According to Ward, TSR felt like oxygen was being pumped out of the room. Sales began to decline. Ward said this new game "was way easier to play than *D&D,* so people started going towards *Magic: The Gathering.*" Typically, two to four hours was needed to play a single session of *D&D,* whereas *Magic* could be played in under an hour. And all of that money spent on *Magic* cards was money that wasn't being spent on *D&D* products. Every hour spent playing *Magic* was an hour that gamers weren't playing *D&D.*

The winter of 1997 was a season of darkness for the company. It had fired dozens of staff and was missing publication dates. Wizards of the Coast CEO Peter Adkison heard the company was in trouble. Working through an intermediary, he purchased the company. TSR, and *Dungeons & Dragons,* was now the property of its fiercest competitor.

This tale, as told by Jim Ward, is one of competition, market forces, and capitalism at work.

In 1997, I was a high school senior in Milwaukee, Wisconsin, and from the hobby shops and gaming tables I frequented, Ward's story seemed about right. I heard game store owners talk about how they could buy RPG supplements that might sell over the course of a year, or they could take that money and buy cases of *Magic: The Gathering* that would fly out the door in a week.

My experience growing up as a nerd was that role-playing games were an outsider hobby played by dorks, dweebs, freak machines, poindexters, and every stripe of pencil-necked geeks. In other words, my tribe. Having been picked last for every game of dodgeball I'd ever been in, it came as no surprise to see the biggest and most important company in role-playing games fall and fail to a younger, sleeker, richer company from the West Coast. It was of a piece with everything else I'd seen of the place reserved for nerds in this world. Unwanted and unloved, it only made sense that even geek hobbies and the companies that supported them were being run down and left like roadkill on the motorway of capitalism.

So from where I stood in 1997, Jim Ward's tale of TSR's end seemed true. The company's failure was a death in single combat. According to the rules of old, it had been felled fairly by the foe.

So when I was assigned to write an article titled "Did You Know that Wizards of the Coast DIDN'T Originally Make *Dungeons & Dragons*?" for Geek & Sundry, I felt like I knew the exact story I was going to tell about the company's fall. I'd lived through it and read Shannon Appelcline's excellent *Designers & Dragons,* which touched on the topic.

Then I started interviewing TSR alumni.

What they told me shocked me. Turned out, I didn't know the story at all. One article became three, but even then, there were fascinating and important aspects of the story that had to be left out. Given how kind and generous all my interviewees were with their time, I felt I had to do right by them and get their stories under the bespectacled eye of the nerd public.

Maybe one day it would be a book?

I continued my interviews and research. I took a sabbatical from Geek & Sundry to write. I dropped my regular Sunday gaming group to write. My short book grew longer and larger, gobbling up time and word count, multiplying in size with age, until the damn thing seemed to have taken over my life. From the glint in its eye, it seemed to be gloating about it.

As I wrote and interviewed, I began to receive secrets. Scans of documents from various sources, one of whom insisted on remaining confidential. Court cases, contracts, notes, and prep binders. The story buried for decades in these hidden sources seized me and would not let me go until I had spoken their truths.

TSR's failure is a tale of misfortune and mistakes kept secret for decades, here given up to the light. It is the story of an unemployed insurance underwriter, an heiress, a preacher's son, and a game like no other.

Jim Ward's story is not the whole truth of what happened. Not even half of it.

THE BIRTH OF TSR, AND THE *D&D* PHENOMENON

> Advanced Dungeons & Dragons *is a fantasy game of role-playing which relies upon the imagination of participants, for it is certainly make-believe, yet it is so interesting, so challenging, so mind-unleashing that it comes near reality.*
>
> —GARY GYGAX, *ADVANCED DUNGEONS & DRAGONS PLAYERS HANDBOOK*

WINTER IN THE American Midwest is merciless, dark, and unending. The role-playing game, like the Russian novel, may be the consequence of such winters.

During Wisconsin winters, the sky is a cold and unbroken slate of gray. Snow cakes the trees and grass. The streets and sidewalks are chalky with salt, and ice crackles across the windows. Winters are so frigid that Lake Michigan steams, sending great gouts of silver billowing skyward, girding the horizon from north to south. During storms, the lake lashes the shoreline. Castles of ice sprout into fantastic shapes with the splash of every wave, and the falling snow and spraying froth fill the world with flecking white. You can't go outside because it's so damn cold, and even if you did, you might hit an icy patch and fall. Where would you be then?

In winter, the world recedes to the circle of warmth around a fire, a heater, or at the side of a loved one.

Or the basement. It's always warm. The furnace is down there after all. There might be games too. Might as well play. What else are you going to do during the endless white-gloom nightmare that reigns between the fall of the last yellow leaf and the spring thaw?

Gamers in the '50s and '60s played war games, miniature games, and strategy games. Games like *Diplomacy*, where players controlled European powers during World War I, or *Gettysburg*, which allowed players to see if they could do better than the generals in re-creating the largest battle to ever take place in the Western Hemisphere. Gamers established hobby groups and published fanzines for each other with names like *Panzerfaust* and *The Domesday Book*.

In short, these men (almost exclusively men at the time) were escaping humdrum lives as insurance salesmen and cobblers by creating a life of the mind in which they were generals, warriors, and leaders of nations. They wanted to be heroes, if only for an afternoon in their own basements.

Gary Gygax was one of these gamers. He cofounded the International Federation of Wargaming and the Castle & Crusade Society. He started a gaming convention of his own called Gen Con. (It was held in Lake Geneva, Wisconsin, and was therefore the Geneva Convention or Gen Con.)

In Lake Geneva in the 1960s and early 1970s, all of that gaming and convention creation earned Gygax a reputation. "He was known as one of the weird guys," said Skip Williams. Williams grew up in Lake Geneva and even went to grade school and high school with Gygax's son Ernie. Williams would go on to have a long and storied career writing *Dungeons & Dragons* and even codesigned the third edition of the game. But before Gygax's epic success cocreating an entirely new medium, Williams said, "he was one of *those people.* He was the sort of person you sort of look askance at. Every neighborhood has those, right?"

First off, he wasn't from Lake Geneva. He was born in Chicago and didn't move to Lake Geneva until he was eight. "In Lake Geneva, that puts you in a weird strata," Williams said. He didn't graduate from high school, and on top of that, "he had all these kids. Sometimes he didn't have a job, and sometimes he didn't have a good job." At one point, "he was the town cobbler." Then there was the fact that "his wife was going around knocking on doors for the Jehovah's Witnesses."

Religion was a serious matter in the Gygax household. Ernie went door-to-door for the Witnesses himself. It was not easy or pleasant. He said that when those doors opened, the faces revealed to him read, "Ugh, you guys."

They took their religion so seriously that they didn't celebrate Christmas, and the children were taught not to stand for the Pledge of Allegiance in school. According to the Jehovah's Witnesses' website, this is because Witnesses "view the flag salute as an act of worship, and worship belongs to God."

This tenet did not go over well in 1960s Cold War Wisconsin.

Despite happening over fifty years ago, both Skip Williams and Ernie Gygax remember the day his second-grade teacher hit him in the face for not standing for the pledge. Everyone in class stood, hands on heart, eyes on the flag, just as every American should do. Except for Ernie. The teacher saw him just sitting there, as though he were too good to rise for the country's colors. This was insult! Outrage! Shameless disdain! She rumbled over to him and said, "Stand up and respect your flag!"

He said, "My mother says I don't have to."

"Stand up!"

She forced him to his feet and swatted him across the face.

Ernie slapped her back.

He was removed to the principal's office, and his parents were called. He was in hot water until his parents learned the whole story, with the pledge and the slap leading up to Ernie hitting his teacher.

In October of 1970, Gygax was fired from his position as an insurance underwriter at Fireman's Fund in Chicago. His boss left the company, and Gygax and another employee named Bruno were up for the position. Bruno got the job, and one of his first moves was to remove his rival. Ernie said, "Dad tended to make either friends or foes. There wasn't anybody on the middle rail." But reasons for the firing may have gone beyond the personal.

Gygax had been using company equipment to help publish a gaming periodical for the Castle & Crusade Society. Perhaps Bruno knew about his personal use of company resources?

In an effort to make ends meet, Gygax took up shoe repair. He continued with game design on the side, but until the success of *D&D,* these endeavors were not profitable enough to keep his growing family from sinking into poverty. Ernie remembered this period as "bad times." His family received government assistance and cut corners wherever they could. For example, there was the problem with Ernie's shoes. The children only got one pair of shoes per year, but Ernie wore holes in his using his feet to brake his bicycle, resulting in swiss cheese soles before a year was up. In a Wisconsin winter, you do not want to be walking around with holes in the bottom of your shoes. He said the solution was to "put cardboard in my shoes before I went to school every day."

Ernie said of his father, "He was stubborn. He had an ego, but he was a hard worker, and creativity just poured out of him into the typewriter."

That creativity would bear fruit. One of Gygax's gaming projects was published in 1971 by Guidon Games. It was a set of medieval combat rules cowritten with Jeff Perren called *Chainmail. Chainmail* introduced a number of innovations to the game table. It provided rules for "man-to-man" combat (instead of combat with massed armies) and a fourteen-page supplement for fantasy that included rules for using elves, dwarves, trolls, and dragons at the table. The game sold well, but was not a hit.

Gygax's game was discovered by Twin Cities native Dave Arneson. Arneson had met Gygax a few years earlier at Gen Con II and began using *Chainmail* to run games in a fantasy kingdom named Blackmoor. In addition to controlling armies, *Blackmoor* players could also choose to control just one character at a time. Arneson had these characters exploring a monster- and trap-filled dungeon. Players did not get new characters at the beginning of every game. Rather, the characters persisted from session to session, growing in power and ability as they gained experience. Arneson's *Blackmoor* was inspired by David Wesely's *Braunstein,* a game in which players took on the roles of characters in a Prussian town under threat of French invasion. The greatest feature of the game was that the characters had near-total freedom to act, unlike in war games, where players were given a defined set of actions they could take.

Arneson wrote about *Blackmoor* in *The Domesday Book*, the periodical of the Castle & Crusade Society. After Gygax expressed some interest, Arneson made a pilgrimage down to Lake Geneva to run *Blackmoor* for Gygax and his friends. The enthralling game ended in the wee hours of the morning.

Gygax was vastly impressed by what Arneson had done with *Chainmail* and asked for a set of his *Blackmoor* rules. About eighteen cribbed and cramped handwritten pages followed, which Gygax set about typing up, expanding, and revising. Soon, he had a much longer rule set, which he began playtesting with his children Elise and Ernie, as well as teenage gamer Rob Kuntz.

He gathered the children in his den for what was likely the first game of *Dungeons & Dragons* ever played. Gary would be the Dungeon Master (DM), the person who portrayed the world and everything in it, from bugbears to barkeeps, that the children would explore. Ernie remembered that first game took place on a weekday after school. The children's characters confronted centipedes and burned their nest. When they did so, a spell scroll hidden in the nest discharged. Ernie remembered his father acting out the sound of the spell scroll's detonation by shouting, "Zing! Zing! Zing! Zing! Zing!" and even admonishing the children afterward, saying, "What a shame you used fire to destroy the nest." Ernie said his sister described the game as "not too exciting," but for him, it was the start of a decades-long career with the game his father cocreated. (You'll hear a few different versions of that first game session, but that's how Ernie Gygax remembered it.)

Guidon Games, which had already published *Chainmail,* passed on publishing *Dungeons & Dragons.* Owner Don Lowry didn't publish the world's first role-playing game because he believed no gamer would ever want to create their own dungeon.

The story of *Dungeons & Dragons* could have ended right there. The game couldn't find a publisher, and without one, what would become of it? Like so many other things in Gygax's life, it looked like *Dungeons & Dragons* just wasn't going to work out.

Unless he took matters into his own hands . . .

_D&D_ TAKES FLIGHT!

Unable to find a publisher, Gygax would publish *Dungeons & Dragons* himself. On October 1, 1973, he formed a partnership with his childhood friend Don Kaye, creating Tactical Studies Rules, or TSR for short. Kaye took out a loan on his life insurance policy to fund the company's start-up costs and the publication of its first game. Ironically, this first publication was not *Dungeons & Dragons* but rather *Cavaliers and Roundheads*, an English Civil War game. Publishing *D&D* would be expensive. It was hoped that *Cavaliers and Roundheads* would sell well and its profits could be used to then publish *D&D*.

It didn't.

Now if the pair wanted to publish the world's first role-playing game, they would need to find a new source of funds. They found them in tool and die maker Brian Blume. Blume was a gamer who believed that fantasy gaming had a future and bought into TSR. The company would now be a three-way partnership. His $2,000 investment allowed the publication of the first thousand copies of *Dungeons & Dragons* in 1974.

The game's wood-grain box held three folded and stapled pamphlets promising, "Rules for Fantastic Medieval Wargames Campaigns Playable with Paper and Pencil and Miniature Figures." It cost $10. That's $54 in 2022 money, which is a hefty price for three short booklets and some reference sheets. The cost was so burdensome that photocopies of the rules were a common sight at gaming tables. Jim Ward, a father just starting a family, had to save for months to be able to buy the game.

Dungeons & Dragons represented a revolution in gaming, one that we are still grappling with decades later. It would be a smash hit, but first, there was tragedy.

Don Kaye, who believed enough in *D&D* to take out a loan on his life insurance policy, died suddenly of a heart attack on January 31, 1975. He was only thirty-six years old. He would not see TSR employ hundreds. He would not see the company warehouse brimming with product. He would not see the mansions, the cars, and the watches that were the fruits of his belief in a new kind of game.

With his death, the company reorganized, and Kaye's shares were purchased from his widow. At the time, Gygax didn't have the money to contribute to the purchase of the shares, and so he became a minority shareholder in the company he founded to publish the game he cocreated. Brian Blume and his father, Melvin, were the company's other shareholders, though Melvin would eventually pass his shares on to another son, Kevin. The Blume brothers and Gary Gygax would be the management team that oversaw the company's golden age.

But it would be impossible for Gygax to manage the company and write every product the company produced. He would need to find other creators to work on *D&D*.

Who would come to Lake Geneva to help grow the brand?

ONE MAN WHO would make an early impact on the game and the company was Tim Kask.

When interviewing subjects for this book, I always tried to find a way to ease them into a conversation. Interviewing can be awkward. I was a strange voice on the phone asking questions about matters from decades past, so I often started with an unrelated topic. *What are you going to have for dinner? Read any good books lately? How are you handling the pandemic?*

Kask mentioned in other interviews that he was a veteran, so I asked him about his time in the service. He unwound a tale that made the hair on the back of my neck stand up. Stationed on the USS *Ranger* during the Vietnam War, it was his job to search for downed navy aircraft. The planes flying missions off the aircraft carrier contained top secret technology that could not be left to the enemy. His task was to find crashed planes and remove or destroy the tech.

One night, he was searching for a plane and discovered he wasn't in Vietnam. He knew he wasn't in Vietnam anymore because of the signage. Vietnamese was written using the Latin alphabet with accent marks, and here the signs were all arcs, arrows, and round curves. Was it Khmer? Lao?

He didn't know. All he knew for sure was that wherever he was, it was night and it was not Vietnam.

At last, the downed plane was located in the treetops. Inside, he found the crew, all dead in their G suits, stinking and foul from sweltering for three days in their plane. Kask took six thermite grenades and wired them together. Then he climbed down the tree, scrambled away, and ignited them. The grenades generated temperatures in excess of four thousand degrees Fahrenheit.

"We gave the crew a Viking funeral," he said of it later.

After leaving the navy, Kask enrolled at Southern Illinois University. There he discovered *Chainmail.* One day, he had a question about the rules, and since this was before the dawn of the internet, there was no quick and easy way to get an answer. But Kask was intrepid and intelligent. He figured out that one of the game's creators lived in Lake Geneva. One night, he called Lake Geneva directory assistance after 9:00 p.m., when the long distance rates would be discounted, and asked to be connected with Gary Gygax. Moments later, he was speaking with Gygax, who did not seem at all upset that some strange gamer was calling him at home at night with a rules question.

The pair hit it off. Kask would call Gygax again to chat, sometimes about war games, sometimes about his service in Vietnam. Gygax talked him into going up to Lake Geneva for Gen Con. Kask attended and played his first game of *Dungeons & Dragons.* He purchased a copy and a set of dice. Gygax also told him that after he graduated, there might be a job for him as an editor at TSR. In the fall of 1975, Kask became the company's first full-time employee outside the owners.

At TSR, he found the birth of an entirely new medium, the bleeding edge of culture, a thing so new it didn't even have a name yet. (The original *D&D* rules didn't use the term *role-playing game* because it hadn't been created!) Was there a smell in the air? A glow from beneath the wind-licked waves of Geneva Lake? Were there portents? Signs? Divine hints?

It is cliché but true that great movements can have humble origins. Acting, and all that has come with it, from Shakespeare to Sally Field can be traced back to one ancient Greek: Thespis of Icaria. He was a singer who would put on masks and actually pretend to be another person. According to Aristotle, it was the first time anyone had affected to be someone they were not for the amusement of others, and his performances were given on the back of a horse-drawn wagon. The dawn of the medium of role-playing had similarly humble origins.

TSR operated out of Gary Gygax's basement. A six-foot-by-ten-foot sheet of plywood resting on two sawhorses served for a table. Above it hung a single naked light bulb. It was clammy and musty and dirty and dark. Most of the company's products at that time were stapled booklets either sold as they were or in the original *Dungeons & Dragons* boxed set. When Kask would go upstairs after assembling product, he said he felt like "a mole being turfed out." Mary Gygax disliked having the business run from the basement. After all, she had children to raise, and now Tim Kask and Brian Blume were stomping through her house all the livelong day. Where was her privacy?

Working in the dungeon of House Gygax was not prestigious, but Kask thought it was damn cool. He described his $100-a-week gig at the newborn company as "the best fucking job in the whole wide world." (That's $500 a week today.) And it didn't hurt that "we were working in a dungeon making things about dungeons!"

Word of mouth on the game was truly outstanding. Sales were such that the company seemed to be constantly assembling and shipping games, then printing games when they ran out of stock. The first printing of one thousand copies sold out in about eleven months. The second printing sold out in five or six months. It was like a rocket ship gathering speed just after launch, a hint of the exponential growth to come.

Sales led to expansion, and soon, the company would be acquiring property all over Lake Geneva. Kask would head *The Dragon,* a magazine run by TSR Periodicals, a new division of the company run out of a gray house on Williams Street.

DESPITE INCREASING SALES, by 1977, *Dungeons & Dragons* faced a number of problems.

First, the game was difficult to learn. This was a challenge that would always bedevil the game, though it may have been severest then. The original *Dungeons & Dragons* boxed set presented an unyielding wall of rules jargon so impenetrable it could have unnaturally aged a new player d10 years for simply attempting to read it. If you actually wanted to learn how to play *D&D,* you probably had to seek out a functioning group and watch a game or two to really get the gist of how it ran.

Second, in the years since the game's publication, the company had released a number of products altering and expanding its rules. For example, *Greyhawk* contained a new character class, the thief, and combat rules. *Blackmoor* introduced the assassin for play. And if people had rules questions, they could write to one of the company's periodicals and get a clarification on the letters page. All this meant that the game's rules were now spread out over a half dozen products with countless clarifications in magazines. This hodgepodge of rules and amendments and caveats meant that running the game could be an exercise in exasperation at the gaming table. One fan wrote that these rules were "confusing as hell!" and asked that "TSR rewrite *D&D* and republish it."

How was the game supposed to grow if people couldn't understand how to play it? Why would players continue playing it if interacting with the rules was difficult and frustrating?

Would everything Gygax and his staff built turn out to be just a fad?

AT THIS MOMENT, just as the company is getting off the ground and facing challenges to its own success, it is worth taking a moment to describe the physical objects it would produce. These new products would solve the twin problems of teaching the game to new players and organizing the existing rules. It would go beyond the production of mere folded and stapled booklets, though it would still make some of those too.

First, it would produce rule books. These were usually hardcover tomes, with a transporting piece of art on the cover, that described the rules of the game. Typically, to play a game of *Dungeons & Dragons,* one needed three of these volumes. There was the *Player's Handbook,* which had all the rules a player would need, the *Dungeon Master's Guide,* which contained the rules the DM would need to run the game, and the *Monster Manual,* which described all the wild and dangerous foes that might be encountered in the game, from aboleths to zombies.

Second, it would make boxed sets, which were boxes containing booklets of rules, setting materials, handouts, and perhaps extra goodies like maps or dice. The original version of *D&D* published in 1974 was a boxed set. New settings were often introduced in stunning boxed sets. What's a setting? If a game of *D&D* is a group-written novel, the setting is the wondrous other world in which you play, in the same way that Middle-earth and Westeros are the settings of fantasy novels.

Third, it would produce adventures. If rule books explained how to play and settings were where you play, an adventure detailed foes, locations, and even plots to overcome. The goal of an adventure is to help players tell the most interesting and exciting story they can. It also saves DMs the labor of creating locations and plots of their own. In the beginning, an adventure produced by the company was a stapled booklet that described a location for players to explore and loot. Over time, they would expand in size, scope, and production quality, until they took characters on epic journeys that shook the foundations of worlds and came in hardcover books like the rules.

While over the course of its life the company would produce vastly more types of media than just these three, such as magazines, novels, CDs, and comic books, none of those were required to play the game called *Dungeons & Dragons.* To this day, if you walk past a table of your friendly local nerd crew playing *D&D,* you will see some combination of rule books, boxed sets, and adventures at the table.

***DUNGEONS & DRAGONS*: NOW BASIC AND ADVANCED!**

To solve the problems of teaching the game and organization, *Dungeons & Dragons* was cleaved in twain. Two products would result, products that in many ways created two lineages of *D&D.* They were the *Dungeons & Dragons Basic Set* and *Advanced Dungeons & Dragons.*

First, novice gamers needed a product that would teach them how to play. Enter J. Eric Holmes, doctor of neurology. He created the *Dungeons & Dragons Basic Set.* Gygax said the *Basic Set* was "designed solely for new players." It was a boxed set that simplified and streamlined the rules, attempting to teach players how to play the game through clear and comprehensible text. It only covered the first three levels of play and then directed interested players to continue their education with *Advanced Dungeons & Dragons.* The *Basic Set* was a hit, selling four thousand copies a month by the end of

1978 and totaling over one hundred thousand copies in 1979 alone. Gygax would credit Holmes's work with bringing over five hundred thousand new players to the game. The *Basic Set* would be revised and rereleased for years to come.

The game contained in the *Basic Set* was zippy and fun. It did not try to be exhaustive, and it left room for Dungeon Masters to make up things on the fly at the table. In so doing, it proved easier to play than *Advanced Dungeons & Dragons*. The *Basic Set* is still considered a hallmark of gaming, inspiring even twenty-first-century game designers to trim role-playing games down to their roots and to make them easier to run and more exciting (and often deadlier) to player characters.

As a product, the *Basic Set* was an answer to the question of how to better teach new players the game.

But what would a new product for existing players look like? Gygax saw that the game, as it was currently constituted, had "too many gray areas . . . too many different books, too many varying approaches offered." He described the solution as "a whole new game," one that would be contained in the first hardcover rule books the company released.

The game described in these volumes would be called *Advanced Dungeons & Dragons*.

If the *Basic Set* was a work of trimming and pruning the game to produce a product that would ease novices into role-playing, in *AD&D*, Gary Gygax let his garden grow wild. The rules burgeoned and bulged, stretching in every direction until it seemed that he was attempting to throw a net around the world and pack it into his game. Consider just these section titles from the first *Dungeon Masters Guide*: Time, Mirrors, Aging, Spying, Death, Lycanthropy, Insanity, Economics, Town and City Social Structure, Listening at Doors, Spell Research, Treasure, and in an appendix, Herbs, Spices, and Medicinal Vegetables. If a Dungeon Master needed to know what the village wisewoman would use to treat pain (belladonna) or cramps (ginger), the new *Advanced Dungeons & Dragons* game had an answer. It attempted to anticipate any situation that could emerge in the game and provide a rule for it. Gygax put it thusly: "What is aimed at is a 'universe.'" The *AD&D* rules reflect the beautiful, noble, if impossible nerd urge to codify and systematize all. The rules bring order. Order brings meaning. That can be a comfort in a real world all too often absent both.

Advanced Dungeons & Dragons was certainly an improvement on the existing organization. The first release in the line, 1977's *Monster Manual,* listed 350 foes for use at the gaming table, ensuring the Dungeon Master knew where to look to find out how many hit dice a black pudding had. The following year saw the release of the *Players Handbook,* followed by the *Dungeon Masters Guide.* (Apostrophes weren't used in the *Handbook*'s or *Guide*'s titles because they were thought ugly, grammar be damned. Pity the poor apostrophe, which wasn't cool enough for *AD&D*!) Before this, if you wanted to know about character classes, you had to look in the original boxed set to read about fighters, *Greyhawk* for thieves, and *Blackmoor* for assassins. Now, happily, all were contained in the *Players Handbook.* Want to know about combat? Those rules were in the *Dungeon Masters Guide.* Sales of *AD&D,* like the *Basic Set,* would blow the doors off TSR headquarters. The *Players Handbook* alone would go through seventeen printings!

AD&D was the great work of Saint Gary, patron saint of role-playing. Reading those books, even today, is hearing the voice of Gary Gygax teaching you how to play RPGs. Its impact has rung down the generations and revolutionized the RPG industry.

TSR EATS A PARENT

You'd think that TSR would have owed Dave Arneson royalties for *Advanced Dungeons & Dragons.* After all, he had cocreated *D&D* with Gygax, and he never sold his rights to the game to the company. In the same way that anyone who wanted to make an incandescent light bulb before 1900 had to pay Thomas Edison for the use of his patent on that invention, you'd think the company would have to pay Arneson for producing an advanced version of the game he'd cocreated.

But TSR didn't see it that way. The company planned to pay Arneson precisely zero royalties for these releases because *Advanced Dungeons & Dragons* was a completely and totally new game. Yes, there were similarities to *Dungeons & Dragons.* In both games, players rolled three six-sided dice to create their characters. In both games, players rolled a twenty-sided die in combat to overcome the armor class of their opponents. In both games, player characters explored dungeons and slayed dragons. But *AD&D* was new, damn it! State of the art! Novel! It was a new thing that Gygax heaved out of oblivion in a unique creative act! Therefore, the company didn't owe Arneson a single red dime in royalties. Any suggestion to the contrary was akin to blasphemy, a denial of the great good that Saint Gary brought us.

Arneson, of course, took issue with TSR's position on the matter and sued the company. An agreement was reached in 1981, which allowed him royalties of 2.5 percent on certain *AD&D* titles, but by 1984, he was back in court suing the company for royalties again.

Much has been written about the rift between the first role-playing game's creators, breathless attempts to paint one as the true animating genius behind it and the other as an opportunistic sneak. The truth, for my money, is as follows. Both were indispensable to the game's creation. *D&D* without Arneson is *Chainmail,* a crunchy, man-to-man fantasy miniatures game. *D&D* without Gygax is *Blackmoor,* a radical and revolutionary style of gaming, but one that perhaps never moves beyond the Minneapolis scene. (It is worth remembering that Arneson had only one publishing credit to his name before *D&D,* and that was another collaboration with Gygax.) *Dungeons & Dragons* is the result of a true back-and-forth between the geniuses of Gygax and Arneson, with Arneson using *Chainmail* in *Blackmoor,* and Gygax taking *Blackmoor* and codifying it in the rules that became *D&D.* What is undeniable is that the game likely never would have been published without Gary Gygax. After all, he created a publishing company to do it. And without that publication, the RPG industry as it is would not exist today.

Let us now pause to pity Dave Arneson, who created a new thing of wonder and was then severed from it in his professional life. He birthed a new medium, but then had little impact on it. He had to watch the ascension of *D&D* and TSR while he remained bound to the earth.

HAVOC, RIOT, AND ANARCHY AT TSR

The company flourished. Operations left the basement and spread out across Lake Geneva. As sales increased, so did the size of the staff. The company attracted the young, men and women often right out of college. It took a special sort to relocate to Lake Geneva for the love of role-playing. For some, it was their first real job. For many, it was the first time they'd been part of a larger community that shared their passion for *D&D*.

One such hire was Lawrence Schick. An atheist since age eleven, he attended Kent State University, where he discovered the game before dropping out to be a writer. In 1979, he was hired by TSR. His starting pay was $2.80 an hour, minimum wage at the time. He was given an office on the third floor of the former Hotel Clair in downtown Lake Geneva. He noted that the building was "a dump."

The Hotel Clair was the shoddy, run-down, ramshackle gem of the company's new properties in downtown Lake Geneva. Here, the nascent culture of role-playing would finally have the space to let it all hang out. The results would be mischief, mayhem, chaos, and genius.

The building made an immediate impression on the company's new hires. It was, they said, a complete pit, the cheapest possible business accommodation, a building waiting to be condemned, one so old and tired, it couldn't even find the strength to fall down.

The third and top floor of the building was the home of the game designers. It was also noteworthy, because there were holes in the ceiling. This floor of the hotel was originally a ballroom, which of course had a high ceiling with rafters. To convert it into a proper office space, walls were put up to create rooms, and a ceiling went up over those.

But if one could get past the new ceiling, one could climb the rafters, jump from beam to beam, and become king of the world, or at least king of TSR, by overtopping all. It was a tempting distraction for the young men of the company.

Game designer Jeff Grubb said that employees' attempts to play flying squirrel on the clock were "not a smart move."

Why in particular?

Grubb said they would "occasionally miss" and fall and smash through the artificial ceiling into the offices below. He said each hole became a story. People would look up at the different holes and say, "Oh yeah, I remember the time Tom Moldvay fell through."

And someone else would disagree and say, "No, no, it wasn't Tom Moldvay, it was Zeb Cook. Zeb Cook fell through there."

And a third person would chime in, "No, no! It was someone else!"

One famous hole was made by artist Erol Otus. One Friday, he decided to climb over Zeb Cook's office and make what was described to me as "a bunch of *ook ook* noises." The office was largely empty, since who doesn't take off as soon as they can on a Friday? And Zeb Cook was down the hall when Otus slipped off a beam and fell through his ceiling. Cook simply heard all hell break loose in his office. It was a tremendous crash. He rushed back to see Otus's legs dangling from the ceiling.

In addition to the holes in the the top-floor ceiling, the floors tilted wildly. Jeff Grubb said they were so uneven that "you'd drop a pencil to see which way it went."

Once upon a time, Steve Winter broke into the offices at the Hotel Clair. Winter, Grubb, and other designers had shown up for work, but there was no one with a key to let them in. They stood on Broad Street in Lake Geneva, huddled on a cement stoop behind the Dungeon Hobby Shop, which led to the door that opened onto the stairs that led to the offices.

They waited.

It was a clear, cool summer morning, and the shining sun turned Geneva Lake itself into a field of diamonds.

A half dozen employees gathered on the cement stoop. They waited some more.

After ten or fifteen minutes, Steve Winter would wait no more. He stood on the railing of the cement stoop, which allowed him to reach a fire escape. He vaulted onto it, then scuttled up to the third floor and his own office window, which he knew to be open. Just as he slithered into his office, Kim Eastland arrived on the stoop below to see him disappear into the building. It was Eastland's first day on the job as the new head of the Role-Playing Game Association, and one can only speculate what thoughts ran through his head when he arrived at this new job at TSR only to see a company employee committing a misdemeanor just to get to his desk. Was every day some form of corporate live-action role-playing event? Was Steve Winter a nerd Evel Knievel?

According to Winter, Eastland "thought it was ridiculous that employees who wanted to start the workday were locked out of the building." He thought it so outrageous that he reported it to Dan Matheson, the head of maintenance and security. Matheson, however, was more concerned about the misdemeanor. Displeased, he went into Steve Winter's office and said, "I'm looking for whoever broke into the office, and if I ever find out who did it, they're in all sorts of trouble! I just want you to know that."

Grubb said, "He didn't want to hear Steve confess or anything." He just wanted to make his point about breaking and entering and move on with his workday.

Somehow, every time a banker or VIP was given a tour to demonstrate that TSR was a serious company that could be trusted with business commitments like loans and contracts and not a bunch of midwestern maniacs whose imaginations were stuck in the Middle Ages, the VIP would inevitably witness some ridiculous shenanigan. For example, frustrated editors formed the Editors Liberation Front (ELF for short) to raid a game designers' meeting. Raid victim Jeff Grubb said, "They kicked open the door and sprayed the room with water pistols and ran away giggling. And of course the bankers were in town that day."

Anticipating retaliation, the editors left sentries, posting Jean Black, head of the Book Department, as guard. Grubb said she "was a sweet little old lady who looked like a librarian with an Uzi water pistol."

Another time, the staff took countless windup toys and set them going down the hall. "And of course," Grubb said, "the bankers were coming by." They came around a corner to see all these toys running and no humans around because, he said, "we had all fled at that point."

What did the bankers think of this company that had an entire hall filled with windup toys, marching and buzzing and glowing, that seemed to serve no discernable purpose? Were company resources invested in this? Was there some wage slave whose only job was to wind the toys and then hide themselves? What sort of kicks did they go for out here in Lake Geneva?

Much mayhem surrounded the creation of *Top Secret,* the first espionage RPG. First, the game's creator, Merle Rasmussen, had to work in the bathroom of Allen Hammack, head of game design. Hammack was working out of what had once been a suite, and the suite of course had a bathroom. The plumbing was ripped out, and Rasmussen was installed in its place. Hearsay held that was why Rasmussen got so much work done, because no one would go to talk to him, because to talk to him, you'd have to get past the boss.

Top Secret also brought the FBI to the Dungeon Hobby Shop downstairs, investigating a possible conspiracy to commit murder. As part of the playtest of the game, Zeb Cook said, "we were playing an office, play-by-message game." Every character was a spy, and this being before the computer revolution, messages would be written on actual paper and handed to the game's coordinator, who would see to it that they got to their intended players. Some of the spies in the game decided that a certain "Mr. Weatherby in Beirut" had to die and began planning his assassination on company stationery. The messages about the assassination were sent and duly dumped into the company trash bins. Somehow, one of these messages escaped from the trash and was found by somebody out in the wide world who didn't see a game move but rather an assassination plot written on company stationery.

Law enforcement was duly contacted.

The FBI appeared in the Dungeon Hobby Shop to investigate. Whoever was behind the counter of the store at the time was shown the disturbing missive and said, "Oh yeah. That's for a game!"

Mollified, the FBI departed.

Then, there was the time the police showed up looking for a sniper. Zeb Cook described the TSR offices as a sort of toy militia, where "we all had Nerf guns." Given the high ratio of Nerf weaponry to staff, Nerf incidents "late in the day, especially towards the end of the week" were all too common. Anyone, at almost any time, could be taken down by a yellow Styrofoam projectile of one stripe or another. Running shoot-outs, moving from office to office and floor to floor of the old hotel, were common.

During one such shoot-out, an employee who was wielding a realistic-looking rifle was hiding behind a door, preparing to fire on a fellow worker. This rifle-wielding employee, who was waiting to unload Styrofoam hell, was somehow also visible from the street. This prompted a local to call the Lake Geneva Police Department, who arrived to investigate. The response of the police, once the situation was explained to them, was, "Those guys again," according to Zeb Cook.

In consequence, management wrote a memo requiring all staff to take their Nerf armaments home and leave them there. Cook said that the staff's response was to start hiding their Nerf weaponry in drawers.

This was the stage of chaos and imagination and goddamn fun upon which much of the great work of TSR's first flowering would be performed.

And sales continued to be strong. The first-ever *Dungeon Masters Guide* was published in 1979, and it proved to be another hit, moving 78,300 copies that year. But for all its success, the company's products were only in hobby shops, not yet in bookstores. If it could manage to get its products on those shelves, who knew how explosive the company's growth might be?

Then, a distributor called Gary Gygax.

Mildred Marmur was the vice president of subsidiary rights at Random House Publishing and her children were *D&D* diehards. With their encouragement, she called to see if Random House and TSR could reach a distribution agreement. Such an agreement would move the game into bookstores from Poughkeepsie to Portland, putting the company's products before the eyes of countless millions of American consumers. Gygax said, "When she mentioned that we could conclude a deal speedily, get into book trade distribution in a matter of months, not a year, I immediately booked a flight to New York City. After a couple of days of meetings, we had struck an excellent agreement."

TSR was so appreciative of the work Marmur's children did in connecting her to the company that the pair were allowed to work at both Gen Con and the Dungeon Hobby Shop, despite being only thirteen and fifteen years old.

The Random House deal was presented to the staff as a publishing coup. It gave the company a new channel of distribution for their products, one that would flow to every mall in America. Gygax said this distribution agreement was "great for TSR."

Six years before, the company operated out of a basement. Now, the Random House deal made *D&D* available to every American who went to a shopping mall. It was a triumph and a sign that hard work had paid off.

The Random House distribution agreement went into effect January 1, 1980.

One might have predicted that the game's increased availability would result in increased sales, which it did. What would have been almost impossible to predict was that it would provoke near-violent frenzy from parents and pastors across the nation. For example, one minister declared in 1981 that he would raise $1,000 to buy *D&D* products and then burn them all to cinders. He said of the plan, "When you play with demonic spirits, that's not a game. When you deal in any way with demonic spirits, they're alive and they've got power."

The Random House agreement launched *D&D* into a mainstream American culture frothing with fears of Eastern religions, brainwashing, drugs, and cults. But how did a game that encouraged young people to stay indoors, sit at a table, and talk to each other become known as a gateway to demon worship, diabolism, satanism, sorcery, and suicide?

SATAN! SUICIDE! AND SALES!

To date, no de-programmers have surfaced to aid worried parents whose children have become D&D *cultists.*

—LOUISE SHANAHAN, "GAMES UNSUSPECTING PEOPLE PLAY: DUNGEONS AND DRAGONS"

IT IS AN irony of history that the game cocreated by Gary Gygax, whose family was so religious that they were knocking on doors looking for converts and getting slapped by teachers for not standing for the Pledge of Allegiance, would be charged with fostering demonism, suicide, occultism, devil worship, and every other sort of dark blasphemy the mind could imagine.

The panic began with the disappearance of James Dallas Egbert III from Michigan State University on August 15, 1979. A mere sixteen years old and already in college, Egbert was a child prodigy. His parents offered a reward, and his uncle hired a private investigator, William Dear, to find the boy. Later, Dear would write a sensationalized memoir about his investigation into Egbert's disappearance, titled *The Dungeon Master.* Dear theorized that Egbert, a *D&D* player, had begun to confuse reality and the world of the game and that "his mind had slipped through the fragile barrier between reality and fantasy." He thought that Egbert "might actually have begun to live this game, not just to play it." Dear said students did live-action role-playing in the steam tunnels beneath campus. Could he have wandered down there in some sort of game fugue?

Then there was the corkboard. A corkboard with pushpins was discovered in Egbert's room. Dear was certain that Egbert, the child prodigy, had left some clue to his fate hidden in the arrangement of the pins. If he discovered the hidden meaning in their pattern, perhaps he would find Egbert. Dear was so certain this was a clue that images of the board were sent to Lake Geneva. Gary Gygax and Tim Kask searched the pattern of the pushpins for some hint, sign, or trace of meaning. Might it be a map? A code? A symbol?

They found nothing.

Practically every one of Dear's guesses would prove, with time, to be completely wrong.

But in those breathless weeks of 1979 between Egbert's disappearance in August and discovery alive and whole in September, the story seized the imagination of journalists. The details of the case were so sensational, they seemed more like a novel than reality. The young prodigy missing, the steam tunnels, the PI, and the mysterious new game so popular with the kids but so hard to understand made for compelling stories. DUNGEONS AND DRAGONS CULT MAY LEAD TO MISSING BOY, panicked the *Sarasota Tribune.* GAME CULTIST STILL MISSING, frighted the *Edmonton Journal.*

The true story of James Dallas Egbert III was both more prosaic and depressing. In August 1979, Egbert attempted to kill himself with quaaludes, but failed. Rather than return to his dorm, he stayed with friends but kept on the move, finally ending up in Louisiana. There, he tried to kill himself a second time and failed a second time. Finally, he reached out to his family, who dispatched Dear to retrieve him, all the efforts of the private eye having failed to find a single clue that he could actually match to the boy's whereabouts.

One might have thought that the return of Egbert, and the fact that his disappearance had about as much to do with *D&D* as it did with pet rocks, would have calmed the nation's fears about this new game.

It did not.

Fears do not run on logic, and the nation's fears of this new game stuck deep. A small industry of investigators, experts, and advocates assembled to educate the world about the so-called dangers of *D&D*. Dear, for all his bombast in linking the game and Egbert's disappearance, would be far outdone in the outlandish and grotesque claims that followed. In 1980, parents in Heber City, Utah, attempted to ban it at the local public school. Faculty who defended the game were accused of practicing witchcraft. One state school board member said that it "brings out murder, poisons, and assassinations, negative kinds of things. It is satanic." The superintendent banned the game. In 1981, a minister named Tom Webster decided to burn *D&D* books because they were demonic. Rumors ran rampant that the books screamed when burned because they contained literal demons. Patricia Pulling blamed the game for her teenage son's suicide. She was so convinced that it caused her son's death that she started an organization, Bothered About Dungeons and Dragons, or BADD, to inform the public. She also wrote a book sedately titled *The Devil's Web: Who Is Stalking Your Children for Satan? 60 Minutes* did a show suggesting that the game was linked to "suicides and murders." Host Ed Bradley interrogated Gary Gygax like he was a pedophile.

Then, in 1982, CBS premiered a made-for-TV movie featuring *Bosom Buddies* star Tom Hanks called *Mazes and Monsters.* It may be the apex of the satanic panic in the culture at large. The film is deeply strange, not so bad it's good but more like a transmission from another reality wherein role-playing games can smash your sanity. Based on a bestselling novel of the same name, the plot involves one Robbie Wheeling, played by Hanks, who suffers a mental break while playing a fantasy role-playing game, the *Mazes and Monsters* of the title, in caves with his friends. He then runs away to New York City. His friends follow clues he left behind and discover him on the roof of the Twin Towers, about to jump off. The film ends with Wheeling totally dissociated from reality, living in his parents' house but believing it to be an inn. He's unable to recognize his friends as his friends, instead seeing them as their *Mazes and Monsters* characters. He is eager to discover what evil lurks in a nearby forest. So his friends play one last session with him. Obviously, the movie is a fictionalization of the Egbert disappearance.

Viewed today, everything the movie has to say about the dangers of *D&D* is drowned out by the image of Hanks clambering over the side of the safety railing on the top of the World Trade Center to jump off. The moment now reads as a sort of foreshadowing of September 11, 2001. How many died jumping from that building, the very action that Hanks acted out? Then there was the fact that in the two decades following *Mazes and Monsters,* Hanks became one of the most famous movie stars on the planet. His name kept the movie in circulation on VHS tapes filling bargain bins at Wal-Mart and gas stations across America. How many saw Hanks's rehearsal for the horrendous events of that September morning?

I won't waste any words explaining that all these accusations about the game are bilge and bosh. This is a history of *D&D.* If you were hoping that this book would initiate you into satanism, you should be reading something by Lucien Greaves or Anton Szandor LaVey. The Satanic Temple has a fine website. While the core accusations leveled against the game were false, the panic had a number of impacts worth mentioning.

First, it made *D&D* cool. Pastors, parents, and periodicals all agreed that the game was unfit for young minds. That elevated it to the outlaw realm of cigarettes, alcohol, pornography, and illicit sex. Of course it made people want the game more, not less. Gary Gygax wrote that the panic "did things for sales you wouldn't believe." Tim Kask recalled a church in Minnesota gathering all their children's *D&D* books and destroying them. In response, TSR doubled the order of the distributor for that patch of Minnesota. And the books sold. Kask said, "All those kids went out and bought their books back, and all the other kids bought one too. Make it forbidden and everybody wants it." The panic and publicity may have had a role in the company's huge sales growth between 1979, when the company had $2.3 million in sales, and 1983, when sales neared $27 million. Gygax himself said that the press's lunatic and lurid obsession with "the *D&D* game and its 'dangers' caused sales to skyrocket. We couldn't print fast enough to fill orders."

Second, while the panic was helping sales, it was hurting distribution. Jim Ward said, "Eight mothers wrote Sears, and a million-dollar sales group disappeared. And the same thing happened to JCPenney. Just a few mothers wrote saying, 'This is demonic,' and JCPenney dropped TSR from their product line, which hurt the company a lot." The idea was put forth that the company should cut demons and devils from the game. Their presence was frequently cited as proof that it was an express elevator to Satan. Remove them, and it at least took a talking point away from the moral panickers. But Gary Gygax refused. TSR's later CEO Lorraine Williams would accede to the idea. Why not remove demons and devils from the game if it helped sales? The second edition of the game, at least initially, would not have demons and devils. Game designer Skip Williams said of the decision, "When somebody is kicking you in the groin, it is really a good idea to at least put on a cup."

Third, while the main thrust of the moral panic surrounding *D&D* was false, buried within it was an observation that has proven true. The moral panicker attacked the game as though it were an evil new religion. While it's not a religion, there are aspects of it that are religious. This idea is expounded on at length in Joseph P. Laycock's *Dangerous Games.* Laycock points out that *D&D* and role-playing games in general can be used to fill a number of human needs often answered by religion. Ritual and myth are obvious examples, but beyond that, role-playing games can fill a need for the sacred, the wondrous, and the numinous that scientific rationalism has stripped from the world. RPGs allow players to step outside of our reality and see it from a different angle. They present a new way of viewing the world. Laycock relates the tale of a gamer who was hit by a car, but walked away from the incident without a scratch. The gamer concluded they had low dexterity, but high constitution. RPGs can even transform people's lives. Laycock tells the tale of a woman with "crippling depression" who claimed that she recovered due to playing a brave character in *Call of Cthulhu.*

Role-playing games were not just games. They were an important new cultural medium. Playing RPGs made life better. Ironically, the civilizational significance of RPGs was seen first by the moral panickers rather than by gamers themselves. For example, players often defended RPGs by saying they were just a game, but any player who ever had a character die and was upset about it for days knew that RPGs were more than that.

This shocking novelty was the foundation of TSR's success. The very thing that provoked outrage and was seen as a threat by many was the very reason *D&D* sold so well.

Ironically, it was all too easy to miss this point if you were an executive in Lake Geneva. It would have been easier to believe that the company's success was built on your special essence and your genius insight. Of course your brilliance was the reason TSR was one of the fastest-growing private companies in America!

That belief would steer the company into disaster.

TSR'S NEAR-DEATH EXPERIENCE

> *TSR and* Dungeons & Dragons, *and I have said this before, have succeeded despite its management, not because of it.*
>
> —JEFF GRUBB, GAME DESIGNER

After years of stunning success, the company was about to fall, and hard. But you wouldn't know it from the coverage the company received in the mainstream press.

In the winter of 1982, *Inc.* magazine proclaimed TSR of Lake Geneva, Wisconsin, the sixth-fastest-growing privately held company. This wasn't the *Milwaukee Journal* or the *Wisconsin State Journal.* No, a nationwide magazine with offices perched among the steel spires that filled the great cities of the east looked west and saw that something special was happening in little Lake Geneva. This was recognition. This was validation. This was a moment.

The article cooed over the company and its managers. "Business is a game to the managers of TSR—and they keep winning," wrote Stewart Alsop II in the subtitle. Chief operating officer Kevin Blume bragged that gamers were simply "intuitively good businessmen." Gygax theorized gaming taught the company's employees "to analyze and cooperate." They were such good businessmen that they "never had a major failure," and "the company only spends money with the greatest reluctance." Kevin Blume mused on incorporating Japanese management methods into their corporate ethos and creating a company compound with a school and food co-op.

The article did note that none of the nine top managers at the company had business experience before their current positions. Instead, they represented "former occupations ranging from biologist to pharmacist to plumber." Alsop said this manifested at times in "odd ways." For example, while Gary Gygax at the time held the title of president, "the company has no real chief executive. Rather it operates under the direction of a 'presidential office' composed of Gygax and Brian and Kevin Blume. The company will not open the door on any new venture without a unanimous decision from these three."

What must it have felt like to have been part of management at the time? The company had moved from the basement of a high school dropout who became the town cobbler to the glossy pages of *Inc.* It had a payroll of hundreds and grossed in the millions. All this had been wrenched out of nothing—a game, a company, and a whole new medium. As human beings are egomaniacs, it must have been so easy for management to believe that they were what made the company such a resounding success. They were outland and outcaste blue-collar laborers who had shown all those college graduates on both coasts that they weren't doing anything a guy from Wisconsin couldn't do better with midwestern common sense and a damn fine work ethic. It would have made a compelling internal narrative.

With the hindsight of history, and knowing what disaster hovered over TSR, all the preening and bragging of management reads like arrogance leading to the great fall in some Greek drama.

Inc. was so taken with TSR that they published a second article on the company, this one titled "Why TSR Hobbies Is So Profitable." They did not cite the genius of management as the reason for the company's success but instead rightfully pointed out that the company had started the role-playing game industry and dominated its competition. In short, TSR was successful because *D&D* was successful. That success allowed the company to paper over problems and failed products, and there certainly were failed products.

Palace of the Silver Princess was an adventure by Jean Wells with rather naughty illustrations. There was an image of a woman under torture, bound by her own hair, and another that seemed to contain caricatures of employees. Finally, the text itself was so Freudian that illustrator Bill Willingham nicknamed the adventure "Phallus of the Silver Princess." Despite the cries from creatives that the product had problems, management didn't seem to care until after the adventure was published and free copies were given to staff. The first print run was confiscated and destroyed. Then the adventure was rewritten by Tom Moldvay and republished in 1981. The original, of course, has gone on to be an incredibly hot collectible.

But disasters like that did not matter, because all iterations of *D&D* were selling so well. The money hid the mistakes.

But what would happen if sales slowed? Or even (gasp!) dropped?

A WORD MUST be said on the rise of the Blume brothers. Brian Blume had been with TSR almost from the beginning, investing money to pay for the first printing of *Dungeons & Dragons*. His father, Melvin, had also invested, and in September 1981, those shares were passed to Brian's brother, Kevin. Like Gygax, neither of them had any formal business training. Brian was senior executive officer and Kevin chief operating officer. Gygax was and remained president.

Like the article in *Inc.* magazine, numerous sources from the time pointed out that the three highest-ranking members of management operated by unanimous consent.

Yet decades later, Gygax would claim that this was untrue. He claimed that he was in a "powerless role" in the early 1980s, as the Blumes could outvote him two to one on any issue. But again, sources from the time said that any one of the three had veto power over decisions at TSR.

What is going on here? Is every source from the early 1980s wrong about how the company operated? Or was Gary Gygax not telling the truth in later interviews?

THE BLUME ERA

In the early 1980s, Gygax stepped back from TSR. Some thought it was so he could focus on new projects. Others said he just wanted to enjoy his newfound wealth. (His best year of royalties grossed him $2.2 million. That's over $7 million in today's dollars!) Others believed the Blumes were consolidating power and did so by removing people deemed loyal to Gygax. Tim Kask, for example.

In 1976, Tim Kask was given five shares in the company. In shareholder meetings, he usually ended up siding with Gary Gygax against the Blumes. Kask believed this was why the Blumes decided to get rid of him.

In April of 1980, he was called to a meeting up in the new offices on Sheridan Springs Road. There, Brian and Kevin demoted him while Gary, Kask recalled, "sat there looking miserable."

Kask could keep the same salary, but he was no longer going to be in charge of periodicals. It would certainly be a fall for Kask. He said, "If you were vice president, would you want to be in charge of building maintenance? It wasn't exactly what they offered, but it wasn't far off."

By then, Kask's Periodicals Department took up the first floor of an entire house. It looked like a real office, stocked with desks, filing cabinets, and typewriters. The second floor was used as a temporary living space for new hires, something that he "resented greatly." He didn't know who these new hires were, and there was no way to secure the downstairs offices from the upstairs living space. But it was a far cry from the dungeon at House Gygax with its worktable set on sawhorses and the single naked light bulb for illumination.

All that would be gone with the demotion.

What may have been worse was the fact that the demotion "would have put me under one of the people at TSR that I absolutely despised." Eloquent in a loathing that seemed to have lost none of its potency since 1980, Kask said of the nameless man who would have been his boss, "He's a dick. He was a dick then; he's still a dick. He's a hack. If he didn't have a good editor, he wouldn't have published much."

And through all of that, Gary Gygax didn't so much as whisper. Kask said, "I was very angry that he hadn't spoken up for me."

Kask was unwilling to swallow the vinegar the Blumes offered him. "I said, 'Fuck you, Blumes!' and I resigned. I still have a copy of my letter of resignation. It's actually too nice."

The March 1980 issue of *The Dragon* listed "T. J. Kask" as managing editor. By the April 1980 issue, the name had disappeared from the masthead. He left feeling "bitter and pissed off."

Finding work was difficult for Kask. When he showed people at other companies his work at TSR, they were either confused or horrified. The bonfires of the satanic panic burned brightly by then, and his time at the company marked him as "one of those crazy gamers."

Lawrence Schick also left due to the Blumes. He said the pair "made a lot of capricious decisions about what products to do and how to do them. They overruled their design managers and made those products worse. It was dumb." Furthermore, he believed the Blumes saw employees as "being interchangeable and not respected." All that turned TSR into "a place to work that was unfriendly to its own employees."

Schick asked for and received a demotion so that he would no longer have to enforce Blume edicts as head of design. However, he did not leave TSR. He was working on a sci-fi RPG named *Star Frontiers* with Zeb Cook. With the royalty rates the company paid employees, he believed the game would be "my ticket to the middle class."

But by the time the pair had finished their work on the game, the Blumes had ended the employee royalty program. Under Gygax, even though employees were already paid a salary, royalty contracts were issued for design work. Given how small the salaries employees received were and how huge the sales of some of these products were, it was completely possible for an employee to make more money on royalties than they did on salary. But Schick believed that to the Blumes, those royalties represented "money thrown away. These were people they were already paying. Why pay them more? This is money they could have kept."

Without royalties, it seemed that Schick would not be making the transition to the middle class while working at the company. He said, "I went off in computer games, and that's where I've been ever since."

TSR's failure to pay its employees what they are worth, and the resulting turnover, is a motif that will occur again and again in the company's history, under different management regimes.

But while old hands were departing the company, new ones were arriving. One of the new hires in the Art Department would leave an indelible mark on the look of the game.

THE DRAGONS OF JEFF EASLEY

No account of the first flowering of TSR is complete without touching on the Art Department. Art is of vital importance to role-playing games because it is both inspirational and instructive. There are accounts of RPG designers seeing a single work of art and being so roused that they created RPGs based on them. Great art also galvanizes Dungeon Masters and players. Great art creates windows to worlds that have never existed outside the imagination, and the role-playing game says, "Would you like to spend time in that world? Right this way . . ." It is a powerful pairing of media. Great art can teach people how to play a role-playing game without words. The first edition *Players Handbook*, for example, showed characters prying the jeweled eyes out of a stone idol on the cover, and inside demonstrated the consequences of failed rolls, such as when a character slipped on a banana peel and fell. The art taught both what the game was about and how to play it. Of course, great art can also impel people to buy games.

The art TSR produced was one of the pillars of the company, no less than game design or fiction writing. Perhaps this is why, when all neared ruin in the spring of 1997, the highest-paid creator was an artist: Jeff Easley. The company could string writers, designers, and editors along on a pittance, but an artist of his capacious abilities had to be kept happy.

The man is, without doubt, a genius.

In the early 1980s, Jeff Easley was living in Massachusetts and working for a popcorn company. O-Ke-Doke Popcorn Company paid the bills, and it had all the free popcorn he could eat while he was on the job, but it wasn't what he wanted to do with his life.

Jeff Easley wanted to make art for a living.

He would go down to New York City with his portfolio to try to get work in the field, but said, "I wasn't having a whole lot of success."

Still, he was getting work. He'd done some pieces for Marvel, including a few covers for *Savage Sword of Conan*. But he wasn't getting enough work to do art full-time, which was his goal.

Born and raised in Kentucky, Easley attended Murray State University and graduated with a degree in art. One of his friends from Murray State got a job at Fort Knox after graduation, where he met an artist working in the Fort Knox Training Aids Department by the name of Larry Elmore. Elmore shared Easley's interest in fantasy art, so Easley's friend introduced the two of them. Soon, Elmore left Kentucky for Wisconsin, having just gotten a job as an artist working for TSR.

When Easley heard about it, he knew Elmore just well enough to call him up and sound him out about prospects at the company. Elmore told him, "They're growing by leaps and bounds and adding staff monthly." He suggested Easley send some art samples in for consideration. Impressed by his art, the company flew him out to Lake Geneva for an interview and gave him a job. He jumped on the opportunity. He was so eager to work there he "probably would have taken a job sweeping the floors."

March 1, 1982, was Jeff Easley's first day of work. While he had heard of *Dungeons & Dragons,* he had never played a single game of it in his livelong life.

What he found was a company in transition.

TSR was still largely run out of the abominable Hotel Clair, and at the time, the Art Department operated on the third floor, working out of the renovated ballroom. There was even a punch clock for the artists. Management, however, had been moved out of downtown to the old Q-tip factory on Sheridan Springs Road, which would be the home of the company for the next fifteen years. In less than a year, the Art Department also moved out to Sheridan Springs Road. There, Easley settled into a work life of drawing monsters, elves, and dragons. His career with the company would span decades, making him one of the most experienced of the old hands. Easley, along with other luminaries such as Clyde Caldwell, Keith Parkinson, and Larry Elmore, came to define the high style of TSR in the 1980s and 1990s.

Easley's art inspired and instructed the viewer; it made the heart bound and the mind dash as he painted windows into worlds that didn't exist. Ornate, detailed, thick with color and action, his art on the cover of a *Dungeons & Dragons* product would make you want to pick it up simply because it was so damn cool. His was a world of grimy undead, red-scaled dragons shining like rubies in the light of their own fiery breath, black-robed wizards staring pensively over stone altars inscribed with forbidden runes, and brave warriors in winged helmets galloping so hard and so fast they might burst off the page. His work bedecked some of the company's most popular products, such as the second edition *Player's Handbook.*

Game designer Bruce Nesmith remembered a demonstration of Easley's skill as an artist. In the early 1990s, Dave Sutherland was assigned to an adventure titled *Web of Illusion,* and for one of the interior illustrations, Sutherland had to draw a tiger's head in perspective on a temple. Sutherland kept trying and couldn't quite do it. Nesmith said, "Dave was a good artist, but that wasn't his forte. He was unhappy and stomping around."

Jeff Easley saw all of this and asked what was wrong. Sutherland replied that he couldn't draw that tiger's head.

Easley took a crack at it, and Nesmith said, "Three minutes later, there was a perfect tiger's head. That's Jeff Easley."

Easley himself did not recall the tale.

At the Sheridan Springs Road location, there was no punch clock, and Easley said that management was not particular about when artists rolled in to work. The artists were all in one large room, each laboring over his own drafting table. Radios played, then CDs when they came into use, and the artists took turns playing what they liked. He described the atmosphere as very social.

"Painting," Easley said, "is an activity where you can actually sit and talk to people while you paint. You don't have to really engage your brain. It's a left brain–right brain dichotomy there. So you can actually talk and interact with people while you're watching the painting happen before your eyes."

Easley would paint until noon, then often go out for lunch. The artists frequented a local Chinese restaurant and a pizzeria across the highway or would march across the field behind the offices to a grocery store to purchase food from the deli and bring it back to the break room. At one point, someone brought in a dartboard. He recalled, "At lunchtime, we would have some pretty spirited dart-throwing tournaments."

Easley and the others would work the rest of the afternoon, and then "knock off around five."

The Art Department took TSR's annual Halloween parade very seriously. According to Bruce Nesmith, one year, artist Clyde Caldwell created a head-to-toe "gold brocade pirate outfit." Jeff Easley, meanwhile, came as some sort of shambling corpse. He'd created a mouthpiece with horrifying teeth, but the coup de grâce was a worm wriggling among the teeth that he could actually move. Easley won that year's costume contest, and according to Nesmith, Clyde Caldwell was "not happy."

When work needed to get done in the Art Department, it got done. Easley said, "I remember coming in one weekend and doing a painting over the weekend because they had to have it on Monday." Artists had card access to the facility, so they could come in anytime.

And how was making art full-time? Easley loved it.

Compared to freelancing, it was much easier. There was no calling around to look for gigs, no networking, nothing but painting. There was no follow-up to make certain that he got paid after completing a job.

At TSR, Easley did not have to be his own PR person, manager, and agent. He could be but an artist, which was what he'd wanted all the time he was prowling New York for jobs and working for the O-Ke-Doke Popcorn Company. He said he'd be given a job to do, he'd paint what he was asked, hand his superior the painting, and he'd be given another job. His work life was the business of creation.

Jeff Easley was not the only new employee in the early '80s. Other core creative staff were drawn to the company.

COLLABORATOR CATS AND THE *POLICE DU CHAT*

The year 1981 saw the arrival of a doe-eyed and brilliant college graduate who would participate in some of the most important events in TSR history, Bruce Nesmith. He was a computer guy who originally found his way to the company from Beloit College, which was forty minutes down I-43 from

Lake Geneva. He spent the summer between his junior and senior years writing accounting software for the college on their new and ultramodern Hewlett-Packard 3000, a computer so advanced it used floppy disks instead of punch cards and could fit on a desk! At night, he used the computer to program a dungeon-crawling video game imaginatively titled *Dragon*. He recalled that the height of the game's graphics was that it used pound signs for the walls, and dots for empty spaces. Numbers were used to signify monsters. "It was as old-school as you can get," he said.

The game was a huge hit with his friends, and even the Hewlett-Packard sales rep played it. He was so impressed that when he went to ply his wares at TSR, he sang the praises of this digital dungeon and its creator.

In 1981, as Nesmith was getting ready to graduate with a degree in mathematics, but "no clue what the heck I'm gonna do" after graduation, TSR phoned him. The voice on the line said, "We would like you to interview for a job as a computer games programmer."

When he was hired, Jim Ward pointed out to him that at the time, there were more astronauts in the world than there were paid game designers. It made Nesmith feel incredibly fortunate to have ended up where he had.

On his first day at the goddamn Hotel Clair in downtown Lake Geneva, which was held together at this point by tape and load-bearing dreams, Nesmith wore a suit to work. He wore a suit because, in his words, "I was an idiot." He immediately felt out of place, as everyone else was dressed firmly in casual wear like faded jeans and T-shirts.

Management installed Nesmith before a TRS-80 microcomputer in a room covered in Post-it notes. Nesmith moved closer to examine the Post-its and discovered mice sporting jackboots and swastikas and cats dressed like French police officers. Each Post-it had a different scene, impressively drawn, of the mouse Gestapo and the *police du chat* (which is French for "cat police"). He described having Nazi mice and collaborator cats for his first work partners at the company as "surreal." It turned out that the gentleman he was supposed to work with had had a dream about Gestapo mice and French police cats the night before, so his friends in the Art Department decided to decorate his work area with the residents of his dreams.

Nesmith would eventually move from making video games to the Games Department.

From that perch, he would witness the disasters to come.

THE CRISIS OF 1983

Under the direction of the Blume brothers and Gary Gygax, from 1979 to 1982, the company grew huge and fat on the success of *D&D.* Sales shot up, payroll increased, and the company expanded, acquiring new offices around the country. The year 1983 was supposed to be even better. Sales were projected to rocket up, perhaps as high as $75 million. In anticipation of such growth, the company expanded even further. By April of that year, RPG historian Jon Peterson reported, "TSR comprised a total of 312 workers. Staffers now sprawled across six buildings in Lake Geneva alone, to say nothing of a warehouse in New Jersey and a licensing office in New York."

By spring and early summer, it became clear that the company's projections were hugely optimistic. It would not meet those sales goals.

The rocket ship of TSR, destined for stars unknown and planets undreamed of, first stalled and then began to plummet earthward. Sales ceased their exponential growth in 1981, crested in 1983, and tumbled in 1984. If one added up all the *D&D* boxed sets and *AD&D* rule books sold in 1983, the company moved 1,885,419 units. In 1984, the company only moved 820,672. Then 1985 would prove even worse, and the company's sales would bottom out in 1986, with combined sales of 397,961, a drop of 1,487,458 units or 79 percent. There were bright spots in those years. As we will see, Margaret Weis and Tracy Hickman's Dragonlance novels would prove to be hits. Rules expansions like *Unearthed Arcana* and settings like *Oriental Adventures* sold well. In 1985, the company sold 301,427 units of setting material. But those sales could not overcome the catastrophic 79 percent drop in boxed set and rule book sales. This was engine failure and hull rupture. Calamity. Disaster. Ruination.

Why did sales collapse? Historian Jon Peterson believes it was mostly market saturation. He pointed out that by 1982, new players had begun to dry up. Soon, unit sales strength shifted entirely to adventures and play aids for existing players, items that were less profitable than rule books.

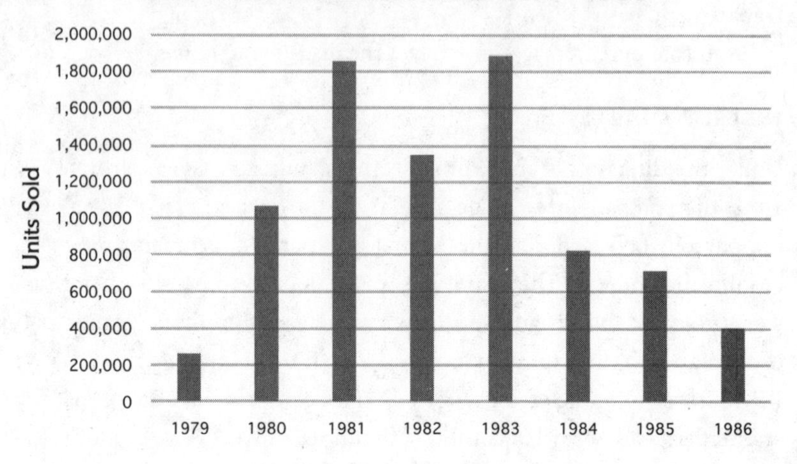

This was further compounded by management decisions that were somewhere between self-serving and stupid. Foremost among them was the purchase of a needlepoint company named Greenfield Needlewomen. The staff was told this was the company reinvesting its profits. Under TSR, Greenfield Needlewomen produced needlepoint kits that allowed crafters to embroider slogans such as "Dragon Power" and "Quiet! Dungeon Zone." With such products, it was hoped that Greenfield Needlewomen would contribute one-fifth of the company's bottom line in coming years.

Suffice it to say, the company failed to meet those expectations. Sales were abysmal. Watercooler scuttlebutt at the time suggested that Greenfield Needlewomen was in fact owned by a Blume relative or friend in need of a bailout. The rumor proved true. The company was owned by Kevin and Brian Blume's cousin, Connie Stano.

But the purchase of Greenfield Needlewomen was not the only error. The company also went on a hiring spree, and being related to a Blume or Gygax was a sure way to move your résumé to the top of the stack. The company also attempted to raise a shipwreck from the bottom of Geneva Lake for no profitable reason anyone could explain to me in my research for this book. Jeff Grubb said all the company ever received for its investment in the project was the ship's boiler, "which sat behind the building for several years until we convinced the Smithsonian to haul it away." The company had a fleet of automobiles. The company purchased *Amazing Stories* magazine even though it had only ten thousand subscribers. The company decided to get into the business of making and selling miniature figures. The company started publishing a line of interactive romance novels titled Heartquest, hoping to break into the teen market. (The back of *Moon Dragon Summer* reads, "You are Summer, a charming, feminine young woman seemingly destined for love and marriage.") The company licensed established properties at a clip, producing games based on Conan the Barbarian, Indiana Jones, and, most improbably, Stanley Kubrick's *2001: A Space Odyssey.* (And yes, you start that adventure playing evolving apes on the African savannah four million years ago. What a tabletop thrill that must be!)

TSR had grown fat. It would now need to be pared to the bone. Given the plunge in sales, frantic hiring, and bad investments, action was needed to avert a total disaster.

Despite such a lengthy indictment of management sins, Kevin Blume's self-satisfaction appeared not to have suffered. When a *Wall Street Journal* reporter inquired about a possible sale of the company, Kevin Blume "jauntily says that there are many prospective suitors, but that TSR won't sell. 'We're having far too much fun, and we make far too much money.'"

Thus spoke the man who had to fire scores of employees and borrow millions of dollars to prevent his company from going bankrupt. To stay afloat, Kevin Blume negotiated a loan of $4 million from the American National Bank, a loan contingent on laying off staff. Thus began a nightmare cycle of falling sales and layoffs that would go on until 1985, when the company was left with under one hundred employees.

Skip Williams, who went to grade school with Ernie Gygax, was fired in the fall of 1983. At the time, he ran Gen Con, the August gaming convention now run by TSR. After the convention that year, he was asked to compose a handbook explaining how to do his job. Being one of the sharper knives in the drawer, he said, "I was wise enough not to finish that project." It did not save him. He was told when he was fired that the company could no longer afford him.

Jeff Grubb recalled that in one of the rounds of layoffs, "they started at one end of the building and they rolled through the building east to west. If someone to the west of you was laid off, you knew you were safe. One marketing guy refused to stay in his office, thinking you can't hit a moving target."

Those that survived the layoffs were not untouched by them. Game designer Bruce Nesmith said, "There's this gut-punch feeling when your friends get laid off. And by round three, you're just numb to it. All the way through that, you struggle to find the will to perform at the level you were performing at before. Because you're not thinking about work. You're just thinking, 'Will I be next? Is this company going to survive? What am I going to do?'"

A WOMAN NAMED MARGARET AND A MAN NAMED TRACY

Despite the layoffs and the dark times, there were products that were selling, most notably the Dragonlance adventures and novels, and the two names most closely linked with that line were Margaret Weis and Tracy Hickman. The pair would forever change role-playing, showing the company that fans were so eager to enter the worlds of *D&D* that they would even buy novels set there. The sales they generated helped keep the company afloat during those black days of layoffs and loans in the 1980s.

Tracy Hickman was bankrupt when he sent two adventures to TSR, hoping the company would buy them, "literally so I could buy shoes for my children," he said. The company ended up hiring him. His game designer wife, Laura, and the kids would move with him to Wisconsin. He said, "It was a terrifying experience. We had no money. My parents begged us not to venture into such foreign territory to pursue such a bizarre career. My father wrote that there was a secure job as a fry cook in Flagstaff (where my parents were living), and he pleaded with me to come and take it."

On the drive to Wisconsin, Tracy and Laura imagined a fantasy setting where dragons were political, magical, and legendary actors trying to conquer the world and who must of course be foiled by brave and doughty heroes. It would come to be called Dragonlance, and the impact of its creation has echoed down the decades. This 1982 road trip was one of the two most important road trips in role-playing game history. (It is rivaled only by the Gen Con road trip that led to the creation of the iconic RPG *Vampire: The Masquerade.*)

The Hickmans brought with them to Lake Geneva new ideas about how adventures should be written. Up to this point, *D&D* adventures were largely descriptions of locations filled with enemies, traps, and treasures. Visit the Caves of Chaos! There behold warring tribes of goblins, orcs, and kobolds! Such adventures were usually about killing monsters in dark places and taking their stuff.

The Hickmans had a higher aim. They wanted to write adventures with objectives "more worthwhile than simply pillaging and killing" and "an intriguing story that is intricately woven into the play itself." These ideas were on full display in the October 1983 adventure composed by the Hickmans, *Ravenloft*.

Ravenloft was a truly brilliant, nigh-perfect adventure. It was set in the misty mountains and valleys of Barovia, a land ruled by the undead and undying Count Strahd von Zarovich. Strahd was an active opponent who pursued characters with all the cunning and hunger of a wolf hunting wounded deer. The players had total freedom to explore Barovia but were magically trapped inside the realm, preventing them from going for help and saving the DM from having to worry about any other locations. The goal of the adventure was to destroy Strahd, free the people of his sad land, and in turn escape his domain. It was about more than murder and pillage, and its story was beyond intriguing. *Mythic* is a more appropriate description. The adventure was even re-playable because the locations of important objects were randomly determined by a deck of cards.

But the project wherein the Hickmans' ideas about adventure design would shine out the strongest was Dragonlance. It set out to tell an epic story over sixteen adventures that would be released over the next four years. For example, the goal of the first adventure in the series would be the rediscovery of the "ancient gods of good," bringing divine magic back into the world. Beyond this deluge of releases, the company also published a series of novels based on these adventures.

Margaret Weis, a freshly hired book editor, was to shepherd the first of these novels into existence. She would find an author to write it, coordinate between the author and Hickman, and of course edit the novel.

But there was a problem.

The author initially selected to write Dragonlance, whose name Weis couldn't recall, was not working out. She said, "He just didn't get the story. And Tracy and I were growing increasingly worried because the game modules were doing really, really well." Furthermore, a short story penned by Weis and published by *Dragon* (the *The* had been dropped from its name by this time), set in the world of Dragonlance, "The Test of the Twins," received more fan mail than any other short story in the magazine's history to that time.

The field had been primed for a Dragonlance novel. Weis said, "We knew we had something really good. We needed to get it out."

The pair decided to try writing the novel themselves.

But Weis had not been hired to write this novel. And Hickman was a game designer. Book Department head Jean Black would need to be convinced that Weis and Hickman were the right people for the job. In the course of a single weekend, the pair produced an introduction and five chapters.

Monday morning, the pair appeared outside Jean Black's cubicle bearing the pages and a request that the two of them be allowed to write the first Dragonlance novel. Years later, Black told Weis that the only reason she agreed to read the pair's effort was because she didn't want to hurt their feelings. She took the pages and stepped into her cubicle, one of the few that had a door. She closed it.

Nervous, Weis and Hickman went to Weis's cubicle to await the verdict. According to Weis, the wait was not long. "Pretty soon she came back." She said one word to the pair: "Wow." The pages were good. So good in fact that the book would go on to launch not just sequels but hundreds of other books set in the world of Dragonlance.

The unremembered author who could have written the first Dragonlance novel was fired. TSR allowed him to keep his advance, as the company was afraid he might sue otherwise.

To get the book into print, Weis and Hickman would have to make a three-month deadline, a short gestation time for a novel. Since Weis was now working as a writer on the project, she could no longer edit it. Jean Black replaced her. Weis said Black "edited it as we went along," and the first novel ever published by TSR, *Dragons of Autumn Twilight,* was completed on time.

Dragons of Autumn Twilight and its two sequels, *Dragons of Winter Night* and *Dragons of Spring Dawning,* were colossal successes. They sold so well the company announced that this first trilogy would receive a sequel, to be called Dragonlance Legends.

Beyond being a huge hit unto themselves, the success of the Dragonlance novels revealed a deeper truth: people loved reading novels set in the fantasy worlds of *D&D.* The worlds were so engrossing, people wanted to spend time in them, but tabletop role-playing has always been difficult to organize. It requires a group of people and hours to play. A novel was an easier way to step into those worlds.

For Weis, the success of Dragonlance was "amazing." She said every writer dreamed of hitting the *New York Times* bestseller list, and the Dragonlance franchise took her there.

But those were times of tribulation for TSR, and just because profits from Dragonlance adventures and novels were helping to keep the company alive did not mean their jobs were safe.

In 1985, a fourth round of layoffs began. Harold Johnson, who was head of the RPG Department at the time, gathered his employees around a table in a conference room. Johnson looked like "somebody had just shot his dog," Nesmith recalled. Johnson had a reason to be downcast. He told his team that he had been ordered to let one of them go, but he had already let everyone go whom he thought he could. The RPG Department had already been flayed to the ribbons. Everyone remaining on the team was crucial. He just didn't know what to do.

It was a moment of dread and despair. Leaving TSR was not leaving just any job. It was leaving the only job in the known universe where employees were paid to make *Dungeons & Dragons.* Leaving did not just mean you'd have to find another source of income, it meant exile from the holy chore of game creation for publication. Jeff Grubb believed the most vulnerable individual was Tracy Hickman. "He was the man on the bubble," Grubb said.

But Tracy Hickman was not fired that day in 1985. He was spared because Bruce Nesmith volunteered to be let go. Nesmith figured he had the computer skills to get a good job somewhere else, so firing him made the most sense.

It was a moment of bright decency. Nesmith took upon himself all the perils of unemployment and the bitter fate of no longer creating *D&D* simply so others wouldn't have to.

Nesmith remembered others in the room being surprised and grateful. He felt good about his decision in that moment. Then he got his papers, boxed up his office, and walked out the door. At that point, his feelings "took a hard left." Two weeks later, he found another job. Four years later, Jim Ward hired him back.

Things were so bad it didn't matter if you were a brilliant creator whose products flew off the shelves; you might still be fired. That meant that literally no one's job was safe. And if sales continued to nose-dive, it was only a matter of time until TSR went under.

As the company he'd cofounded struggled for life, where was Gary Gygax?

D&D AND LIVING THE RIOT LIFE IN LA

Did I see piles of cocaine, prostitutes, spank-movie actresses, bikers, and people who may or may not have been psychotic? Yes. All present. But there is always an asterisk to any scene.

—FLINT DILLE ON WHAT HE SAW AT THE D&D MANSION, FROM HIS MEMOIR, *THE GAME MASTER*

IN THE EARLY 1980s, Gary Gygax attempted to turn *Dungeons & Dragons* into a marketable Hollywood property. Movies and television were the lifeblood of mass culture at the time. Inject *D&D* into that current, and who could even predict how successful it might become? To achieve that goal, he would begin spending large amounts of time in California, away from the headquarters of the company he'd cofounded and away from the Blumes. Though a promised movie would not materialize until much later, Gygax did get *D&D* on TV as a Saturday morning cartoon that ran from 1983 to 1985 and was aptly titled *Dungeons & Dragons.*

Gygax was divorced, rich, and powerful. California had much to offer a man of that description, and he indulged in all of it. He met Hollywood luminaries like Universal Studios president Sid Sheinberg and actor/director

Orson Welles. He moved into a mansion in the hills with his sons Ernie and Luke, a mansion once owned by producer/writer/director King Vidor. The mansion was so high up in the hills that you could see both downtown LA and the San Fernando Valley from the property. A sand table was set up for games of *Chainmail.* There were women. There were drugs. It was Hollywood.

Upon first hearing about this side of the story, it sounded like some strange Wisconsin spin-off of *The Beverly Hillbillies.* A poor family strikes it rich and moves west to live the sweet life, but brings their sand table and role-playing games with them.

Flint Dille was an eyewitness to what happened when the Gygaxes went west. As for Dille, well, where to begin? Years before I interviewed him for this project, I'd been hearing stories about Flint, tales whispered from geek to geek, and handed down over the years in the gaming community. The man was half-rumor and half-myth. One could say he was larger than life, but that comes off as understatement when paired with the man himself. One could say he was a Hollywood guy, but that doesn't compass the whole of him. After all, he wrote novels and comics and worked on video games. Dille was the inspiration for Dilios, the tale-telling narrator in *300.* (*300* in its comic book form was dedicated to Flint Dille.) He also said that Flint from the *G.I. Joe* cartoon was "sort of" based on him. The producers of the show named a character after him so he'd have to take a job working on it. He said, "My fictional life is far more interesting than my real life."

He grew up in Glenview, Illinois, with his sister, Lorraine, and by the 1980s, he had become a cartoon writer. He has been described in print as "the man who wrote your childhood," and if you're between forty and fifty, that's about right. He worked on iconic Saturday morning fare like *G.I. Joe* and *Transformers* and was hired to write by both George Lucas and Steven Spielberg. He met Gygax in 1982 and even helped him pick out the mansion that would serve as TSR's base of operations in California. He cowrote the Sagard the Barbarian books with Gary and an uncredited Ernie.

Flint Dille saw it all. Gary's $1,500 blue jeans. *Playboy* models in the jacuzzi. He was unaware of the Gygax family's membership in the Jehovah's Witnesses until later. He said, "In that period in the mansion, Jehovah was looking in a whole new direction."

A young Jim Lowder standing outside the Dungeon Hobby Shop in Lake Geneva in 1983. Photo by Debra Lowder. © 2022 James and Debra Lowder.

Jim Lowder in his office at TSR in 1990. Photo by Debra Lowder. © 2022 James and Debra Lowder.

The Guardian by Brom. An early piece for *Dragon Magazine*. Courtesy Brom.

Enchanter by Brom. One of the images created for the Dark Sun setting. A clear demonstration of his growth as an artist while at TSR. Courtesy Brom.

Jim Ward and Jeff Grubb at a TSR event in the early 1990s, with Julia Martin in the background. Courtesy Sue Weinlein.

Downtown Lake Geneva in the early 1990s. Courtesy Sue Weinlein.

The TSR castle at Gen Con in the 1990s. Courtesy Sue Weinlein.

Bill Connors demoing a game in the TSR castle at Gen Con 1992. Courtesy Sue Weinlein.

Sue Weinlein in her cubicle at TSR in the 1990s. Photographer unknown. Courtesy Sue Weinlein.

Behold the TSR slush pile! In the early 1990s, TSR was one of the few companies that accepted submissions from unagented authors, and those submissions awaited consideration in this pile. Courtesy Sue Weinlein.

The exterior of Sue Weinlein and Monte Cook's home, which had a prior life as a church. TSR employee and Christmas ghost Bruce Cordell haunts the door. Courtesy Sue Weinlein.

The interior of Sue Weinlein and Monte Cook's home, decked out for Christmas. Sue Weinlein stands on the stairs. Photograph by Monte Cook. Courtesy Sue Weinlein.

LEFT: Jim Lowder has gone on to a long career in the industry, and is currently executive editor at Chaosium. Photo by Denise Robinson.

BELOW: An iconic red dragon as painted by Jeff Easley. One can see why he was the highest-paid creative at the company in 1997. Courtesy Jeff Easley.

Blue dragons as painted by Jeff Easley. Courtesy Jeff Easley.

Dille said the time was less like *The Beverly Hillbillies* and more like a 1980s sitcom. "Think *Cheers* or *Seinfeld.*" There was a "central cast of ridiculous and compelling characters." Gary, the rich, middle-aged nerd newly freed from marriage and the Midwest. His thirteen-year-old son, Luke, whom he described as "the normal center" to the D&D mansion. There was Jim Johnson, Gary's "mysterious chauffeur/bodyguard."

Ernie was there too. His life had changed significantly since the days of shoving cardboard into his shoes to cover the holes in his soles. He had remade himself as an LA scenester, hitting the Troubadour and Madame Wong's, cruising West Hollywood, prowling English pubs, eating hot curry, and watching belly dancers. He dated Peggy Wilkins, an actress described as "an elegant rock and roll dream girl." Ernie remembered "bringing Peggy to California in my company Trans Am and finding her an agent." The agent landed her an audition for a South American hairstyling commercial, and she beat out two hundred other "beautiful ladies" to score the job.

Then there were the cameos. For example, Frank Miller, a friend of Dille's who would go on to revolutionize comics with titles like *300* and *The Dark Knight Returns,* would drop by the mansion to hang out.

One of the strangest episodes in Gary Gygax's adventures in LA was the company's attempted funding of a "hard R" movie—*hard R* meaning there was going to be a lot of nudity. Dille said of the concept, "Given that TSR was in the business of making products for children, this seemed like a very bad idea to me. Nobody cared that I thought it was a bad idea." The home video market was exploding. There was money to be made. When he saw the script for the proposed film, he said, "it wasn't filth; it was just kind of eighties cheese with aspirations to be more." But what he found truly amusing were the notes someone had written in the script, which included suggestions such as "More spankings" and "Good scene for a spanking."

Actress Edy Williams, known for films like *Beyond the Valley of the Dolls* and *Nudity Required,* was attached to the project. When Dille first met her, "she seemed like a fun cross between [a] businesswoman and sexy actress, which is exactly what she was." He met her again at the 1984 New Year's Eve party held at the D&D mansion. He and his girlfriend strode through the front door of the mansion and walked "straight into Edy Williams. She was wearing what can be best described as a doily dress with nothing under it. That didn't surprise me. What surprised me was what she did after." Williams removed the lampshade from a lamp, put the lamp on the floor, and stood over it. Ernie recalled another guest remarking, "I see the carpet matches the drapes."

Suffice it to say, the project was never completed. And soon, the entire LA run of the Gary Gygax Flying Gaming Circus would end.

One day, Dille showed up at the mansion when it was still dark. He went to the sunken bar in search of coffee, but found Ernie instead. Dille said he had "a look of shock on his face. It stopped me in my tracks. Something was wrong."

TSR's line of credit had just been stopped by its bank, and Gary Gygax had returned to Lake Geneva.

Was this the end?

GARY GYGAX AS UNRELIABLE NARRATOR

We must now confront an ugly fact, one that may even hurt the hearts of gamers everywhere. But it is a fact. We must throw it on the table and dissect it, or this will be no true history. Simply put, Gary Gygax did not always tell the truth when describing his time at TSR. Given the awful fate that awaits him at the hands of the company he cofounded, it is easy to see why he might play fast and loose with the facts, why he might deepen the shadows of others, such as the Blume brothers, and absolve himself of mistakes to better light the aura of Saint Gary. Because the truth is that the company's management in the first half of the 1980s made a number of disastrous errors, but by later claiming to be both out of power and ignorant, he freed himself of any responsibility for them.

Here is the tale of the crisis as related by him after the fact: The Blumes were mean-spirited and incompetent, but also so Machiavellian that they boxed him out of all major decisions at the company where he was president. Because of all of that, he went west and got the *Dungeons & Dragons* cartoon made. There, he negotiated big deals with big names, while entirely unbeknownst to him, the Blumes were burning down the company, wasting cash on idiocy and nepotism while firing staff and watching sales circle the drain. But because he was in California, which was somehow unreachable by telephone, letter, or messenger pigeon, Gary Gygax didn't know any of this was going on. In 1985, he learned that Kevin Blume was trying to sell the company. He raced back to Lake Geneva, discovered all the terrible things the Blumes had done, and made a heroic choice. He would present all of Kevin's misdeeds to the board of directors. Yes, the board consisted of the Blumes and people put on the board by the Blumes. This meant the board was more likely to remove Gygax for speaking the truth than Kevin for his mismanagement, but that didn't matter. Saint Gary the Martyr would do the right thing because his alignment was neutral good.

And then, a miracle occurred.

According to Gygax, he went to the board and was so convincing that Kevin Blume was removed, not Gary Gygax. Not even Brian Blume voted to keep his brother! Instead, he abstained. So Saint Gary, with bravado and brains, actually saved TSR!

There are certainly elements of this story that are accurate, but the truth, as it so often is, is more complicated and leaves Saint Gary much less the hero. The most salient difference is that he knew of and participated in many of the company's mistakes as they were happening. He did not live in ignorance and discover them all in a single swoop in 1985. The nepotism, the bad investments, the overextension of the business, the mistakes go on and on, yet later, he would claim not to know anything about them as they were occurring. Never mind that he was on the record defending a number of these decisions, such as the purchase of Greenfield Needlewomen. (He pointed out that "crafts is a larger field than hobbies.") Never mind that the problems were so well known that *The Wall Street Journal* ran an article in November of 1983 titled AFTER SUCCESS OF DUNGEONS & DRAGONS, TSR FIGHTS POOR MANAGEMENT, UNEVEN GROWTH, giving a fine summary of the issues that Gygax will claim to know nothing about for over a year. Never mind that this article, which discusses the problems with hiring, Greenfield Needlewomen, miniatures, and Heartquest, *includes a picture of Gary Gygax,* smiling at the reader, bespectacled in a suit.

In later interviews, he simply asks us to ignore all of that, as though a person can get their picture in *The Wall Street Journal,* detailing how the company they'd cofounded is struggling financially due to "poor management" and just not notice.

Ernie said of this portrayal of his father, "I do not necessarily agree with all the Gary Gygax comments that you've made."

While the idea that Gary Gygax did not know of these problems is nonsense, it does seem clear that in the spring of 1985, he believed he had to again take control of the company. We can surmise this based on what he did when he returned to Wisconsin. He didn't go to the board and have a dramatic showdown that resulted in Kevin's removal. Rather, he exercised an option to buy seven hundred shares of TSR stock. This, combined with his previously existing shares, and the forty shares belonging to his son Ernie, gave him 51.1 percent of all stock.

Gary Gygax was back in control at TSR. On March 29, 1985, he was named president and CEO. He was now piloting a company in dire straits. Sales were still crashing, and the company was in at least $1.5 million of debt.

He approached Flint Dille about possibly investing in the company. Flint was a successful screenwriter, and his family owned Buck Rogers. Debuting in 1928, Buck Rogers was the first sci-fi phenomenon to hit pop culture. Buck was a twentieth-century man transported five hundred years into the future, where he fought space foes such as Killer Kane and the Tiger Men of Mars. Ray guns and spaceships and derring-do abounded. His story was told in novels, comic strips, films, and radio dramas. Buck Rogers tie-in merchandise was popular. In short, Gygax needed money, and he thought Dille had it.

Flint suggested Gygax speak to his sister, Lorraine Williams.

It was an introduction that would reverberate for over a decade and change the entire future of *Dungeons & Dragons*, for good and for ill. Dille said, "As I analyze that moment, my guess is that I was just trying to dodge the issue of me or my family lending him money." Also, there was the fact that his sister was "a business type." He said she'd been working to "turn around a hospital" and had helped their father prepare to sell his company.

Gygax spoke to Williams about investing in TSR. She said that putting money into the company would simply be "money down a rat hole." Still, she was interested. She said, "I looked upon it as another great experience."

She took a position at the company as general manager and hoped to "help Gary get the ship righted."

And the ship was still in need of righting. He proposed a slate of new releases to get the company back on its feet, a rules expansion titled *Unearthed Arcana,* a Far East setting in *Oriental Adventures,* a Greyhawk novel, and several adventures. He also cut lines that weren't profitable, such as their western RPG, *Boot Hill.*

The rightsizing of the company brought Lorraine Williams and Gary Gygax into conflict. Williams said that when she proposed cuts, he had a "temper tantrum." (Many former employees agreed that he had a temper.)

Gygax, in enumerating what he saw as Williams's sins decades later, said, "She held gamers in contempt, that they were socially beneath her." He also charged "when I stated that I planned to see that the employees gained share ownership when the corporate crises were passed in recognition of their loyalty, Williams had turned to my personal assistant Gail Carpenter (now Gail Gygax, my wife) and said: 'Over my dead body!'"

Out of power at a company with shrinking sales, the Blume brothers wanted to depart. On July 22, 1985, they offered to sell their stock to Gygax at $500 a share. He refused. According to historian Jon Peterson, he did so because he considered that price to be "unreasonable."

However, the Blumes did manage to find a buyer for their shares: Lorraine Williams.

Even with all the Blumes' stock, Williams would still be a minority shareholder in TSR. To her, this was unacceptable, as it kept Gary Gygax in charge. They had clashed mightily over the direction of the company since she'd come on board, and if she was going to buy in, then damn the fact that he'd cocreated *D&D,* and damn the fact that the man had cofounded the company. He would be taken down.

The Blumes exercised an option to buy seven hundred more shares, and Williams likewise bought fifty. After these purchases, and the sale of all the Blumes' stock to her on October 21, 1985, she was left the majority shareholder in the company, a fact that was kept secret from Gygax until the following day, at 5:15 p.m., when a board meeting began. In a cruel coincidence, Gygax chaired the meeting where he was deposed. Over the next hour and a half, he would lose control of the company, be voted out as CEO and president, and be replaced by Lorraine Williams. A non-gamer had captured TSR and, with it, *Dungeons & Dragons.*

Luke Gygax said his father felt "anger and disbelief" that he'd lost control of the company he cofounded and the game he cocreated. "His life's works were in the hands of a non-gamer who didn't understand the community or what it was all about," he said.

Gygax challenged the sale in court, and the judge noted that he had been given the opportunity by the Blumes to buy them out months before their sale to Williams. Some would say that what happened on October 22, 1985, may have been legal, but that doesn't make it right.

Others might point out that the reason TSR was in such dire financial straits in 1985 was because of business decisions and failures that Gygax and the Blumes had made along the way and that if Williams hadn't purchased the company, it might not have survived.

Ernie countered that hypothetical with his own, saying, "Of course others may have said that with Kevin Blume gone and with Brian leaving as his interest waned that creativity may have spawned once again at a TSR returning to its roots, its gamer inception."

Gary Gygax was done working at TSR, but Williams and TSR were not done with him. Once ejected from the company he birthed, he became the target of unremitting and merciless legal warfare. The company threatened to sue or sued him no fewer than three times. Why? To Luke Gygax, Williams appeared to have "a personal vendetta" against his father. "Anything he did was immediately bogged down in litigation," he said. Gygax started another game company, New Infinities. It was sued by TSR and soon went bankrupt. (That said, the company had a number of problems beyond this lawsuit that contributed to its fall.)

He sold a new role-playing game, originally titled *Dangerous Dimensions* (would it have been abbreviated *DD*?), to another role-playing game company, GDW. TSR sued GDW, upset over the title, arguing that the game was derivative of first edition *Advanced Dungeons & Dragons.* Soon, GDW likewise failed. Luke said that after that, not many wanted to risk working with his father. Watching the company hound his father with a pack of baying lawyers was "dreadful," like watching the good guys get butchered on *Game of Thrones.*

TSR was sending a clear message. It would fly at him with lawsuits anytime he had the temerity to step into the role-playing arena.

Let us now pause to pity Saint Gary, who gave us so much and had so much taken from him. The game he cocreated and the company he cofounded had both passed from his power. His fate was now that of Dave Arneson, to watch the life of *Dungeons & Dragons* carry on from below and without him.

Let us also consider that this vendetta against Gygax served neither TSR nor Lorraine Williams in the long run. While the Cult of Saint Gary that has burgeoned since his death in 2008 did not exist at the time, he had stock and credit with the fans as the cofounder of role-playing. How much better would it have been to retain him within the company as a creator? Now the bad blood between the pair and the fact that Gygax had enough money to start his own company makes such a what-if unlikely. But it is an early example of a problem that will be one of the original sins of the Williams era: letting the personal come before what might be best for the company.

Williams was now the sovereign of Sheridan Springs Road. She would oversee years of growth, the release of a second edition of *Advanced Dungeons & Dragons,* and the expansion of the company in the fiction market. She would also bring about the company's death.

How would she be different from Gygax and the Blumes?

Part II

◆

THE WILLIAMS ERA

SYMPATHY FOR LORRAINE

I learned a lot from Lorraine, both the good things she did and the bad things she did. She was not always in touch with what we did, but she was very loyal. I think I'm a way better manager for having worked for her. In the end, I think she really wanted to make things work. She wanted to take the company to the next level. I think she just didn't have the capacity to understand it, and people were so afraid of her. One thing I think she gets short shrift on is, her reputation was so great and almost mythologized where people were afraid to say no *to her. I think maybe one of the reasons I lasted as long as I did there was that's one thing I did do. She once said, "Fallone, he's an acquired taste." If I thought it was wrong, I would tell her, and she appreciated me in a weird way for that, by not being a yes-person. Though she would yell at me a lot, you just got over it.*

—JIM FALLONE, TSR DIRECTOR OF SALES AND MARKETING

LORRAINE WILLIAMS DID not talk to me for this book, and I don't much blame her. The assembled hosts of geeks have been straight-up cruel to her in the decades since the fall of TSR. If you can imagine a negative quality, like as not, someone has ascribed it to her in the past decades. She has been portrayed as the schemer who stole the company from Gary Gygax and the fool who plowed it into the ground.

A persistent scurrilous rumor states that she was the model for the Lady of Pain, a character from the Planescape *AD&D* setting. The Lady of Pain is a powerful and capricious being, akin to a goddess. The Lady never speaks. She has an unknown agenda, which she violently enforces. The scuttlebutt is that you should always stay out of the Lady of Pain's way, as the few people foolish enough to worship the Lady end up flayed to death by her. But despite her cruelty and unknown ways, she is the "uncaring protector" of her city.

Those looking to link her and the Lady of Pain would point out Williams was a distant manager. Some creatives might have only had one or two encounters with her over years of employment at the company. Others only passed her in the hall. There was a perception that the closer one worked to her, the closer one was to trouble. Whether the rumor is true or not fact-checking would not reveal. But the fact that the Lady of Pain rumor has taken hold in the geek community reveals an emotional resonance. Employees and fans felt like she could have been the model for the Lady of Pain. (If true, it also seems a bit much, a sort of phantasmagorical and hysterical overreaction to a boss employees had problems with.)

She was famously purported to loathe gamers, the accusation having been read into the record by Gary Gygax himself. TSR employee Kate Novak also pointed out that Williams "wasn't a geek."

The only person to get Williams to speak on the record about her time at the company in the past twenty years was *Of Dice and Men* author David M. Ewalt. In that volume, she specifically addressed the charges against her. When discussing why she wanted to buy the company, she said, "I had grown to really like the people, and I had a lot of respect for the product. I may not have understood it 100 percent, but I understood intellectually that it was the right product for the right time."

Since Williams doesn't know me from Cain, I can understand why she wouldn't want to be interviewed for this book. But I find it frustrating because the story of TSR will always be unfinished without her telling her part.

History is thirsty for her words, and the idea of never hearing from Williams about her time at the company fills me with a profound sense of loss.

Furthermore, she was the female CEO of a predominantly male company making products for a predominantly male hobby. She was a trailblazer. And as I read some of the most intense and vicious attacks on Williams, I could not help but wonder what role misogyny might play in her villainization. Because while she made mistakes and the death of the company in 1997 is her responsibility, there were achievements during her reign that simply go unmentioned in the record.

In short, the legacy of Lorraine Williams needs reconsideration.

First, it is necessary to point out that she saved TSR from financial disaster when she took over the company in 1985, and by extension, she saved *D&D.* Some staff, weary from years of layoffs and pay deferments, were relieved to have her in control. Jeff Grubb welcomed her arrival. He said, "When she came on board, we were about two paychecks away from closing the doors. We were all on pay deferments. We were skating the thin edge right there." He said she "pretty much saved the company" because she was "a grown-up" and could "talk to banks." She even paid the staff back the money they were owed, "with interest," according to him.

This reaction by staff was not uncommon. Editor John Rateliff said, "Every single person I talked to who worked under Gary and the Blumes and then worked under Lorraine preferred working under Lorraine. With all the respect people had for Gygax and for all the stories people tell about how Lorraine mismanaged things, I never met a single person who was under both who didn't prefer being under her."

Many products created during her reign were dazzling, a high-water mark for the company in terms of quality. Those of us who were buying TSR products during the Williams era can easily be teased into waxing nostalgic over the many game worlds and boxed sets that were a feature of the time. Gamers could explore gothic horror in Ravenloft, Arabian Nights–themed adventures in Al-Qadim, interplanar scheming (and the Lady of Pain) in Planescape, and more standard fantasy in the Forgotten Realms. The list of settings produced at this time rolls on: Birthright, Greyhawk, the Council of Wyrms, Dark Sun, Mystara.

And by Arneson's beard, the boxed sets that introduced many of those settings were breathtaking! Full-color maps, posters, player guides, dice, miniatures, video cassettes, and CDs made them a feast at the gaming table. Each was masterfully completed by brilliant designers who had birthed a whole world out of nothing, making their own imaginations real for thousands of gamers.

From a fan's point of view, these products are incredible. They are storehouses of story and playgrounds for dreams. They are undeniably awesome in breadth, depth, and production value. Thanks to PDFs, gamers continue to have them as options for play, perhaps forever.

Then there was the simple fact that Williams saved William W. Connors's family.

THE EMPLOYEE WHO WASN'T ALLOWED TO QUIT

Bill Connors was a game designer hired by TSR who moved to Lake Geneva in the 1990s. One day, his wife, Kathy, attended a guided meditation session, and something happened. Connors said the meditation instructor asked Kathy to think back to when she was a child, to find some distant memory to focus on. Connors said his wife "got relaxed, and mellow, and freaked out."

Memories started coming back to her, rising up in her mind like bubbles humming to the surface. Memories of traumatic sexual abuse stretching back before kindergarten, like her father using her body to pay off his bar tab. Connors said the things that happened to his wife were the sort of things one would see on *Law & Order: SVU.*

Connors said oftentimes repressed memories come back when the person finally feels safe enough to remember them and that perhaps the move to Wisconsin and their new life with friends in Lake Geneva finally allowed her to feel safe.

Kathy's mental state began to deteriorate. She started having panic attacks. Connors described them as "crippling." During a camping trip, fireworks set her off.

Things for Kathy got worse and worse. Finally, she required hospitalization, for fear that she would hurt herself.

It is worth mentioning that during our interview, Bill Connors wore what appeared to be the One Ring on a chain around his neck. As we spoke about his wife and her troubles, he clutched the ring and chain with both hands. Tightly. But he kept talking. Later, he told me it was his wedding ring and was inscribed with the words TOGETHER FOREVER.

Eventually, his wife was cleared for release from the hospital, but Connors said, "It became really clear that she was going to need a lot of help at home." He decided he would quit to take care of his wife. He went in and resigned.

But Lorraine Williams would not accept his resignation. He was too important to the company. The treatment Bill Connors received over the coming years was nothing less than royal. He was advanced vacation time as needed so he could be at home and take care of his wife. He was advanced paychecks to cover medical expenses. He devoted the vast majority of his time for the next few months to his wife's recovery, sneaking in once or twice a week to work. But in all of that time, the company never delayed a paycheck or even decreased his pay. Furthermore, his coworkers stepped up to help finish projects, and no one ever so much as whispered a word of criticism about Bill for being unable to give 100 percent at work.

So while Williams made mistakes as CEO of TSR, and the bulk of this book is devoted to discussing them, it is important to balance out that ledger. She likely saved *D&D* when she bought the company, and she produced games that are still cooed over and emulated today. Furthermore, while she made mistakes in business, that does not mean she was a bad person. Perhaps no story highlights this fact quite like that of William W. Connors.

BUCK ROGERS IN THE LATE TWENTIETH CENTURY

As a businesswoman, Williams had limitations. At times, she seemed to treat the company like a speedboat. It was an impressive and gorgeous thing, and it was hers. Therefore, she could do with it as she pleased.

One apparent example of this sort of thinking involved Buck Rogers. After her ascension as CEO, she ordered the company to begin producing Buck material. Novels, board games, and role-playing games vomited forth to spiritless fanfare and craptastic sales.

Yet the company kept making Buck Rogers products. At the GAMA Expo trade show in 1993, after announcing a new iteration of the Buck Rogers RPG, Jim Ward said, "We're going to keep making it until you buy it." It sounded more like a threat than a sales pitch.

Further down the ranks, the production of Buck Rogers material was met with general scorn. The staff saw that the public wasn't interested. Likewise, the staff knew that because the property was owned by Williams and her family, the company would keep making Buck products. Some thought it was to help retain copyright, others thought it was so the company would pay for the rights to use Buck and his associated characters (payments that would have been made to the Dille Family Trust), while others believed it was an attempt to make Buck Rogers cool again.

Perhaps there was some brilliant reason for the production of Buck Rogers material, but I can't see it, and Williams refused to speak with me for this volume, so I am left believing that the decision to keep publishing these products may be an example of the speedboat thinking that would lead the company to financial ruin. It was likely a decision made in spite of sales data, not because of it. It was a decision to create products Williams wanted to make, not what their customers wanted to buy. It seemed to be a decision to use the company to further her own interests.

And because the company was hers, who could tell her no? It was her speedboat. If she wanted to make high-velocity turns, even if people spilled their drinks or the kids fell overboard, who could tear the wheel away from her?

Another ultimately destructive practice of Williams's time as CEO was the inability to retain genius-level staff at the company. This was seen early on with the departure of a pair whose sales had helped keep the company afloat during the worst of the dark days . . .

THE DEPARTURE OF WEIS AND HICKMAN

And I will show that whatever happens to anybody it may be turn'd to beautiful results.

—WALT WHITMAN, *LEAVES OF GRASS*

TSR WAS A company that discovered geniuses and paid them to create worlds for the rest of us to live in. The company knew it needed brilliant minds to do this work. It went to great lengths to find creative souls to employ. Yet it was less than careful about retaining them. Once these worlds were created, management's attitude seemed to be that these great minds could be replaced with cheaper labor. So *New York Times* bestselling authors and pioneering game designers would be discovered, nurtured, and then allowed to leave the company. It happened to Dave Arneson and Gary Gygax. It was a fate that would also befall Margaret Weis and Tracy Hickman.

Margaret Weis said that the success of Dragonlance "changed my life," because it allowed her to leave TSR.

Why did Weis want to leave? Her work at the company transformed her from a book editor to a *New York Times* bestselling author. And why couldn't the company convince her to remain? It had discovered her, nurtured her, and marketed her as an author for years. The company had a vested financial interest in keeping Weis right where she was, producing Dragonlance novels. Why couldn't it do so?

When I asked Weis why she left, she immediately spoke of Lorraine Williams. She clearly felt that Williams took the company in the wrong direction. She said, "The creative spirit in the company seemed to die when Gary was gone. He truly cared about *D&D.* After he was ousted, management seemed to care only about making money, though without any real idea of how to do it. All the while spending money on wasteful projects such as remodeling offices and promoting self-interests, such as Buck Rogers." Weis added, "I never really interacted a whole lot with Lorraine, but when I did, I really didn't like it."

Furthermore, TSR was simply not paying Margaret Weis what she was worth. Weis and Hickman proposed another book series, titled the Darksword Trilogy. The books would tell the story of a man born into a world where everyone has magical powers, but he was born without them. The company decided to pass on it. Weis and Hickman then took the Darksword Trilogy to Bantam Books. A few weeks passed, and the pair's agent, Ray Puechner, called Weis to say that Bantam wanted to make an offer.

Weis said, "Oh, wow! That's really cool."

Puechner said, "And they want the whole trilogy."

Weis said, "Great."

"And they're going to offer you thirty thousand dollars." (That's almost $75,000 in today's money.)

Weis was excited by that number. She said, "We'd been getting a pittance from TSR," for the novels they'd been writing, so $30,000 for the trilogy seemed like a great deal of money.

Enthused, Weis said to Puechner, "Thirty thousand for three books!"

And Puechner said, "No, no, no. That's for *each book.*"

Weis said, "Oh my gosh!"

At the time, Weis said that even though she was a bestselling author whose work had helped keep the company afloat during troubled times, she wasn't making $30,000 a year. The company was paying her like a freight handler or entry-level graphic designer.

She called Tracy Hickman to tell him the good news, and that was when they decided to leave the company. The capitalist calculus of it all was brutal and swift. Bantam was offering them more than their annual salary per novel. It was more money for less work. Who wouldn't take that offer?

Success at TSR meant that Weis and Hickman could leave TSR.

When artist Larry Elmore heard that Weis and Hickman would be departing to write fantasy novels for Bantam, he wanted a piece of the action. Could they get him the job of painting the cover of the first novel?

It is worth noting that to the artists working in Lake Geneva, painting fantasy covers for the New York publishing houses was seen as the big time. Doing their novel cover would be a real step up in terms of prestige for Elmore.

The publication of a book by Bantam was a similar step up for Weis and Hickman, and when she responded to Elmore's request, she had skyscrapers and Times Square on her mind. She said, "I don't know, Larry. This is a big New York publisher."

But she wouldn't forget his request.

Later, the pair were flown to New York by Bantam. There, in the city where shining towers touch the sky and the subway trains rumble like dragons in their dens, the bigwigs at Bantam took them out for lunch.

Margaret Weis of Independence, Missouri, was meeting with a major publisher in a city so absolute and grand and final that on the East Coast you can simply say *the City,* and everyone knows you're talking about New York. She described her emotional state at that moment on the day she was taken out for lunch in New York City with a single syllable of onomatopoeia: "Woo!"

But despite the majesty of her surroundings and the corresponding majesty of the bigwigs taking her out for lunch, she didn't forget Larry Elmore, who was stuck back in Lake Geneva, Wisconsin, painting in the former Q-tip factory on Sheridan Springs Road.

But the skyscrapers and the food and the suits! What would the bigwigs say about Larry Elmore? Would they say they never heard of him? Would they laugh at her for being a mid-country rube to think that her friend who painted elves and dragons in outstate Wisconsin could make the grade in New York City?

Weis recalled that "with fear and trepidation, I said, 'You know, if it would be at all possible, Larry Elmore would really love to do the cover . . .'"

One of the bigwigs replied, "Oh my God. We were going to ask you if there was any way you could get Larry Elmore to do the cover!"

Elmore was hired, and not long after, he left the company as well.

The Darksword Trilogy was published by Bantam in 1988, along with a role-playing game called *Darksword Adventures.* Each had a cover by Larry Elmore. One can see in these books the outline of the product that might have been if it had been picked up by TSR. Clearly, a trilogy of novels would have been written, along with a series of adventures set in the world. But it was not to be. Weis and Hickman were gone.

Yet as was so often the case, TSR was not done with them.

Years passed. Weis and Hickman went on to write another trilogy, titled Rose of the Prophet, again published by Bantam, again with covers by Larry Elmore, but set in a fantastic ideation of the Middle East, with sheikhs and djinns and a pantheon of twenty gods.

Weis doesn't remember at what convention or in what year Lorraine Williams threatened to sue her, but it was definitely at a convention. It wasn't Gen Con, of that much she is certain. But it was at a convention, and Williams was there.

Weis was in the middle of a conversation when Williams appeared. She had a simple message to convey: She was considering suing her and Hickman over Rose of the Prophet. She believed that the pair had worked on material for the trilogy while at TSR. If so, it was company property under their contracts, and she had standing to sue.

With that, like a bad dream, Williams was gone.

If she had threatened to sue over the Darksword Trilogy, it would at least have made sense. The Darksword Trilogy was obviously developed while the pair had been at TSR. The company, after all, had turned the project down. The acceptance of the trilogy by Bantam and their commensurate pay raise was the reason the pair had left. The idea that Williams and her baying pack of lawyers could have found any hard, tangible proof that the pair had worked on Rose of the Prophet at the company years after they left was at best unlikely. Furthermore, given the pair's talents and proven sales track record, she should have been trying to woo them back by hook, crook, love, or money. Instead, she was haunting them at conventions to make illogical threats of legal action. That was likely to irritate Weis and Hickman, not win them back into the fold. And from the point of view of the bottom line, that was the winning move here: Get them back writing Dragonlance. After all, the pair were still making money for the company, selling tens of thousands of copies of their novels every year.

For their part, neither Weis nor Hickman took the threat to heart. Weis said, "It didn't mean a whole lot. We actually thought it was just kind of funny."

Yet to approach one of them at a convention to threaten a lawsuit seemed so excessively aggressive. Why would the CEO of a multimillion-dollar company do that?

Weis said, "You had to know Lorraine."

The break between TSR and Weis and Hickman seemed complete. Why would the pair ever come back while she was casually threatening frivolous lawsuits against them?

It is worth pausing for a moment to measure the caliber of disaster that the departure of Weis and Hickman represented. You couldn't swing a vorpal sword in the company offices without beheading a genius. Every department was thick with them, women and men whose minds sparkled like obsidian in firelight. Given the success of Dragonlance, Weis and Hickman were certainly geniuses. But I believe I have interviewed dozens of company alumni that I would rank as creative geniuses for this book. So curiously, the quality that might make Weis and Hickman stand out against the general populace was not what made them stand out at the company.

They were—there is no other word for it—stars. Perhaps the first the company produced after Gygax himself. They had fanatical devotees who knew their names, even if in confusion they misgendered Tracy Hickman. The company sold fourteen million copies of Dragonlance novels, settings, and adventures by 1997. At conventions, people would crowd their table for autographs. For years at Gen Con, Tracy Hickman hosted two-hour sessions of what he called "Killer Breakfast." Fans came onstage with *D&D* characters, and Hickman killed them as amusingly as possible, sometimes dispatching up to two hundred in a go. Other fans have taken their books to war with them. One wounded veteran returned from Afghanistan and gifted the pair his Bronze Star and Purple Heart, saying they deserved them because the Dragonlance novels helped him earn those medals.

To call the people faithful to the works of Weis and Hickman a fan base is to damn with faint praise. The pair reached out with their words and touched something elemental and profound within their readers.

Yet TSR seemed to believe that sort of allegiance from an audience could be replaced. It acted on a theory of interchangeable creativity, as though a novel or adventure would sell equally well irrespective of who produced it. Writers were machines that made words to sell. Other machines would make words if they would not.

Acting on this theory set a pattern that would recur again and again during the Williams era: The company would discover and support talent. That talent would mature, make amazing products, then leave, often due to low pay or perceived disrespect.

Once Weis and Hickman were gone, along came a crisis: What fantasy setting would replace Dragonlance, and what author would replace them?

LOST REALMS FOUND AGAIN

Elminster came up the path, a grey spectre in his cowled cloak, looked around the garden, pipe in hand, nodded thoughtfully, and said, "Let's go in." The cozy corner where he is wont to sit was much warmer; Elminster sank down with a sigh of contentment and accepted a mug of cocoa. "Thank'ee," he said, and swung his feet up onto the clawed footstool—and the footstool clawed him back! It was Stardust—the one of our cats black as night save for the four white hairs that gave her her name.

—ED GREENWOOD, "NINE WANDS OF WONDER," *DRAGON* #102

SETTINGS HAD BECOME a reliable way for TSR to make money. For example, 1983's *World of Greyhawk Fantasy Game Setting* sold very well, moving over 120,000 copies in its first year of release, while 1987's *Dragonlance Adventures* sold over 130,000 copies its first year and marked the last significant work for Margaret Weis and Tracy Hickman at the company in the 1980s.

But Greyhawk was a world created by Gary Gygax, and Weis and Hickman were now gone from Dragonlance. It would be handy to publish a game world whose creator was still on good terms with the company.

Jeff Grubb would find the next big setting, one so popular that material for it is still being produced today. He grew up in Mt. Lebanon, Pennsylvania, just a trolley ride away from downtown Pittsburgh. He trained as a civil engineer, but was hired by TSR as a game designer. There, he would prove himself a Jim Thorpe of creativity. (Thorpe is widely considered one of the most versatile athletes of all time, winning Olympic medals in the pentathlon and the decathlon, as well as playing football, basketball, and baseball professionally.) Over the course of his career, Grubb would create settings, adventures, novels, comic books, and video games. And like Thorpe, he excelled in writing each and every one.

When looking for a new setting, Grubb noted that a Canadian librarian named Ed Greenwood had been writing articles in *Dragon* for years using a mage named Elminster. Typically, the articles would be framed as though Elminster came to visit Greenwood at home in Ontario, as in the example above, and the rest of the article would be the mage holding forth on a topic such as "The Ecology of the Ochre Jelly." His pieces were lushly written, wry, and informative. The framing device was particularly enchanting, allowing the reader to pretend that the world of the fantastic was so close to our own that wizards could stop by for cocoa.

But where did Elminster come from? Did Ed Greenwood have more material on Elminster's world? That might be the start of something. Grubb called up Greenwood and asked him if he had more information on that world, and if so, would he be willing to sell it?

Greenwood replied, "Well. You've been publishing my stuff all along. I thought you already owned it."

Grubb said, "I'm not going to tell anybody that. Let's buy your stuff."

And so in January of 1987, the company purchased the Forgotten Realms universe from Ed Greenwood. The company acquired the Forgotten Realms in exchange for a lump sum payment of $4,000 and $1,000 for "the Author's services as a design consultant." In the contract, Ed Greenwood gave up to TSR, absolutely and forever, all his rights, title, and interest throughout the world in and to the Forgotten Realms. Grubb described the deal as a relatively modest amount of cash, a Macintosh II computer, and a promise to publish novels Greenwood wrote. Grubb said, "Later, when we were very happy with him, we bought him a hard drive to go with the computer." Given the value the Forgotten Realms has accrued in the decades since, the purchase seems a steal.

Grubb, as Greenwood's primary contact in Lake Geneva, said he became the setting's "de facto product manager." Shaping Greenwood's twenty years of background material into a boxed set would be a journey. He said the material arriving in Lake Geneva from Greenwood was "rough." It needed an editorial hand. Greenwood would cut up pages he'd already typed up, paste them together in a new order, and then photocopy them. At one point, the *T* key on his typewriter died, so Greenwood filled in every *T* on his work by hand. Grubb said, "It was like reading a graveyard on every page."

Every package from Greenwood was, of course, shipped from Canada, and Grubb said he would wrap packages "within an inch of their lives." If Greenwood was sending a floppy disk, first he would wrap it in foil. Then, he would wrap it in "heavy Canadian cellophane." He would then pair the disk with a manuscript and then wrap that in heavy Canadian cellophane. This would then go into an envelope, which would again get the cellophane treatment. He wrapped up his words with a care verging on paranoia of the sort one would imagine is reserved for moon rocks and artifacts from King Tut's tomb. Anne Brown, who worked in the cubicle next to Grubb, told him she always knew when Greenwood had sent him more of the Realms, because he would spend fifteen minutes unwrapping the damn thing, and all she'd hear was "the rustle of heavy Canadian cellophane and mild cursing."

Despite this, Grubb said there was "beauty" already visible in Greenwood's Realms. Between the handwritten *T*s and photocopied pages, he would find drawings and maps. Grubb asked Greenwood to send him a map of the entire Realms. He received from Canada a twenty-four-sheet, A4-size, loose paper map that Grubb taped together and hung on his wall. (Research suggests the map may have been fifty-five sheets, but either way, it was big.)

Because the map was hand-drawn by Greenwood, transcription errors did occur. For example, a site labeled on Greenwood's map as "cavemouth" was misread by Grubb and became "the Lost Empire of Cavenauth." He said that Greenwood was "accommodating" about the changes made to his maps, which included draining half of the Great Glacier, redrawing the Moonshae Isles, and adding the Ten Towns.

Greenwood also sent a map of Waterdeep, the City of Splendors and possibly the most important metropolis in the Realms, which was even bigger. "It was impossible to hang anywhere but the stairwell," said Grubb. When Sales and Marketing saw the map hanging there, they decided a product had to be based on it. What resulted was *City System,* a product that contains twelve full-color maps of Waterdeep, ten of which go together to create a massive map of the city, including over two hundred locations. Years later, out in Seattle at the AFK Tavern, Grubb saw all the maps of Waterdeep from *City System* put together and on display. It covered the height of a two-story wall.

The name Forgotten Realms came from Greenwood's idea that "the Realms were always there, right next door, but we had forgotten them." We fools had eaten of the tree of knowledge and been cast into this gray, low world while they still lived in a highland of gods and magic.

What are the Forgotten Realms? They are a world akin to thirteenth-century Earth, which, as the *Forgotten Realms Campaign Set* described, had

> until recently been covered by wild forests and unsettled grasslands. Civilization is still a novelty in much of this world; even the oldest of cities on the Inland Sea, or the founding of Waterdeep, the greatest City of the North, are within the memory of the oldest living elves of Evermeet. City-states are common, and nations on the increase as more of the wild lands are pushed back and gathered under a single king or government.

It seems almost a generic setting for an *AD&D* game, presenting obvious themes of civilization against the wilds, with plenty of dangerous locales for adventurers to explore.

The foundational secret to the success of the Forgotten Realms was the team of Greenwood and Grubb. Greenwood had been setting stories in the Realms since 1968. The setting actually predated *Dungeons & Dragons*! Imagining the Realms for all of those years gave Greenwood a vast knowledge to deploy in Forgotten Realms products. Meanwhile, Jeff Grubb was a creativity machine and lovely writer who knew TSR and *AD&D.*

The first Forgotten Realms game product was a boxed set, the *Forgotten*

Realms Campaign Set, and it has not grown old in the three decades since its release. Rather, it has ripened. Despite the passage of years, it is still fresh, intriguing, and fun. It makes you want to spend time in the Realms with the characters created by Greenwood and Grubb. Great gaming products have a density of good ideas that inspire DMs and that can be turned into encounters at the gaming table. This quality of density is more important than being complete or making total sense. And good ideas abound in the *Forgotten Realms Campaign Set.*

Let's start on page 17 of the *DM's Sourcebook of the Realms,* a booklet from the 1987 boxed set, wherein Greenwood and Grubb introduced readers to characters such as Masyr, an illusionist who uses his powers to make shoddy equipment look serviceable and then resells it during times of trouble at inflated prices, and Elminster of Shadowdale, whose age is unknown, and "may be the most knowledgeable and well-informed individual in the realms, though this may be only his own opinion."

Giving such intriguing characters a prominent place was wise, as it is often characters that bring players back to the gaming table. Such characters are a delight for the DM to portray, and it's easy to see how both could be used to inspire an adventure. For example, Masyr, who has finally been caught for his crimes, needs to be transported to trial and keeps using his illusion spells to try to escape. Or the PCs have a question, and they must travel through all manner of danger and devilry to reach Elminster, the only mage wise enough to answer them. Or is he?

The book goes on to describe "Recent News and Rumors in the Realms." It is a chapter of gossip and chin-wag, and the rumors it lays out are trampolines for the imagination, allowing DMs to jump on them and make adventures of their own. For example, there are whispers of a dragon near Archendale that is eating whole herds of cattle by night. The chapter also breathlessly tells us, "Rumors are rampant in the North that there is a new Beast Lord."

Lastly, Keith Parkinson's art must be mentioned. He painted a world of mottled grays and mists, hidden castles, and lone horsemen. One cover shows a man in white being attacked by some foul creature on horseback; the only splash of color in the piece is the blood on the edge of the creature's axe, which is about to plunge into the man's exposed neck. It seemed a world where good would have to face down the darkest evil, and good might not win out in the end . . .

The Forgotten Realms seemed like a hit, and creatively, it certainly was. But sales numbers tell a different story. After selling 79,759 copies in its first year, the 1987 boxed set settled into selling a comfortable 20,000-ish copies a year until 1993. The Realms were updated in 1990's *Forgotten Realms Adventures*, which outsold even the first edition boxed set in its first year, moving 81,904 copies. (In fairness, though, *Adventures* was released in March and the boxed set in July, giving *Adventures* an extra three months to move those numbers.) The boxed set didn't stop selling until 1993, when it was replaced by the *Forgotten Realms Campaign Setting, Revised.* That revision only moved 36,186 units its first year.

TITLE	FIRST YEAR SALES	TOTAL SALES BEFORE 1999
Forgotten Realms Campaign Set (1987)	79,759	207,016
Forgotten Realms Adventures (1990)	81,904	116,343
Forgotten Realms Campaign Setting, Revised (1993)	36,186	106,782
Total Core Setting Sales:	197,849	430,141

Even though the Forgotten Realms was so absorbing and wonderful and inspiring that adventures are still being produced for it today, the sales numbers pointed to a problem: TSR wasn't selling product like it used to. The *Forgotten Realms Campaign Set* sold less than *Dragonlance Adventures* or the *World of Greyhawk Fantasy Game Setting* before it, and the *Forgotten Realms Campaign Setting, Revised* represented a crash from even those lesser numbers.

If creating new settings was a way for the company to bring in money, it was a trick that was growing less profitable over time.

Looking over the history of sales at TSR, the bestselling products were always *AD&D* rule books or boxed sets for the more basic *Dungeons & Dragons* game. Was there some way to remake those products and sell them again to the fan base?

What about novels? The Hickman and Weis books sold terrifically well. What if the company went out and found more great authors? Could novel sales help keep it afloat?

HOW TO FIND A BESTSELLING AUTHOR

IN THE LATE 1980s, the search for something to replace Dragonlance and Greyhawk in the Games Department was mirrored in the Book Department, which had to find new talent akin to that of the departed Weis and Hickman. Mary Kirchoff would be the woman to do it because Mary Kirchoff had an eye for writing talent. She could go through a stack of unpublished authors' manuscripts and pick out the one with the chops to write novels so popular, so unputdownable, that they land on the *New York Times* bestseller list.

A graduate of Badger High School in Lake Geneva, Kirchoff found employment at TSR in March of 1982 through fellow Badger alumnus Ernie Gygax. She worked on the second floor of the converted hotel in downtown Lake Geneva that served as the company headquarters at the time, and while others found the building as wretched as some forgotten circle of hell, she said, "It had a lot of character." In the Games Department, she found something else of interest to her, an Iowa boy who'd moved north to Wisconsin to design games: Steve Winter. The pair would be married in 1985.

Kirchoff left the company to freelance in 1984. She wanted to spend her time writing books, and that was what she did until 1987, when Book Department head Jean Black approached Kirchoff about coming back to the company.

Much like when Black hired Margaret Weis specifically to shepherd the Dragonlance fiction line into existence, Black hired Kirchoff with a mission in mind: She was to find the next Margaret Weis and Tracy Hickman, but instead of writing in the world of Dragonlance, they would be working in TSR's newest setting, the Forgotten Realms. She was told to go into the slush pile and find this next bestselling author. When unsolicited queries and manuscripts are sent to a publisher, they end up in the slush pile. Given that the submissions are usually from un-agented and unpublished authors looking for their break, the slush pile is often large, and thick with work of spotty quality. But un-agented first-time authors had written many books for the company, and unlike many larger publishing houses, TSR saw the slush pile as a legitimate source of talent.

Kirchoff would bundle thick novels home with her at night, plumbing the depths of the slush pile looking for talent. After a month, she found nothing and no one of note.

One night, she was lying in bed reading with her husband, Steve. The manuscript was titled *Echoes of the Fourth Magic*. It was about a submarine sucked into a postapocalyptic future that resembled a fantasy world. She leaned over in bed and said to Steve Winter, "I don't particularly like this story, but I like this writing."

The book was written by one Robert Salvatore.

She said, "What I found in [Salvatore's] manuscript was compelling characters, and his narrative was fast-paced. I mean, you wanted to keep reading it."

When asked to recall what stood out most about meeting R. A. "Bob" Salvatore for the first time, with decades to look back on the moment, Kirchoff said, "He was a quintessential Boston, Massachusetts, guy."

With that, we need to take a look at the man who would go on to be the next breakout star to burst from the Book Department: R. A. Salvatore.

A MASSACHUSETTS MAN

To say that someone is a Massachusetts man is to summarize a book's worth of ideas and principles into two words. The Massachusetts man is unyielding as stone in defense of his values, sometimes even to the point of stubbornness. The Massachusetts man is a loyal and eternal friend, although he will not stand being taken advantage of. Like a street fighter checking the layout of an alley before throwing the first punch, the Massachusetts man sees the world as it truly is and discerns how to move to his advantage.

Robert Salvatore was a Massachusetts man, Leominster-born and -raised. He was the youngest of seven children and had five older sisters. He was shy as a child and said he would skip school to read, until "school beat the reading out of me."

A Christmas gift when he was in college would bring the world of books rushing back to Bob Salvatore. By then, Salvatore said he was a "math / physics / computer science guy" who saw a future career in one of those fields. But that Christmas, his sister Susan gave him a copy of *The Hobbit* and *The Lord of the Rings* by J. R. R. Tolkien.

His Christmas wish that year was for money, not books about short and hairy thieves and evil jewelry. He needed cash because his car was breaking down every day. He threw the books to the side of the room because, he said, "I was upset with that Christmas gift."

Then, on February 7, 1978, a record-setting nor'easter hit Massachusetts. Flood tides peaked at over fifteen feet, destroying thousands of homes. High winds of over ninety-two miles per hour were recorded on Cape Cod. Two to four feet of snow buried Massachusetts, and it was made worse by the wind. Plows would clear roads only to have the winds cover them again. Route 495 was shut down. Countless cars were abandoned in drifts of snow.

Bob Salvatore was stuck at his mother's house. Trapped, and after days of boredom, he put on Fleetwood Mac's *Rumours* and opened *The Hobbit.*

Love for reading swelled inside him again, as it had before school had beaten it out of him.

Salvatore switched his major to communications media and started reading again. He said, "I read every fantasy book I could get my hands on." He tore through the fantasy canon of the time. "Then when I ran out of books to read, I wrote one," he said. "I was working in a plastics factory all day, and I was working as a bouncer at night. And when I came home, I was too amped up to go to sleep. I put candles on. I put on an album, usually *Tusk,* and I just started writing in a three-ring binder."

Meanwhile, he got married, had kids, and moved on to be a financial specialist at GenRad in Concord, Massachusetts. But his passion for reading, writing, and fantasy continued.

By 1983, Salvatore had completed a novel he titled *Echoes of the Fourth Magic,* and he sent it to a number of agents and publishers and received back nothing but rejection letters, which, he recalled, "really pissed me off."

In 1987, Salvatore sent *Echoes of the Fourth Magic* to Lake Geneva, Wisconsin, where it landed on the desk of Mary Kirchoff.

A few months after sending the novel off to the company, Salvatore came home from work, and his wife told him Mary Kirchoff from TSR called.

"Somebody called?" he responded. He was used to rejection coming in the form of a letter. People who were rejecting you did not call you. And he had been called! She left a number and wanted him to call her back. Because of the time difference, he could still phone her!

His wife said, "Take the dog out."

Salvatore said, "He can wait," dialed Lake Geneva, and got Mary Kirchoff. She said she enjoyed the novel, but she didn't have room on the publishing schedule for any books that weren't based on a *D&D* setting. Could Salvatore possibly turn this into a Forgotten Realms novel?

The dog, tired of waiting, urinated on Salvatore's foot.

"What," Salvatore asked, "is the Forgotten Realms?"

The first Realms fiction release, Douglas Niles's novel *Darkwalker on Moonshae,* which predated the release of the setting's boxed set by a month, hadn't yet come out. (*Darkwalker* came out in June of 1987, followed by the boxed set in July.) The only way to hear about the Forgotten Realms in 1987 was in *Dragon* magazine, and Salvatore was not a regular reader.

Once Kirchoff brought Salvatore up to speed on the Realms, he said that he couldn't make the book into a Realms novel because *Echoes of the Fourth Magic* began on Earth and then went forward into a postapocalyptic future that resembled fantasy. The novel starts with a submarine caught in the Bermuda Triangle during a storm being sucked into Earth's far future, making a translation to the Realms a difficult project at best. (Though it is fun to imagine: "Elminster shook his beard, turned, and said to Submarine Commander Mitchell, 'Dive!'")

Still interested in Salvatore's writing ability, Kirchoff offered to let him audition for the second Forgotten Realms novel. To brief him on the setting, they sent him *Darkwalker on Moonshae.* Salvatore loved it. He wrote a synopsis and sample chapter of a novel titled at the time *The Tyrant of Icewind Dale.*

On July 11, 1987, Salvatore received a call from Mary Kirchoff. She said, "Well, Bob, I've got good news, and I've got bad news. The good news is you've won it. You're writing the second Forgotten Realms novel, and you're going to be a published author."

"Wow," Salvatore said. "What could possibly be the bad news?"

"The bad news is we need it on October 1."

At the time, Salvatore was still working full-time with an hour-long commute each way to his job as a financial specialist. Compounding matters, at home he had a three-year-old and a two-year-old, and his wife was pregnant.

What did Salvatore say? He told Mary Kirchoff, "No problem." He took the gig "because I wanted to be a published author, and I went and I wrote *The Crystal Shard.*"

Salvatore was "very colorful by midwestern standards," Kirchoff said. "I remember thinking of him like Tony Danza. This extroverted Italian guy was writing our books now. He was affable, with not a lot of attitude. Especially in the early days, he was thirsty for feedback and very receptive. To be honest, I think we taught each other how to do publishing. I didn't have much more experience being a book editor than Bob had at being a book author at that time. We taught each other how to have a great collaborative relationship."

When Kirchoff was hired by Black, the bulk of her experience had been in magazines and in writing. Now, she took on the task of editing Salvatore's upcoming novel.

In magazines, she'd been a copy editor, and copy editors, Kirchoff said, "are like the accountants of publishing." Copy editors look at accuracy, readability, and the matching of a piece with house style. It is a mechanical, by rote, task. Now, Kirchoff was being asked to be a manuscript editor. A manuscript editor, Kirchoff said, was like an artist. Manuscript editors looked at plot, character, and style.

Over decades of writing and editing books, Kirchoff would come to realize that "editors are just readers with opinions. Developing those opinions is partly instinctive and partly it's practice." She would come to believe that good editing was not about getting an author to write the book that she wanted them to write but rather to help and encourage the author to produce the best version of the book that they wanted to write.

One of her first notes to Salvatore was about his characters. He had used some of Doug Niles's characters and settings in his pitch, and they all had to be removed. He had to write a new corner of the Realms. She wanted to differentiate the Forgotten Realms books from the Dragonlance books that had come before. The Dragonlance saga was about a central group of heroes, and whenever novels strayed from them, sales suffered. The Forgotten Realms, though, was a gigantic world. Authors could claim pieces of the geography and develop them with their own characters and stories. The company could then watch which authors' series did better and double down on those. This also set up an opportunity because there was now room for a sidekick to Salvatore's hero, the barbarian Wulfgar.

This news came to Salvatore in another call from Mary Kirchoff. He was happy not to use Niles's characters and said he would get back to Kirchoff with some ideas for a sidekick in a few days.

Kirchoff said, "No, Bob, you don't understand. I gotta go to a meeting to tell the marketing team about your book. I need to get them excited, and I need a sidekick for Wulfgar."

Salvatore looked at the clock. It was nearly noon.

He said, "Look, I won't take lunch. I'll work for you, and come up with a sidekick for Wulfgar—"

"Bob, you're not understanding. I'm standing across the hall from a room where I'm late for a meeting with the sales force. And I need a sidekick for Wulfgar."

Salvatore, panic hitting him, said off the top of his head, "A drow."

There was a long pause in Lake Geneva as Kirchoff digested the idea.

Salvatore continued, "A drow ranger that fights with two swords. Yeah, that'll be cool."

Kirchoff said, "A drow? A drow ranger?"

"Yeah, it should be cool. Nobody's ever done that before."

"Bob, there is probably a reason why nobody's ever done that before."

Salvatore said, "No, no, no, no, that'll be cool. Drow ranger."

The pair bickered over it a bit more until Kirchoff relented. "Since it's a sidekick character, I'll let you get away with it. What's his name?"

Recalling the moment decades later, Salvatore said, "Off the top of my head, I have no idea how or why, or whatever, I said, 'Drizzt Do'Urden of Menzoberranzan.'"

She said, "Can you spell that?"

"Not a chance," he replied.

Thus one of the icons of *Dungeons & Dragons* was created. The drow, also known as dark elves, are a subterranean race of spider-worshipping elves. They are, of course, evil.

Except for Drizzt.

Drizzt was neither evil nor cruel, but marked by the color of his skin, the outside world would see him as such. Drizzt would react to their hatred and fear and prejudice not with violence but with peace.

Salvatore described Drizzt as "the classic romantic hero—misunderstood, holding to a code of ideals even when the going gets tough, and getting no appreciation for it most of the time." As of this writing, Drizzt Do'Urden has been featured in thirty-one novels, and Salvatore has regularly landed on the *New York Times* bestseller list.

In a miracle of speed writing, Salvatore turned in the first draft of *The Crystal Shard* in mid-September, beating his October deadline.

In reading the first draft, Kirchoff couldn't help but notice that while the novel was supposed to be about a barbarian character named Wulfgar, he was being overshadowed by a member of the supporting cast. In a long phone call to give notes on the novel, she told Salvatore, "Wulfgar is not your most interesting character. You gotta bring out this dark elf. So in the revision, give me more Drizzt."

According to Salvatore, one of the biggest changes she asked for was the inclusion of a female character in the book. He said that at the time, "fantasy was chicks in chain mail and damsels in distress as far as female characters went."

Salvatore said of Kirchoff's request for inclusion, "Thank God. That was the big missing ingredient in my writing." He added Catti-brie, a human adopted by dwarves, to the novel. The character would go on to be a love interest for Drizzt. Fifteen days after he turned in the final draft of *The Crystal Share,* his daughter, Caitlin, or Catti-brie, was born.

Salvatore's first three books for the company, the Icewind Dale trilogy, were a huge success. The first two volumes sold over 1.5 million copies combined worldwide, and the concluding volume, *The Halfling's Gem,* hit the *New York Times* list of paperback bestsellers on March 4, 1990, in the twelfth slot. In celebration, he got a phone call from fantasy author Terry Brooks telling him how his life was never again going to be the same.

The man who wrote as R. A. Salvatore would go on to be the next star to emerge from the company. Years later, at a restaurant outside of Gen Con, I stumbled on an R. A. Salvatore event. On the way to the bathroom, I found a line stretching halfway across the restaurant. At first, I worried it was the line for the bathroom, so I asked someone waiting in it what it was for.

"R. A. Salvatore is signing books," she said.

Sure enough, at the front of the long, long line was the man himself. Pen in hand, he joked with his fans.

So it happened that Mary Kirchoff discovered a new star author, while for Bob Salvatore, the company provided a gateway to the world of publishing.

Perhaps this was where the company's future lay: bestselling novels. If so, TSR should have done everything it could to keep the authors it had developed and sought out new talent to augment the department.

Regrettably, the company seemed to learn nothing from the losses of Arneson, Gygax, Weis, and Hickman. It would repeat them with all the regularity of a scratched record.

Meanwhile, the Games Department had its own problems. *AD&D* rule book sales were not even a quarter of what they were in the early 1980s. Was there some way to revitalize the game and improve sales?

D&D, NOW ADVANCED AND 2.0!

The ten years of experience I've had in game design has shown me what works and what doesn't and sometimes even why.

—DAVID "ZEB" COOK, *ADVANCED DUNGEONS & DRAGONS SECOND EDITION PLAYER'S HANDBOOK*

EXPERIENCE TAUGHT TSR that putting out a hardcover book of new rules was good for the bottom line. Gamers bought these books, and money flowed into the coffers of the company. Books like *Unearthed Arcana,* which provided new classes and races, and *Oriental Adventures,* which took *AD&D* out of a European backdrop and transplanted it to Asia, sold well.

A new edition of the game would mean TSR could produce and sell at least three such books: a book for players, a book for Dungeon Masters, and some sort of monster book. They would make the company a fortune if they sold.

Would they sell? If the company produced a second edition of *Advanced Dungeons & Dragons,* would people buy it? The first edition of the game sold fantastically and drove much of the company's early growth. A revision of *AD&D,* perhaps an improvement as well, could drive the thousands of gamers who purchased the game before to buy it again. If they did, it would mean huge sales for the company.

But Gary Gygax was no more. Who would write the next edition? What if they lacked the genius of Saint Gary and produced a version of the holy game that the fans didn't like? The impact on the company would be disastrous.

Producing a second edition of the game was rich with both risk and reward. The man to do it was David "Zeb" Cook. He and his team were the first men to produce a version of *Advanced Dungeons & Dragons* untouched by Saint Gary.

By the late 1980s, Cook was a grizzled veteran of the Games Department, though he'd first adulted as an English teacher in the wilds of Nebraska. After two years of students and papers and grades and tests, he noticed an advertisement in the pages of *Dragon.* TSR, it seemed, was looking for designers.

Cook applied for the job. He was sent a number of forms to fill out and then wrote a sample adventure. On that basis, he was flown up to Lake Geneva, where he was interviewed by Lawrence Schick and Gary Gygax himself. He was hired and given an office in the ramshackle Hotel Clair, where men fell through the ceiling with all the grace of cattle shoved out an airplane without a parachute.

Cook's work at the company shone. He expanded the realms of *Dungeons & Dragons* by providing rules that took characters to the fourteenth level. He created a number of games based on preexisting properties, such as Indiana Jones, Conan the Barbarian, and even Rocky and Bullwinkle. *The Isle of Dread,* an adventure he cowrote with Tom Moldvay, brought the hex crawl to the world of *D&D.* (If you've ever played a game where you're exploring and when you enter a new area, something happens, that's a hex crawl.) In short, he was doing work that is still influencing game designers in the twenty-first century.

When Lorraine Williams took over the company, Zeb Cook said he had no idea who she was. He just knew that she was this woman who had money and somehow finagled her way into TSR and outmaneuvered Gygax. Now she was in charge. "Frankly, her arrival meant the departure of the Blumes, and that was not a bad thing," he said. "It brought some sense of stability to things. The company started acting a little bit more like a company. And so, it seemed like it might work out. She didn't know anything about games, and so consequently, she tended to leave the Design Department alone. She knew that we made stuff, and it theoretically made money."

Zeb Cook was gifted the choice but fraught task of creating the second edition of *Advanced Dungeons & Dragons.* He would have to step into the sacred robes of Gary Gygax and Dave Arneson, go out into the wilds of design, and come back bearing the rules that would glow at the table and grow *AD&D.* Succeed, and he'd be a hero. Fail, and he'd . . . No, no. Best not to even think about it.

Zeb Cook doesn't remember how the task of designing the second edition fell to him. He said, "I was certainly the most senior designer they had at the time, and I worked with Gary." Furthermore, before Gygax was forced out of the company, he had had "initial discussions" with him about a possible second edition of the game. He said without Saint Gary at the company, the question became: Who understood the "spirit" of *Dungeons & Dragons*? And the answers were Cook, Steve Winter, and Jon Pickens. He said, "Steve was the editor, and I was the designer. And Jon was the 'Oh, by the way, we need all sorts of other stuff done' guy, including playtest coordination and making sure these two other guys, but mainly me, don't go off the rails. Jon was the master of trivia too, and he was really good at organizing."

These three were the elect. The holy chosen. Those who would bring about a new birth of *Dungeons & Dragons.* But holiness exacts a price: isolation.

The holy chosen were exiled from the Games Department and moved one floor down, into the belly of the Marketing Department. The police were never called because the Marketing Department was having a Nerf battle that got out of control. The FBI never dropped by because the Marketing Department was running a spy RPG at the office. Nobody ever fell through the ceiling of the Marketing Department because they were trying to pull a prank.

Cook said the point of the move was to isolate the chosen three in the hopes that they would get more (and better) work done. Steve Winter said on the second floor, "we'd have fewer distractions, and be able to focus on the huge amount of work ahead." After all, the holy chosen had the future of the game, the company, and, to some extent, role-playing itself looming over them.

The new edition would be an opportunity to address problems that had grown up in the game. The amount of material that had come to exist was problematic, both for gamers and designers. For gamers, there were now simply more rules than one could comfortably keep in one's head. And Saint Gary forbid you should forget a rule and forget what book it was in! Was the Wandering Monster Table in the *Dungeon Master's Guide,* the *Dungeoneer's Survival Guide,* or *Unearthed Arcana*? Nothing kills excitement at the gaming table faster than poring over rule books. It was a repeat of one of the problems that drove the creation of the first edition of *Advanced Dungeons & Dragons* back in the late 1970s.

For designers, these rule books were a challenge because they could not design adventures that presupposed DMs owned and read all of those books. Even though the game now included drow, a subrace of elves, as a character race, to assume that DMs had anything beyond the three core rule books would be to decrease the number of people who might buy the adventure. Therefore, even though designers were creating new rules for the game, they couldn't use them when writing an adventure.

The first question that had to be answered was: How different will a new edition of the game be?

Back in 1985, in *Dragon* #103, Gary Gygax laid out a number of expectations for the second edition. He wrote, "A Second Edition is a major undertaking. There are corrections to be made, parts to be meshed, material to be deleted or shifted, and new rules and information to be included in such a work." It is worth noting the order in which he listed what needed doing for the second edition. He wrote of corrections, meshing, deleting, and shifting material. Only after all of that does he mention new rules.

And while Gygax was gone, there was still a push within management to view a second edition as a chance to revise and edit, but not produce astounding or fundamental changes to the rule set. Cook said such an effort would allow the company to "incorporate the good stuff and fix a bunch of the bad problems." This would hopefully allow the rule books to become more "accessible" and "reach a broader market."

After all, the organization of the first edition books was problematic. Steve Winter described reading the original books as "having a one-on-one conversation with Gary Gygax. They were charming but not much help when a question arose in the middle of a battle." Reorganizing, rearranging, and editing would produce a second edition that was easier to digest and use for experienced players, while not making any of the many, many, many adventures the company had already produced obsolete.

But mere editing and rearranging would not make a better game. Cook said one could not "cut and paste and rearrange" the game's problems away. Improving *the game* would mean rules changes.

Furthermore, dread began to wrap its cold, mucky fingers around the hearts of management and marketing regarding the new edition. Steve Winter said they were afraid of "a disastrous drop in sales when we announced we were working on a new edition. Backlist sales were a big part of TSR's business. If customers, retailers, and distributors stopped buying existing *AD&D* material out of fear those titles were becoming obsolete, the company would take a huge financial hit."

What resulted was an in-between, twilight time. Winter said it was a moment when executives were caught between saying, "No way" to another edition of the game and saying, "Second edition is go."

As paralysis gripped management, sales continued to fall. The first edition *Players Handbook* and *Dungeon Masters Guide* moved a mere 90,515 copies combined in 1988.

It fell to Steve Winter to act and spur the company forward.

POKING AT DYNAMITE

Steve Winter decided to see how many problems reorganizing the game would solve.

He acquired physical copies of the first edition *Players Handbook* and *Dungeon Masters Guide.* He attacked them with a pair of scissors, cutting, slicing, slitting, and lacerating the pages until the books looked like a pair of butchered chicken carcasses. Then he taped the severed bits of text back together, but this time, they were organized, Winter said, "the way they belonged," creating "a big, fat, three-ring binder with clippings of rule books, all taped together like some insane kidnapper's ransom-note manifesto." He combined material from both books into one section, and some material that had been joined was split. He even rearranged some sections sentence by sentence to reassemble them in a more logical order. "It was terribly tedious work, but it was also something I'd wanted to do for a decade," he said.

The exercise was a test of how many problems a mere reorganization of the existing rules would solve. His goal was to arrange the volumes in such a way that they made sense as a rules reference, and while the company was using word processors by then, the first edition *PHB* and *DMG* did not exist in digital form. Therefore the cutting and the slicing and the taping.

The effort, according to Winter, "demonstrated to those up the chain of authority that the job was too big to be handled by a simple reorganization."

A true second edition would be produced.

The twilight time would end. The holy three would be the first allowed to rearrange and bravely but carefully rewrite the sacred rules of *Advanced Dungeons & Dragons* since Gygax himself. While working on the second edition, Cook said, "we knew we were poking at dynamite." A poor reception could lead to a backlash, reduced sales, and perhaps even wreck the company.

The changes in the game were a combination of orders from management and a decision-making process. Cook said that before anything, he and Steve Winter would thoroughly chew over any alterations. Once a change was decided on by the pair of them, Cook would march back to the Games Department and run it by the worthies there and then present it to upper management. This process made sure that other principals in the company were buying into the modifications Winter and Cook were making to the game and relieved them somewhat of their sacred isolation. The monk's elimination as a character class, for example, followed this process. Other character classes, like the assassin, would also be removed. Monsters, like demons and devils, would be excised.

Steve Winter's goal for the second edition was "to put everything the players needed into the *Player's Handbook* and everything else into the *Dungeon Master's Guide.* Players needed the rules on creating and equipping characters, on magic, and on combat. The DM needed the rules on world building, running adventures, and all the little things that crop up often enough to need rules but not often enough to deserve space in the *Player's Handbook.*"

Yet that design goal would prove contentious.

Believe it or not, in the first edition, Gygax intentionally kept a number of important rules, like combat, out of the *Players Handbook.* According to RPG historian Shannon Appelcline, "Back in 1978, Gygax had decided that it was best if the players did not know the rules." Given that *Advanced Dungeons & Dragons* was a game that centered around combat, it seemed absurd not to put it in the *Players Handbook.* Doing so, however, would mean overruling the blessed precedent of Saint Gary, and doing so in the first edition of the game that he did not write. It was easy to imagine what an irate fan might say about that. "That was a big issue for a while. Where do you put all the combat information?" asked Zeb Cook. After deliberation, he said, "we decided it was better to have it accessible to the player as much as possible."

Jon Pickens, meanwhile, was organizing playtest groups, sending out the newest drafts of the rules, receiving feedback, and compiling it into useful forms for Winter and Cook.

In the end, Zeb Cook ended up writing the second edition *Player's Handbook* and *Dungeon Master's Guide.* However, he emphasizes that the writing of those two volumes was "very collaborative" and that "Steve Winter made my writing legible."

Did upper management in any way intervene in the nitty-gritty scrum of the creation of the second edition of *Advanced Dungeons & Dragons*?

Somewhat, but not a lot. Zeb Cook couldn't remember one example of a diktat from above when I interviewed him, though he said, "Probably at the time I could have mentioned ten million of them, petty little things. But mostly because our upper management were not gamers as a rule, they did not say, 'Oh, this must be done.' Jim Ward was the filter through which all of that stuff went. They were much more concerned about, 'Don't fuck up. By the way, our entire livelihood depends on this.' Jim was the one who would say, 'No, you're going too far. We can't do that.' He was the pushback, but we respected him because he was a gamer. He understood the game and what was going on."

Management's issues were concerns like backward compatibility (*What's going to happen to all of those first edition adventures in the warehouse?!*) and, Cook said, "reducing the amount of controversy that we generate among the anti-TSR moms." Hence the removal of demons, devils, and assassins.

The second edition sold well when it was finally released. Combined, the *Dungeon Master's Guide* and *Player's Handbook* sold over 400,000 copies in their first year. That's a lot of books. Not the most ever sold by the company, but a lot. To give some historical comparison, the 1981 *D&D Basic Set* sold over 650,000 copies in its first year. To compare to previous editions of *AD&D*, the first edition *DMG* and *PHB* together sold over 146,000 copies in 1979. (That's not the first year those books were released but rather the first year for which I have sales data.) Putting those numbers together makes *AD&D* second edition look like a solid hit. But it hides a deeper problem.

The second edition didn't have the legs that the first edition did. Combined sales of the first edition *DMG* and *PHB* actually went up at first, perhaps swelling with the rising tide of the satanic panic, to peak in 1981 with over 577,000 copies sold before dropping. The second edition would never match those sales numbers. It just wasn't selling like its predecessor.

What had changed? Was the problem that it had been forged without the holy hands of Saint Gary? Was a rule altered that shouldn't have been? Was it too complex? Not complex enough? Were RPGs a fad that had faded? Should the *AD&D* lines be canceled entirely to focus on the historically better-selling *D&D*?

These numbers should have been an occasion for self-reflection and correction all over the company.

But they weren't.

SALES KEPT SECRET

At TSR, sales numbers stayed in the offices of upper management. Zeb Cook himself said he never saw any concrete sales numbers for the second edition. Skip Williams, who had been rehired at the company, said of this time, "Some of us at TSR had a decent idea about what was selling and how fast, but it was all based on anecdotal information and the occasional bit of hard data that slipped out."

The decision to keep sales numbers hidden behind the veil of management must be seen as a mistake. The inability of the game designers to know how their product was selling cut them off from economic feedback on their product. Zeb Cook didn't know how the game sold, so how could he make changes to improve his craft in the future?

Why wasn't the second edition selling like the first? Theories abounded.

It was possible that the problem facing the game wasn't any rule changes Zeb Cook made. The name *Advanced Dungeons & Dragons* itself might have been working against the success of the game. There was an unresolved contradiction at the heart of TSR—namely, the company was famous for making a game called *Dungeons & Dragons*, but they kept producing and pushing a different game named *Advanced Dungeons & Dragons*.

The idea that *Advanced Dungeons & Dragons* was its own worst problem was put forward by John Danovich. He was director of sales and marketing, and he saw the strength in *Dungeons & Dragons*. He said that the non-advanced version of the game was "the most valuable intellectual property that TSR ever had." Looking at sales, he certainly had a point. By 1999, the company sold 5.4 million *D&D* boxed sets, but only 4.6 million copies of the *Player's Handbook* and *Dungeon Master's Guide*. He said that *D&D* was "where the power is. It's where all the money is. It's the thing that we can get the most licensing for." He said that it was the default in the marketplace, like Kleenex was to facial tissues or Xerox was to photocopying.

Danovich believed that the reason for the pivot to *AD&D* was because Dave Arneson was cocreator of *Dungeons & Dragons* and still had extant royalty agreements with the company. He said, "So every time *Dungeons & Dragons* was sold, a royalty was generated for Dave Arneson. The management led by Lorraine Williams at that time period did not want to pay Dave Arneson any money at all. Zero. So *Dungeons & Dragons* was put out as a separate product to keep the trademark active, to keep our ownership of it, to make sure that it would still be out there, but do as little as humanly possible to promote it."

Danovich wanted to bring back *Dungeons & Dragons*. His solution? "Buy out Dave Arneson. We should just take some money, and buy him out. What would it take? Is it one million dollars? It's worth it. Is it two million? It's worth it. Four million? Guess what? It's worth it." But according to him, Williams utterly refused to consider it. "It's not something that she would ever, ever entertain. It was not a trademark that she owned, like Buck Rogers. It was not something that she wanted anyone else to make money off of."

The best Danovich could get for his trouble was a change in the *AD&D* second edition logo. He got *2nd Edition* removed entirely and *Advanced* shrunk so that a reader moving quickly only saw *Dungeons & Dragons* in large red letters on a black background.

So perhaps the very name *Advanced Dungeons & Dragons* engendered customer confusion, the word *advanced* telling new players that the game was not for them.

But there were other theories to explain the decreasing sales.

THE RPG CONSUMPTION PROBLEM

A $4 comic book can be read in a half hour.

A $10 movie can be watched in a couple of hours.

A $30 hardcover novel can be read in a couple of weeks.

A $50 video game might take forty hours to play through.

But if you spend $150 on a few RPG rule books, a setting, and some adventures, you could be playing for years, and everyone has heard of RPG campaigns lasting for decades. Yes, hard-core fans will purchase much more than they could ever play in a lifetime, but the RPG fan has the option of buying nothing new ever again, unlike a comic book fan. If a Superman buff wants to know what's going on with the Man of Steel, they have to buy a comic book every month, perhaps more. If the RPG fan wants to play in the Forgotten Realms, they can buy the boxed set and never have to buy another Forgotten Realms product ever again.

This is the RPG consumption problem.

Another director of sales and marketing, Jim Fallone, put it this way: "You just needed the rules. Early on, there [was] zero product in the marketplace, so you are filling the bucket with gamers and customers. By the time you're in the late 1980s, the bucket is kind of getting full, and you've got early adopters who are still playing" versions of the game from five, ten, or fifteen years earlier. People were even making up their own house systems.

Furthermore, the power the RPG medium gives players and DMs to create their own stories, which is one of the most important and addicting parts of the form, also meant that once the game was purchased, a customer didn't need to buy another product from TSR ever again. Fallone said, "Once you know how to play *D&D,* you don't have to buy our adventures anymore. You can tell your own stories, which was both an innovation and killed the game to some degree." He also said that competition from other games was a factor in the decreasing sales.

New editions were an attempt to solve these problems. Fallone said, "That's where editions started to become an important model for sales at TSR." Once you have a customer base, "you have to get them to rebuy everything. We would have to make the next edition, and after about five years, we'd have to do it again, and then you just timed all the core settings to slow-walk them in the upgrade so that by the time you got the smallest one upgraded, then you do the next edition."

The second edition showed a flaw in that business model: Not every player and DM was going to transition to the new edition. And while the second edition was my first experience of *Dungeons & Dragons,* and flipping through the second edition *Player's Handbook* still makes my heart flutter as I recall adolescent summers spent examining that tome of wisdom to discover how to make a better character as though that might also teach me to be a better man, the edition itself must be viewed as a failure both because so many existing players did not make the transition to it and because it did not bring large numbers of new players to the game.

But this fact was kept from the literal geniuses in the Games Department. Management did not inform them of the lackluster sales and together search for an answer. What solutions might a company-wide soul-searching produce? A re-embracing of ye olde *Dungeons & Dragons*?

Management did have ideas. For example, according to Skip Williams, they wanted the Games Department "to reach for an ever-younger audience." The push resulted in products like *Dragon Strike,* which was intended to bring the game to eight-year-olds.

In the search for new customers, the company even attempted to break into the field of comic books. It opened an office in LA and called it TSR West. The saga of this branch of the company is a tale worthy of a chapter unto itself.

It is a story heretofore entirely unknown . . .

THE SAGA OF TSR WEST

Ben Riggs: I want to know what role TSR West played in the failure of the company.

Scott Haring: You mean other than losing a boatload of Lorraine Williams's money?

—INTERVIEW WITH THE AUTHOR, OCTOBER 18, 2018

TSR West was an attempt by the company to break into comics in the late '80s and early '90s. At the time, the comics industry was griddle-hot. A successful expansion into the field would bring the company another revenue stream, perhaps one to equal the growing Book Department. Comics might also be a new path for people to discover *D&D*, and the company needed to expand its fan base. Finally, film and television were the searing-white nexus of mainstream culture at the time, and comic books are much easier to adapt to those mediums than role-playing games. Get a good Forgotten Realms movie or TV show made and the future of the company might know no bounds . . .

These were all logical, laudable goals for the company.

But it would amount to less than nothing. The company would repeat in LA mistakes it already made in Lake Geneva, but now in offices with higher rent. And in the end, it is likely that this attempted expansion simply added to the pile of debt that the company was accruing.

The tale of TSR West is broad and deep, so much so that it is hard to know where to start. The story could begin with DC Comics. In the late 1980s, TSR licensed a number of its properties to DC, which made comic books based on them. The comics did well, selling on par with popular titles like *Wonder Woman*.

One of these series was *Forgotten Realms*. It was written by that river of creativity in human form, Jeff Grubb. From DC's point of view, it was advantageous having a TSR employee writing the book because it meant the scripts would essentially come preapproved, as it was unlikely Grubb would do something that broke genre, like having a spaceship descend on Waterdeep or writing a dimensional travel story involving Nazis and the Harpers. The book's editor was comics stalwart Elliot S! Maggin. The story of how Elliot S! Maggin broke into comics is legendary in the field. While a student at Brandeis University, Maggin wrote a paper titled "What Can One Man Do?" It received a grade of B+. Irritated that he hadn't made the A, he decided to rework his paper into a comic book script. When it was finished, he put it in an envelope and sent it off to DC Comics. The script was so well received by DC that it became *Green Lantern* #87 and was illustrated by the great Neal Adams.

Forgotten Realms and the other *AD&D* comics did well at DC. Grubb said, "The books were a success, placing in the mid-list of the superhero books." He said the *AD&D* books were "just inside the top one hundred, around the *Captain America* / *Wonder Woman* / *Aquaman* levels." Maggin said of the books' performance, "They did better than they needed to do to stay at DC."

In short, the comics deal appeared to be a hit for TSR. It was exposing their brand to a new market and selling well for their licensee, DC Comics. DC put out a *Gammarauders* comic and a *Spelljammer* comic and was working on producing a Ravenloft comic written by Jim Lowder.

Perhaps this was the answer to TSR's dropping sales. Perhaps it could become a company that created fantasy worlds and then licensed them to others. As the twenty-first century has taught us, comic books are ripe for translation into film and television. Perhaps DC Comics could have been a road back to the screen.

Of course, management would find a way to muck it up.

From Grubb's point of view, TSR decided to go into competition with DC Comics over Buck Rogers.

Lorraine Williams, as we know, was one of the owners of the Buck Rogers copyright. Now that TSR was working with DC to produce comic books, management wanted to see them make a Buck Rogers comic book. According to Grubb, the reaction of DC to the offer was a sarcastic, "Oh yeah, we'll get around to that."

Grubb said that with no Buck Rogers comic in sight, TSR decided to get into the comics business themselves.

But Flint Dille tells a different story . . .

To TELL THE story of TSR West, one might have to start with the meeting of Flint Dille and Steven Grant.

Steven Grant has a writing résumé long as a rope. In comics, Grant is well known for taking the Punisher and transforming him from a minor character to one of the most recognizable in Marvel's stable with the 1986 miniseries *Punisher: Circle of Blood.* He also wrote a number of Hardy Boys novels in the 1980s. Grant said that at the time, "one-man war on crime" books were tremendously popular in the adult market. A publisher decided to resurrect the twee teen sleuths as "a two-man war on crime." When Grant started writing the books, the publisher wanted the Hardy Boys to be tough, edgy, and ready for action, more Sylvester Stallone than Sherlock Holmes. But as the publisher became increasingly uncomfortable with novels that featured teens firing Uzis, every time Grant went to write a new novel, his writing guidelines would tighten. First, they couldn't use guns. Then, they couldn't use knives. It was much different from writing the Punisher, who was known for his take-no-prisoners, kill-'em-all-let-God-sort-'em-out ethos.

And Flint Dille we have, of course, already met.

Dille and Grant, as it turned out, both lived in Westwood, and they were both writers. As a result, Grant said the pair "started having lunch periodically.

And it was during lunch we casually started floating around the idea of starting a comics company." And according to Grant, "then he said, 'You know, I should ask my sister about this . . .'"

This was, of course, Lorraine Williams. It seemed like an echo of when Dille recommended his sister to Gary Gygax years before. He said of that connection, "Gary didn't talk to me for a long time afterwards because he thought I knew something about Lorraine taking over the company, and I certainly didn't, and I certainly didn't think it was a good idea. No part of me was happy about it when it happened."

Dille had done some work for his sister's company, and he now returned to the hope of *Dungeons & Dragons* ascending to film or television, the same hope that brought Gygax out to California years before. He wanted to get the company's intellectual property on television or in the movies.

But how would TSR move from novels and games to movies and TV? All Gygax had to show for his trouble was the *D&D* cartoon. That lasted three seasons, then got canceled before a final episode wrapping up the story could be completed. Why would this work out now?

Dille's answer was, "We have to develop properties. And the cheapest platform to develop on is a comic book." He knew comic book people. He said, "Frank Miller is probably my best friend."

A TSR comic book division could be used to develop properties that could then be sold to film and television. Comic books were essentially storyboards already. Comic books were a visual medium, like film and television. Instead of handing the *AD&D* second edition rule book to some tanned, slim, and sleek executive vice president of very important things in a corner office in Studio City, California, and asking said executive to translate those words into wizards hurling lightning bolts with all the fury of Zeus, a comic book could show it to them. It simply asked less of the minds of executives. Maybe, just maybe, comic books would allow the company to succeed where it failed before and seal a deal with Hollywood that would take the company into the big leagues.

Thing was, TSR was already in comics. They'd licensed their best intellectual property to DC. The comics were selling well, but not spectacularly. A market was there.

What DC was not doing was making a Buck Rogers comic book. This meant that if TSR did start a comic book division, they would have one established intellectual property to anchor them in the public consciousness, even if it was unfortunately Buck Rogers.

So TSR would do it. They would go forth and create comic books in an effort to break into broadcasting or film, even if it meant alienating DC. One could sell this as a bold move to grow the company, but Jeff Grubb saw this as TSR of Lake Geneva, Wisconsin, going to war with DC, a division of Time-Warner Communications.

Elliot S! Maggin added that from where he sat in the DC offices, TSR might have had a good reason to be upset. He said that DC never supported the *AD&D* comics the way they should have, and rumor held that DC head Jenette Kahn thought them to be of low quality.

Back in California, plans were taking shape. Steven Grant said that "in the space of a month," discussions with Dille went from wild talk over lunch to concrete plans. Brad Munson, a writer with ten years' experience in the magazine and book publishing industry, was hired to assist in the development of a business plan.

On overstuffed couches in Dille's living room, the group laid down the bones and guts of what would become TSR West. The company's business plan was developed jointly by Munson and Grant, though Dille was deeply involved in concepts. The plan was to create an overall comic book universe with shared characters and settings, just like Marvel and DC. The comics could not feature *Dungeons & Dragons* material since DC Comics had that license.

In retrospect, Brad Munson believed that the fact that TSR West was not going to be able to use the company's A-list intellectual properties in their comics "should have been the first moment where we said, 'You know what? Maybe this isn't such a wonderful idea.' But we were young and hungry, what can I tell ya?"

Instead, the TSR West team came up with their own slate of characters and would use other TSR properties. Dille created *13 Assassin*, a comic about a perfect human weapon. Also, there would be a time travel book called *Warhawks*, a horror comic called *R.I.P.*, a sci-fi comic called *Intruder*, and, of course, Buck Rogers. Flint Dille said, "And we did Buck Rogers because we had to do Buck Rogers." The intention was to show Hollywood how to do Buck Rogers right and overcome the strong, fecal stench the 1979 TV show left wafting over the property.

The business plan called for TSR West to start by publishing five comic books. Every issue published was to have a main feature and a secondary feature. The secondary feature would be thematically related to the main feature and provide an opportunity to try out new settings and characters, as well as test reader reactions to them. For example, Steven Grant pitched a concept he titled "Raiders of Mars," about radicals fighting to overthrow the Martian government, to go along with the Buck Rogers comic book. New comics would come out of the backup feature. If people particularly liked a character, they could be spun off into their own book. Then, the new book would also have a backup feature, allowing the comic line to continue growing.

Also according to the business plan, every comic was to be published in four-issue story arcs. This would allow editorial flexibility on the part of the company. If there was a comic that was not selling well, it could be wrapped up in four issues and then replaced with a character from the backup features that fans enjoyed.

The four-issue arcs were then to be packaged as trade paperbacks and sold in bookstores. This would give TSR West a chance to broaden their audience and provide the company with another revenue stream. According to the business plan, the company's primary sales outlet would be specialty comic book stores, not bookstores.

Grant said that the business plan put together by Munson, Dille, and himself was "very good." Munson described it as "visionary."

The TSR West working group presented an estimate of costs to Lake Geneva, detailing how much money would be required for production, setting up offices, salaries, benefits, and so on. Dille convinced his sister that the venture was feasible. Williams, according to Grant and Munson, then convinced banks to provide TSR with loans to finance this expansion of their business. The money flowed, and suddenly, TSR West popped into existence. TSR committed to funding TSR West for "two to three years," according to Brad Munson. Grant said that "comics were taking off at the time, so it was getting fairly easy to interest people" in moving into the industry.

It is worth lingering for a moment over this loan. No one I spoke to could pin down the loan's amount. Grant did not remember how much it was for, but did know it was "quite a bit of money." When Flint Dille, who would soon come to run the entire LA operation, was asked about whether a loan was used to fund it, he said, "That stuff was invisible to me."

But Munson and Grant both agreed that a loan was used to finance the operation. And that loan wasn't small. Which meant that if TSR West didn't become a viable entity, TSR back in Lake Geneva would be responsible for paying back the loan that made possible the offices in LA, the salaries of the staff, and their insurance.

In a bare handful of months, Munson, Dille, and Grant had gone from spitballing ideas over lunch to renting offices on Sepulveda Boulevard. Their thoughts had become real enough to touch, and in no time at all. Grant had an office! And insurance!

The endeavor roared forward, and it would carry Grant, Munson, Dille, and the rest with it. Movies, television, money, awards, success, fame, and glory were all possible outcomes of this endeavor.

Flint Dille was sitting in his car one day when it hit him. He thought, *This is really happening.* TSR West was going to be a thing. He became "dizzily excited." Yet he was not surprised. He said starting a comic book company "seemed like a cool and normal thing to be doing."

It was August of 1989, and the world could not know what TSR West had in store for it.

THE REVENGE OF DC COMICS

The old gods at DC Comics saw what TSR was doing and seethed.

Lawyers began to unfreeze their joints and gaze with mechanical eyes upon the contract they had made with TSR. The company licensed their properties to DC for use in comic books. Now, TSR was making comic books, thereby going into competition with DC.

Was this a breach of contract?

The slow juicing and greasing of lawsuits commenced. While TSR was not going to publish any comics using *AD&D* or other properties that DC had the license to, DC was still apparently furious. Steven Grant said that the comic book behemoth was "very pissed off."

We now enter a new phase in the history of TSR West, one where the management in Lake Geneva would make decisions outside or even contradicting what was in the original business plan that Grant, Munson, and Dille composed. So far as I can tell, these changes were never for the better, but my sources for this are of course Grubb, Grant, Munson, Maggin, and Dille. Lorraine Williams would certainly have her own side of these events, but as she refused to speak to me, we are left with the tale as it is.

One of the changes imposed on TSR West by Lake Geneva was an attempt to placate DC Comics, and it went thus: TSR West would no longer make comic books. Instead, they would make "comic modules." A comic module would be sequential graphic art, which is of course the definition of a comic book. But it would also contain a small game or role-playing material as well. (*Module,* by the way, was the word TSR used for adventures in the '70s and '80s.)

Looking at a comic module today, you might think it looks exactly like a comic book. Hell, you might think it *is* a comic book. After all, it is ten and a half inches by six and a half inches in size. It has a cover with eye-catching art. But according to TSR, you would be wrong. The addition of that game material transmuted it into an altogether new thing—a comic module!

The company metaphorically suggested that comic books were like a cheese pizza. Cheese pizza is a fine thing, no doubt, but the addition of pepperoni makes it into something totally different—namely, a pepperoni pizza—and a pepperoni pizza is not the same as a cheese pizza, for it has pepperoni. These things are not the same. Unalike. Dissimilar. Two entirely separate and distinct Platonic categories. One titled cheese pizza. The other entitled pepperoni pizza. Therefore, the company was not going into competition against DC Comics because it wasn't making comic books. It was making comic modules. This was a distinct category!

(I cannot help but remember TSR's claim that *Advanced Dungeons & Dragons* was a completely new game birthed by Gary Gygax that had nothing to do with *Dungeons & Dragons*, and therefore Dave Arneson was owed zero royalties.)

But the old gods at DC did not grow old by being fools. Though they saw through the flimflam of the comic module, they did not sue. They trod a different road to revenge.

DC canceled every single *AD&D* comic book line, from the original eponymous comic to Grubb's *Forgotten Realms* title and the still-in-production Ravenloft book.

This made DC a freshly hated enemy in the cubicles and corridors of the old Q-tip factory on Sheridan Springs Road, apparently without much reflection on the actions the company had taken to bring matters to this pass.

This first change imposed on TSR West by Lake Geneva concerned the product it made. The next would change how its comic modules would be sold.

The business plan called for TSR West's products to be distributed through comic book specialty stores. But now Lake Geneva decreed that the distribution and marketing of comic modules would be run through Random House, TSR's book trade distributor of long standing. On the surface, using Random House in this capacity made sense. TSR had a relationship with the company stretching back to the reign of Gygax, and it made lots of money having its games and books in every mall in America.

The rub was that Random House was not steeped in the comic trade, so when crates of what looked like comic books arrived at Waldenbooks and B. Dalton labeled as comic modules and published by TSR, employees put them in the gaming section of the store. It made sense. They were gaming material published by TSR. Not comic books, as the company's lawyers would have insisted in court if sued by the old gods at DC. And the comic module moniker was very successful in preventing that lawsuit.

But out in the wide world, no one knew what a comic module was. And now they were in bookstores, in the gaming section, a place that comic book readers did not go to buy their comic books. The twin decisions of naming TSR West's products comic modules and distributing them through bookstores meant that the company had, literally and physically, isolated their product from the audience they wanted to buy it.

Dille said that the decision to distribute through Random House was made by TSR HQ, and while "it seemed like a good idea at the time," lived experience proved it was not the way to go.

But if TSR West was now making comic modules, and a comic module was defined by the inclusion of gaming material, who would generate that content?

Enter Scott Haring.

WARHAWKS, INTRUDER, BUCK ROGERS, R.I.P.

Scott Haring started out working at Steve Jackson Games, but was eventually hired by TSR. Haring said he was "working away in my cubicle like a good little editorial drone at the old abandoned Q-tip factory in Lake Geneva, Wisconsin," when vice president Mike Cook marched into his office with an offer for him. Would he move to Los Angeles?

Management wanted Haring to head west and become the gaming guy at the TSR West office. He would be in charge of the module part of the comic modules that TSR West would produce instead of comic books in their effort to placate the old gods over at DC Comics.

It can be hard to pry Wisconsin folk out of the state, but Haring wasn't from Wisconsin. He didn't have tradition and clan binding him to the soil. After two years at the company, Haring said, "I'm not going to say I was a lonely boy, but I didn't really know anybody that well. So this chance to move to Los Angeles seemed like a big deal."

Moving to LA seemed risky to Haring for other reasons. He knew Flint Dille was in charge of the West Coast operation, and Haring said Dille already had "a reputation" among the staff. Haring told Mike Cook that he really appreciated the opportunity on offer, but he also saw how things on the West Coast could "really blow up." Haring wanted to know, would he still have a job back in Lake Geneva if things didn't work out in LA?

According to Haring, he was told that coming back to Lake Geneva would present "no problem" in the event that TSR West went bust.

With that assurance, Haring decided to head west. He said, "The company was making a major commitment to the West Coast office. Someone who attached themselves to it on the ground floor and saw it become successful had a good chance at some sort of advancement. TSR offered me a nice raise and paid all my moving expenses, and you know, who was I to complain? I took a shot."

Scott Haring ended up getting an apartment in the San Fernando Valley north of the TSR West offices just off the 405 and became the office "game guy." He worked on a Buck Rogers role-playing game and *A Line in the Sand*, a board game.

Haring also resolutely produced game material for the comic modules. He said, "Whenever there was a comic book with an interesting character or a weird MacGuffin, I would write *D&D* game stats for it. I made up little tiny board games." One game Haring compared to Parcheesi, "using pennies and a map of the world that came in the comic book, with all of these mystical sites from our mystical comic book. It was a simple 'roll the dice and move your mice' kind of game." But Haring said that the game didn't need to blow the world away with its addicting originality. Rather, the game material simply needed to be; it needed to exist to demonstrate that what TSR West was producing was not straight-up comic books but rather comic modules, which are of course totally and completely different, so DC Comics should not consider suing the company.

To provide one specific example, the premiere issue of *R.I.P.*, written by comics legend Marv Wolfman, had an essay by Scott Haring on adapting the content of the comic to the *Top Secret / S.I.* role-playing game, and a complete game titled *The Battle for Smithville* by Flint Dille and Scott Haring. According to the game, "The tiny town of Smithville has a problem—it's being overrun by all sorts of horrible monsters!" One player takes on the role of the human residents of Smithville, and the other portrays the monsters. The game is a bit like war, where players turn over cards with numbers on them, then roll dice and add the card to the die total, and whichever side rolled higher wins.

You may ask yourself how a comic module can include cards. Well, they were printed in the comic. "The Battle for Smithville" instructed players to "carefully cut out the 30 cards printed on these pages."

Now try to imagine any true comic book aficionado you know picking up a pair of shears and *actually cutting up pages of a comic book*. Yes, it is an action that could take place, in theory, in the same way we all know we could be hit by lightning or killed by a falling satellite. But to try to imagine it actually happening, in reality, and in front of you? It's . . . Well. Imagine a nun spitting on the pope. Imagine Red Sox fans burning down Fenway Park. These things could happen, yes. But actually seeing them occur in our reality? Impossible.

Comic book fans are archivists. They seize and preserve. They value for the future. I've seen comic fans put on gloves before handling issues, use tweezers to turn pages, and abhor the slightest white fluff on a comic cover's corner. And collecting comic books in the hopes that they one day accrue in value is part of the fun of the hobby. It's a feature, not a bug. Of course, the condition of the comic is vitally important to determining its value. Yet here was TSR West, asking their readers to violently violate the sacred pages of a comic, to commit a taboo act.

The company heard from fans about this. In *Intruder* #3, Dille wrote an editorial titled "Trash This Book" to answer these fan concerns. He wrote:

> We've been getting complaints about our Comic Modules. The complaints center around the fact that we—GASP—ask you to tear up the books to pull out the game components. "The collectors will hate that. They like to keep their books 'pristine.'" Well, these books aren't for collectors. They're *meant* to be mauled. Our goal is to see our books returned to their natural state: shredded pulp . . . We want our books to be read until the covers fall off, sliced apart for game materials, used to hold up beds, jammed into drawers—and finally, returned to nature by either mom or the wife. Just call it our little contribution to ecology.

TSR West compounded their initial error of asking comic buyers to commit a taboo by slicing up their comics for game components by not listening to their audience. The people who bought comic modules apparently wanted the games in the back, but they didn't want to have to cut up the comics for them. Audiences don't lie. They give honest feedback. And TSR West responded by telling the people who were good enough to buy their products that what they wanted was wrong. Even in its LA incarnation, TSR was a company that didn't listen enough to the market or its audience, even when the latter was kind enough to write them letters telling them exactly what they wanted.

Furthermore, the management structure became an issue. According to Munson, he was the guy who knew publishing, Grant was the guy who knew comics, and Dille was the guy with a strong creative background and family connections at TSR. The three of them were to be coequal managers in the endeavor that was TSR West. (Like Gygax and the Blumes during the long, long ago back in Lake Geneva.) Conflicts over creative direction, writing, and stories emerged as the lineup of comics firmed up. Brad Munson said, "Grant and Dille and I were having daily disagreements about what to do next." But since the three of them were coequal managers, no one could resolve these conflicts. The question was, who would have the final say in these decisions? In short, within the offices of TSR West, who was the boss?

Lorraine Williams reached down from Lake Geneva and raised up her brother. Flint Dille was in charge. Munson said he vividly remembered her telling him, "This is Flint's operation. You work for Flint."

Steven Grant began to be uncomfortable with the direction of TSR West. He saw elements of the business plan "get whittled away one by one." The business plan was a good plan. It convinced banks to front the money to start TSR West. Why mess with it? A concerned Grant gave notice that he would be leaving the company in December of 1989. Since he'd created a number of properties that the company still intended to publish, it wanted to purchase the rights to these properties from him. Grant took a few weeks to mull over how much money he should ask for, but before he reached a decision, the company sent him what he described as an "insane demand." It insisted he hand over all the rights to the intellectual property he'd created while at TSR West for a certain amount of money or they'd see him in court.

Grant was stunned. He said, "I think they thought I was going to hold them up or something." However, the tale had a happy ending. The certain sum that TSR insisted that Grant take under threat of full-on legal blitzkrieg, that certain sum for properties like *Warhawks* and *Intruder,* was so much more than what Grant ever imagined asking for that he told the company, "'Okay, you win,' and I signed off on it and cashed the check."

Grant went on writing *Intruder,* but his management involvement was at an end months before the company's first comic module was ever published. He would be missed, since he was the only member of management with a background in comic books, and as Brad Munson pointed out, creating comic books before the heyday of computerization and the internet was "hideously complicated." He said, "We were naive to think we could start a comic book company" without a deeper bench of comic book professionals. Art, lettering, editing, proofing, and dealing with printing was all time-intensive and simply difficult. Munson cited the simple problem of lettering all the comic books. He said, "Computer lettering was ten years away," so the company had to hire someone to come in and physically write letters on every page of every one of their comic books. Furthermore, they had to do this in Los Angeles. LA was not a comic book hub. Marvel, DC, and most independent comic companies operated out of the New York metropolitan area. There, you could find a letterer, no problem. But in sunny LA? Big problem. Finding a letterer was a nightmare.

While we have already discussed the problems TSR West had distributing its products through bookstores, it had similar problems getting its comic modules in comic book shops. First, you have to know that running a comic shop is a brutal business. Every item that a store owner orders is nonreturnable, so if ten issues of *Squirrel Girl* #9 are ordered, but only two sell, the owner eats that loss. This makes comic shop owners incredibly risk-averse in putting new titles on their shelves.

Moreover, Brad Munson believed the *comic module* moniker further hurt the company's sales to comic book stores. The name was damn confusing. Comic book stores sell comic books, not games. TSR made games that often came in modules. Therefore, comic store owners might look at the "comic module" and think it was not a product their customers would be interested in, because it sounds like some sort of gaming product.

Further complicating matters was the fact that Steven Grant was the member of management that knew comics, and he had vamoosed. Neither Munson nor Dille were familiar with the intricacies of sales to comic stores. Munson said they should have hired someone from DC or Marvel to join management, but due to a lack of interest in the idea from Lake Geneva, they never did.

TSR West did get an infusion of talent from DC Comics in their stable of writers. Elliot S! Maggin, who had edited Jeff Grubb's *Forgotten Realms* comic, was happy to hear that the company was looking for help. He wanted to get out of comics and into TV and screenwriting, so when Maggin "heard through the grapevine that Lorraine Williams was thinking about pulling the contract for the next renewal and publishing comics herself, I called Flint Dille, and I said, 'What can we do?'"

Dille was certainly interested in having Maggin come out and work in LA. However, Maggin also had personal considerations to deal with. He was divorced with a son. He asked his ex-wife, Pamela King, if she would move out west with him. Amazingly, she said she would, but they had to move before September. Their son would be entering first grade, and understandably, she didn't want the kid to have to switch schools in the middle of the year.

So with son and ex-wife in tow, Maggin moved to LA. Flint Dille promised him he would be made an editor eventually, but he started out by simply writing comics. *R.I.P.,* TSR West's horror comic, was his first assignment, and Maggin said, "I did a story on Nikola Tesla that I thought was cool."

Even though he'd quit DC and moved to California for TSR West, Maggin was not a salaried employee at the company. Rather, he found himself working for stipends for "four or five months." The pay, he said, "was not very much." Even though Steven Grant's departure meant that Maggin was the only guy with comic book experience physically present in the office, and even though he was something of a storied name in the comics industry (his middle initial had an exclamation point after it, for the love of all!), Maggin had an extended period where he was being tried out. Maggin said TSR West "had a habit of having people come in and testing them out before they'd hire them, which was kind of medieval, I thought. But I wanted to be in LA, so I went along with it."

The comic modules were a wildly mixed bag. Beautiful art was paired with work that was sloppy and ugly. Some comics had fine writing, and other comics felt amateur or even hammy. The best of the bunch were likely *Warhawks* and *R.I.P.* In *Warhawks,* a band of über-fascists called the Zetans discover time travel. They test it out on prisoners, the first of whom perishes bloodily when only his head goes back in time. The Zetans readjust the settings on their time travel device and then escape into Earth's past. It is up to the Warhawks to hunt down the enemies hiding in our history.

R.I.P. was unapologetically morbid, gruesome, and packed with the liveliest awfulness. Its first cover portrayed a shambling parade of the dead shuffling toward the viewer with menace in their lifeless eyes. The tie-wearing corpse in the center of the cover had the top of its skull blown out and a drill stuck in its brain at a jaunty angle. The image was offensively unnecessary—and rather delightful for it. The comic module itself was about the murdered dead coming back to the mortal plane for revenge and a homicidal succubus that finds her prey on a dating show.

Other comic modules were not as strong. *Intruder*, which almost precisely copied the concept of the TV show *Quantum Leap*, unfortunately stands out for art that moves between the amateur and the ugly, with writing that leaves the reader bored and puzzled. *Buck Rogers* had far stronger art, but spent too much time on exposition before giving the reader anyone or anything to care about.

It all ended as quickly as it began. Brad Munson said, "The orders for the first three months were not all that great. And when the actual sales figures came in off the orders for the first two or three months of these comic modules that nobody understood, they pretty much killed the project." In Munson's diagnosis of where the company went wrong, he fingers the decision to produce comic modules instead of straight-up comic books as "one of the things that led to TSR West's ultimate and rather rapid demise." The moniker caused confusion, discouraged purchases by comic stores, and channeled product into the wrong section of bookstores. It is logical for Munson to cite that as the foundational error. It didn't matter how good *Warhawks* was, because it would never be discovered by comic book fans if it wasn't purchased by comic stores and if bookstores shelved it with gaming material. The decision to call the products comic modules ended up severing the company from the very fans it sought to seduce.

Munson also faulted the company's mediocre product as a reason for its collapse. He said, "The quality of the books themselves suffered from the very outset. I think if the books had been *really* good and the stories had been *really* strong and the art had been *really* hot, a lot of the other things that kept distributors away would not have mattered as much."

Munson left disappointed. This was supposed to be his big break. His time. His chance. His moment. But it wasn't.

It was no doubt a disappointment to all involved. If TSR West had worked, they could have strode like giants across the geek landscape, towering over city and field, and scratched their names for all to see on the mountainside. In years to come, when TSR West was as big as DC or Marvel, people would want to hear their story. The countless huddled fans of *Intruder, Warhawks,* and *Buck Rogers* would want to know how it all happened. Their names would hold eternal in the nerd firmament as though written in stone, contesting famous names like Mary Shelley, Jack Kirby, Jerry Siegel, Joe Shuster, and Osamu Tezuka. People would stalk them at conventions, phone them at odd hours asking obscure questions about *R.I.P.,* and go through their trash hoping to find some glimpse, some hint, into the inner beings of the great men who glimpsed TSR's future and saw it was in comics. Maybe one day a writer would come along to write their story down for future generations to learn about them.

And here I am, writing, but it is a much different story. That said, one can learn more from failure than from success.

Maggin remembered the day everyone at TSR West was fired except for him. He said, "A couple of guys from Wisconsin showed up in the office unannounced, and they told everybody that everybody was gone except me. I could stay and be the editor in chief. And they wanted to absorb the company into the Wisconsin operation, whatever that meant. At one point, someone said to me, 'Do you wanna move to Wisconsin?' and I said, 'No!'"

So Maggin soldiered on in the now very empty office. There were still bills to be paid, artists to communicate with, and comic modules to push out the door. But four months later, two guys from Wisconsin materialized in Maggin's doorway to inform him his time at TSR West was at an end.

Maggin's reply was, "Okay, let me get my data off my computer."

Alarmed, the Wisconsin suits said, "No! You cannot have the data off the computer!"

Maggin explained it was simply contact information for his family and the like.

The Wisconsin suits proffered him a severance check. Maggin sniffed at the amount. He had a nine-day-old daughter. The money they were offering him to walk away was wholly inadequate. He told the Wisconsin suits exactly that. They were unyielding as ice on the subject of the amount.

So Maggin called his ex-wife, Pamela King. King was a formidable woman. When younger, she'd been New Hampshire's state tennis champion. King and Maggin had married in 1983, divorced in 1988, and gotten married again in 1991. (They divorced again in 2011.)

King, Maggin knew, would annihilate these Wisconsin suits. There would be no fingerprints, not even any teeth left over for identification when she was done with them. Maggin felt compelled to warn the pair. "Batten down the hatches," Maggin said. "Pam's on her way."

King burst into the office with her nine-day-old daughter. After placing her baby carefully on the couch, King extended her claws and teeth and sank both into the tender flesh of the suits from Wisconsin.

Maggin said simply, "She tore them new assholes."

The scene was so gruesome that Maggin at one point had to call her off, telling his (ex-)wife, "That's enough."

The bitter scene at its end, Maggin picked up his daughter.

Maggin was allowed to go on the computer and get his personal information. When finished, he formatted the computer's hard drive. The computer purred and sent every bit of data it contained shrieking into the ether. He said there was nothing "valuable or incriminating" on the computer, but rather, "I just wanted to wipe the hard drive clean. I'd never done that before."

In the collapse, Scott Haring got screwed over hard. When he first took the job, it was with the understanding that he could move back to Lake Geneva and return to his old position if everything in LA melted down. A few years later, everything had indeed melted down with such intensity that the offices on Sepulveda Boulevard were sinking through the Earth's crust. Could Haring return to his position in Lake Geneva?

It turned out not.

Haring called Mike Cook. He told Haring, "'I just can't do it. I know I said it, but I can't do it now."

Haring said of the experience, "I've been fired before. I try not to let it get to me." He was abandoned, cast off, and adrift. To make ends meet, he drove a shuttle bus to LAX for Prime Time. He did freelance writing and editing for game companies on the side.

Looking back, Munson is not sure that TSR West ever would have worked. The comic book industry went bust in the 1990s anyway, and the fact that the company had already licensed its most valuable properties to DC made TSR West seem like a venture that would probably fail.

Unless they had stuck to the business plan.

Munson said that from the perspective of the twenty-first century, the TSR West business plan still seemed sound. Furthermore, strategies included in the business plan were used by other comic book companies to stay alive during the lean years. For example, Dark Horse Comics collected their comics in trade paperbacks and sold them in bookstores. Dark Horse Comics also sold movie rights to their characters. Nineties flicks like *The Mask, Timecop,* and *Tank Girl* were based on Dark Horse properties. If those tactics helped Dark Horse survive, maybe they would have worked for TSR West too.

Elliot S! Maggin said that, ultimately, the venture needed "more time to catch on." He said, "Lorraine was a good manager, but mostly she understood money. She didn't understand product. I think she lost interest in TSR West."

In reflecting on why things didn't work out, Flint Dille returned to the theme of time. He said, "I don't think we did the world's greatest execution, and we only really existed for a year. And it's hard to get involved in an industry and master that industry and really make a name for yourself inside a year. It's just a tall order. It was everything from the reality that the product just wasn't what it should have been to we just didn't have enough time to really do it. I would argue that they actually started getting good by the time TSR West went under, but that's just my opinion. It was this world of huge possibility, and we thought, *This is really cool.* But when it ended, it ended, and everybody moved on."

TSR West is now dead and mostly forgotten. You can find the company's comic modules for cheap on eBay, Amazon, and a half dozen other online comic book stores. They have not become valuable with time.

Every once in a while, Brad Munson will be driving down Sepulveda Boulevard, and among the concrete and the traffic and the infinite sprawl, he will see the former offices of TSR West. He'll gaze at the redbrick building and wonder who now sits in the corner office that was once his.

TSR West was an attempt by TSR to break into the wider world of comic books, television, and movies in the late 1980s and early 1990s. This effort wound up costing the company significant monies, with little to show for it other than a balance sheet in the red. However, the mistakes the company made are instructive. They comprise a negative blueprint, a list of things a company working in a creative field should try not to do. With all the arrogance and perspective of hindsight, it is hard not to look at the tale and think the company should have never alienated DC Comics.

At the time, the collapse of the DC Comics licensing arrangement followed by the failure of TSR West was bad. It left the company burdened with debt, with no exposure in the realm of comic books, and denied them monies from DC.

With thirty years of hindsight, this double failure looks like a disaster. Given that comic books have become the spawning ground of movies, and movies are such a leviathan of twenty-first-century popular culture, it is easy to imagine how things might be different if this deal had not collapsed.

Consider these two touchstones: Marvel Comics was sold to Disney in 2009 for $4.2 billion, and *Wonder Woman,* which Jeff Grubb said was selling about as well as the *AD&D* comic books, was made into a hit film that made $821.74 million.

This is what could have been.

If TSR had simply kept on with DC Comics, the *AD&D* lines could have served as templates for movies. If the movies did well, this would have increased the value of the company's intellectual property and, thusly, the value of the company.

Yes, there was a *Dungeons & Dragons* movie. But it's worth noting that it was a movie based on a game. In our putative future, our *D&D* movies would be based on comic books, a much easier medium for adaptation.

The decision to alienate DC Comics bore bitter fruit. It is an example of a moment when cooperation between all parties, rather than competition, would perhaps have netted the greater benefit.

In the end, TSR died because it wasn't making enough money. Given what a cash cow the comic-book-to-film road has become, the failure of the company to step on to it due to the decision to break faith with DC Comics seems in hindsight a calamity. Fans are left to imagine what stories might have been with decades of DC-made *AD&D* comics for Hollywood to draw on.

With the failure of the company to break into comic books, it needed to find a way to generate more revenue.

Perhaps another new setting? Could new settings bring in new fans?

THE FISH-BAIT STRATEGY

Bruce Nesmith is someone who's not fully appreciated. As good as people think he is, he's even better than that.

—JOHN RATELIFF, GAME DESIGNER AND EDITOR

THUS FAR, TSR's game worlds had hewed closely to heroic fantasy. The genre's knobs and dials were obviously leveled and tuned differently depending on the world, with Dragonlance blasting up the dragons and *Oriental Adventures* clicking the setting to East Asia. But in 1990, the company experimented with genre. It debuted Ravenloft, the *AD&D* setting of gothic horror, a world where desire curdled into evil, which led to general doom. It would prove a critical darling and fan favorite. Could it also bring new fans to the game?

This departure from high fantasy was an intentional bid for new players. Jim Ward described it as a fish-bait strategy. Earthworms are a fine bait if you're fishing for trout, but if you want walleye, you have to use nightcrawlers or leeches. It was the same with RPG settings. The company had captured hordes of fantasy fans with their existing settings. Now they would set out to find new fans by creating settings in new genres. Ravenloft, of course, would feature horror.

The man in charge of this setting was Bruce Nesmith, the computer whiz kid hired right out of college who volunteered to be fired in 1985. In 1989, he was hired back, and one of his first new projects would be Ravenloft.

Why Ravenloft? Because TSR had nothing in the horror genre and because, according to Nesmith, the bestselling adventure in company history at that point was Laura and Tracy Hickman's *Ravenloft.* Bruce Nesmith thought it was a masterpiece. By my lights, he's right. It remains the greatest *D&D* adventure ever written, so much so that sequels and remakes are still produced to this day, many stretching on for hundreds and hundreds of pages. For all of that ink, none of the retreads have yet equaled the original adventure, which changed tabletop role-playing forever in a spare and stunning thirty-two pages. So it made sense to take the adventure and expand it into an entire setting. The sales numbers said people wanted *Ravenloft*, and giving the public what it wants is a good way to make money. It is an example of the company doing something right—in this case, listening to its audience.

The original idea for expanding *Ravenloft* into a setting was Jim Ward's, but Bruce Nesmith said that when he heard about it, "I fell all over myself trying to get assigned to that." (Jim Ward said the idea was a group effort and that he had the greatest team of game designers in the world.) Nesmith was given the task of writing it, and Andria Hayday would edit the work.

Nesmith began with research. He described himself as a "research junkie." He read *Ravenloft* several times. He played through parts of it, though not the entirety of the adventure, as it is rather long. He delved deep into the lore of vampires, horror, the occult, and the gothic.

Then, he began writing. He said, "At the time, I was a passable writer. I would hesitate to say I was a good writer at all." But when his pages passed to Hayday, she transmogrified them. He said she was a strong personality with good ideas and a fantastic grasp of gothic horror who "added flavor and color that I was really struggling to hit the right tone for." The prose became evocative and inspiring, and games must always be inspiring so a DM will want to run them. In recognition of the effort Hayday put in, which went above and beyond what editors were usually expected to do, she was given a design credit on the *Ravenloft: Realm of Terror* boxed set, which came out in 1990.

The Ravenloft setting was for telling tales of mystery and menace, ghosts and gallows, sordid sins and the crimes committed to keep them secret. *Dracula, Frankenstein,* and *The Haunting of Hill House* would all be touchstone texts for the setting.

Because the default *D&D* setting is heroic fantasy, it would take some design finesse to make Ravenloft work. First, it was located on a different plane of existence, the Demiplane of Dread. Using the *Ravenloft* adventure as a starting point, Nesmith posited that somehow Strahd and his entire country were sucked into the demiplane and stuck there. This fit the Hickmans' adventure nicely, because in *Ravenloft,* once characters entered Barovia, they couldn't leave. Mysterious mists kept them imprisoned. But Nesmith would need more room for gamers to play in than just Barovia. So he made the mists even more powerful. They could suck characters from other worlds into the Demiplane of Dread. When other powerful (often evil) individuals were brought there, new lands would spring up for them to rule, the trick being that their domains were also their prisons, which they could never leave. For example, one land is ruled by a ghost in a castle. Another, Lamordia, is ruled by a sort of Frankenstein's monster. Rules would have to change as well as setting to allow for gothic horror in the game. Fear and horror checks were added, forcing characters to flee whatever terror they are confronting rather than just slaughtering it and taking its stuff as they would in most adventures.

The product was reviewed by the up-and-comers over at White Wolf Publishing in issue #23 of *White Wolf Magazine.* Stewart Wieck, who was editor in chief of the magazine at the time, began his review by praising Laura and Tracy Hickman's original adventure, then saying of *Realm of Terror,* "I expected a hack product trying to make good on a ripped-off name, so I was pleasantly surprised to find the authors making a real attempt to maintain the integrity of the setting and characters." It goes on to praise the product at length, especially the advice on running gothic horror adventurers. The only reason that *Realm of Terror* was not given the "coveted rating of five stars" was because thirty-four domains, the number of realms run by evil beings in Ravenloft, "make the whole product a bit clumsy." He would have liked the product better if it was restricted to a mere dozen domains, each fleshed out in greater detail.

Sales of Ravenloft products were "through the roof," according to Nesmith. "Other than the Forgotten Realms boxed set, it was the bestselling setting that we had. And it had legs. It just kept selling and selling and selling."

A look at the company's actual sales numbers revealed that not to be true. The boxed set was outsold by a number of other settings, such as Dragonlance and Greyhawk, and it's worth mentioning again that management did not inform creatives about the sales of their products. The *Realm of Terror* boxed set sold 36,491 copies in its first year of release and 103,820 copies between 1990 and 1999. That first-year number is particularly troubling, as it was part of a continuing downward trend in sales.

The Ravenloft setting is a personal favorite of mine. I bought the boxed set and the adventures, and I read the novels. But despite the exceptional quality of the product, the sales of settings were dropping down, down, down, down . . .

How did management not see this? The trouble here may have been the very reason TSR was producing so many different settings to begin with, the fish-bait strategy. If one imagines the approximately 36,000 copies of *Realm of Terror* sold in its first year as bringing 36,000 new players to role-playing, people who will buy game products and novels from the company for years, it obscures the falling sales.

And if Ravenloft brought 36,000 new players to the fold, why not make another setting that would appeal to another audience? The company had so many brilliant artists. Why not bring them in early in the process and make a sort of collaboration with the game designers?

THE CHARACTERS OF BROM

In the late 1980s, on twenty-four-hours' notice, Gerald Brom appeared in the Art Department, but he is no Gerry. He was and remains simply Brom. That single syllable enfolds within it the man's capacious style for the brooding, the gothic, and the über-cool. Brom proved himself an artistic genius while at the company, though of a different sort from Jeff Easley. He would not paint windows into other worlds but instead birth characters, men and women of startling darkness struggling to survive in lands where wonder was equaled by peril, and there was no guarantee of escaping unharmed, or even alive.

Gerald Brom's first love had always been fantasy art. He aspired to a career creating shambling horrors, armor-bedecked warriors, and the like. But work was sparse. There was a small cadre of top artists who managed to score all the major book covers, leaving less than crumbs for up-and-comers like him. Like Easley before him, he had a day job paying the bills. He worked in Atlanta, "doing commercial art and hating it." He concluded, "I needed to paint monsters. I needed to create imaginative characters and creatures or I wouldn't be happy."

He heard TSR was hiring fantasy artists, so he sent his work to Lake Geneva.

He heard nothing back.

He followed up with a phone call. The artist liaison told him he was just not what they were looking for and added, "You just don't really have what it takes yet."

(It is worth noting here that from the point of view of today, Brom is obviously an artist of immense prowess. Telling him he doesn't have what it takes is like telling Einstein to keep trying for a promotion at the patent office. The lesson to be learned may be that for the young artist, hard work and persistence are of more value than listening to summative critiques of their work.)

The artist liaison also told him there was a position as a staff artist that would soon be opening up. Perhaps he could do some new work and send that for them to take a look at?

Like a wolf on a wounded deer, Brom moved on the opportunity. He would not merely send them more work. He would go up to Lake Geneva and visit.

Looking back on this moment over twenty-five years after the fact, Brom said, "I was twenty-three years old and not that good at self-evaluating my work. I thought I was perfectly qualified for any position. So I jumped right on that. I gathered a couple more paintings, and I actually called up TSR and said, 'Hey, I'm going to come see you guys!' They were like, 'Huh? What?' You know, they weren't encouraging at all."

Brom flew up to Wisconsin and drove out to the offices on Sheridan Springs Road. He showed his portfolio to the art director and the other artists on staff.

Their response to all his effort and enthusiasm was at best underwhelming. He said that the artists were "incredibly generous and kind, but nobody was very impressed with my work." The art director gave it to him straight. According to Brom, he said, "Look, kid, we have ten other people that we are talking to right now about this job, and on that list, you're number eleven."

Defeated, Brom returned to Atlanta and put all thought of TSR out of his mind. Instead, he focused his efforts on New York City. This being the dark times before the rise of the internet, he would have to live near the major publishing houses if he wanted to get any work with them, and the nucleus of American publishing was of course New York City. Brom and his wife flew up north and found an apartment in New Jersey. Having secured residence, they went back down to Atlanta to pack their things.

The moment came when Brom and his wife had crammed every stick of furniture, every box, book, photo album, pot, pan, lamp, and bath mat into a U-Haul. He said the only things they hadn't packed were the cat and the phone, which proved a lucky break. The telephone sat on the bare floor of their empty apartment. He left it plugged in because the last thing he was going to do before setting off for New Jersey was call his parents to tell them he was leaving.

The phone rang, echoing through the hollow spaces of the apartment.

Figuring it was his parents, Brom ran over and picked up the receiver.

It was the art director from TSR. The same art director who told Brom that his name was eleventh on a list of ten. The art director asked him if by any chance he was still interested in that job.

Brom's internal reaction was, "Oh my God!" but he said, "Yeah, of course I am. Of course I am."

The art director went on to tell him that of the other ten artists, precisely zero were interested in relocating to a microscopic town in southern Wisconsin, so would Brom take it?

He said, "Oh yeah. Hell yeah, I'll take it."

The art director replied, "Well, I know that it's probably going to take you a couple of months to finish up your work and get out of your lease before you can leave Atlanta. Roughly, how long will it take you to get up here?"

Brom looked at the U-Haul, packed to the roof with everything he owned except for the cat and the phone, and said, "I can be there in twenty-four hours."

ARTISTICALLY, BROM HAD a difficult time fitting in at TSR, at least at first.

A word is necessary here about Brom as a creator. His art is powerful. His style is stark, jarring, and lovely, with all the beauty of a dead moor, a skeleton bleaching on the side of a road, or a spider scuttling across its web to feast on the trapped fly. His canvases bloat with grays, blacks, and whites. He paints with the palette of gloom. Both alluring and horrifying, his work demands attention.

Meanwhile, Clyde Caldwell, Keith Parkinson, Jeff Easley, and the other established company artists were painting Technicolor fantasies. The apex of the style may well be Easley's red dragon, which is an eyeball feast of lush, deep reds. The dragon seems so slick it might slide off the page to begin tearing up the local bookstore.

To a management class accustomed to the rich, varied, and bright style that had become the hallmark of the Art Department, Brom's stygian phantasmagoria would prove difficult to swallow. He said, "My style did not jell well with the house look for Dragonlance and Forgotten Realms." He pointed out that the art produced for those two settings was scene-driven. The artists endeavored to show the viewer a world that never was but that was complete and consistent and worthy of experiencing. He described this approach as "perfect for role-playing." But Brom enjoyed painting figures. He said, "My paintings are much more character-driven and less about background."

A further obstacle to his integration at the company was that his choice of colors contrasted sharply with what Easley, Caldwell, and those who preceded him had shaped for *D&D*. Brom said, "The early established look of *Dungeons & Dragons* was very colorful. TSR often felt like you were cheating them if you didn't use all the colors, and I had more of a stark palette. So there were some conflicts there. A lot of my early work did not go over well with management."

Brom remembered a higher-up approaching him to talk about a particular painting. The man told him that the painting was really important, so he should make sure to use all his colors when he made it. Another time, he was told to use all his most expensive colors in a work. Telling Brom to use more colors in his paintings is like telling J. R. R. Tolkien to make his novels more realistic. It entirely misses the artistry of the work. He said that he looked back on such moments as "laughable" and "comedic." He described a company where management simply did not understand the language, habits, or practices of the artists they employed. Management consisted almost entirely of businesspeople who didn't understand how to work with creatives. "If you were managing a cardboard factory, these were the people that could help you with production, but that type of management doesn't work with creatives," he said.

Brom remembered art directors trying to get people to "paint faster" or to goad him into creating paintings that looked more like Larry Elmore's work.

One of the results of these crossed lines of expectation was that art directors came and went at TSR. Art directors were much easier to replace than artists when management was unhappy.

While Brom received a torrent of direction from management, he built relationships with other artists at the company. Jeff Easley said that when Brom appeared in the Art Department, he was a vision in black. He dressed like a goth, but was interested in old toys, Halloween, and weird movies. In other words, he was a man right up Easley's alley. The two of them had a lot in common.

Easley said Brom showed up in Lake Geneva already making great art, but that he would grow a lot during his time on Sheridan Springs Road. He stepped into the role of mentor to Brom. It was Easley who taught him how to gesso a canvas. (Gesso is a white paint mixture used by artists to prepare a canvas for painting.)

Brom said that when he arrived, he didn't know how to paint with oils, but the other artists taught him. Jeff Easley was largely humble about any part he may have played in mentoring Brom. He said that as far as painting in oil went, "I tell everybody who's trying to paint with oil that it's just a matter of pushing it around on the surface and seeing what it will do. It's just pretty obvious if you just practice a little," which is a bit like Shakespeare saying that writing a play is just a matter of putting a pen to paper and scribbling words on it.

Easley did say that if he had any influence in helping Brom become the artist he is today, that it is one of the most significant accomplishments of his career.

Brom, having learned from his fellow artists and weathered the criticisms of management, was about to show everyone what he could do.

A DARK SUN RISES

Brom would prove his genius working on a new setting named Dark Sun.

Dark Sun was a postapocalyptic world where sorcerer-kings vied for power, and the scarcity of resources meant that the daily life of characters would be a struggle. It was a world dark and gritty and deadly. In standard *D&D*, halflings were merry and jolly little folk, always ready to laugh and enjoy a meal. In Dark Sun, the halflings were cannibals! It would certainly provoke a new player experience. It was created by a team that stretched across departments and included Tim Brown, Troy Denning, Mary Kirchoff, and Steve Winter. Kirchoff said that they didn't want to come up with just another world. She wanted this setting to produce a new kind of player experience, one that would "break the mold" of what *D&D* was. Cannibal halflings certainly were a break from tradition.

The way artists were incorporated into the design process also broke the mold. Typically, artists were told what to produce for TSR products. Writing and design were captain to the art. But the Dark Sun team was so enamored with Brom's unique style, so sure that it would prove an excellent fit for the gritty, savage setting they were creating, that he was incorporated early in the design process. Furthermore, designers and writers would look at art he had already created and write backgrounds for the characters within, an inversion of the usual process. He said he was allowed "free rein to explore the world. So, you know, how could I not love that?" The process was a true collaboration between words and art, wherein "ideas went back and forth."

Brom's vision of Dark Sun was a somber and cruel landscape where a yellow sun beat down on deserts like a hammer on an anvil, where men and women were twisted by the land's harshness into knots of bone and muscle that seemed almost inhuman. He painted a setting where the question was not whether good would prevail but rather who would survive. A full-color painting of his leered off the cover of the first Dark Sun release, and his black-and-white drawings bedecked the interior.

Mary Kirchoff said she believed it was Brom's art that made Dark Sun so memorable in the minds of the fans. Brom was so pleased with the result that he described the Dark Sun setting as his favorite RPG project. With Dark Sun, he made his mark as an artist of significance working in the field of fantasy.

The setting was another creative peak for the company and remains a fan favorite to this day. Furthermore, the integration of artists early in the design process would become a hallmark at the company and bore fruit in the excellence of the final product.

The 1991 *Dark Sun Boxed Set* would do better than Ravenloft did the year before, selling 50,065 copies in its first year of release. Viewing that number through the lens of the fish-bait strategy, the product was an unalloyed success. It added tens of thousands of new players to the fold.

Unless of course there was a fundamental problem with the fish-bait strategy . . .

While TSR did not so much discover Brom as stumble over him and then realize what they had, the man clearly developed into a major asset for the company. He produced work that drove sales. His work appeared on the covers of games, novels, and magazines.

New hands were not only brought on board the Art Department. The Book Department also saw new hires move the company forward.

SALVATION SALES IN THE BOOK DEPARTMENT

Moments like this are buds on the tree of life.

—VIRGINIA WOOLF, *MRS. DALLOWAY*

TSR WAS ESTABLISHED to create and publish games, not novels. Consider the company's very name: Tactical Studies Rules. Where does one use rules? Games. Yet the company would find that their audience was so thirsty for fiction set in their game worlds that book sales would come to be approximately half of its profits as time went on.

This was not a natural growth. Game designers and fiction writers are very different animals, and skill at the first means nothing for the second. It is to state the obvious to say that for authors, craft at writing is the most important skill. For game designers, this is not true. Yes, they may describe their games and lay down their rules using the written word, but for them, words are the instructions for their creation, not the thing itself. One can be a writer of questionable ability and still be a hugely successful game designer. Saint Gary himself comes to mind as one such example. His prose was labyrinthine and bombastic. The man never used a simple word where he could instead use one so obscure it would send Ph.D.s racing to the dictionary. (Was the high school dropout proving his smarts?) His turgid prose often congested whatever it was he was supposed to be explaining.

Yes, there would be fits and bumps and hiccups as fiction grew. Two people who helped the fiction lines grow strong and tall in the late '80s and early '90s were Mary Kirchoff and Jim Lowder. Jean Black, who had shepherded the Dragonlance novels into existence and tasked Mary Kirchoff with finding a bestselling author, left the company. Kirchoff was promoted to replace her.

Jim Lowder, who would go on to edit and write novels and games for TSR, was another Massachusetts man, who had attended Marquette University in Milwaukee to study English. Marquette was a neo-medieval splotch of spires, stained glass, and dormitories on the western edge of downtown Milwaukee. It featured a chapel where Joan of Arc once supposedly prayed, shipped to Wisconsin stone by stone from France, and the papers of J. R. R. Tolkien, purchased by the university for less than $5,000 in 1957. After graduating, Lowder received his master's from the University of Wisconsin–Milwaukee, but rather than pursue a job in academia, he landed a job at TSR.

Kirchoff hired Lowder to be a copy editor with the opportunity for advancement, and advancement there would be, because in the Book Department, there was much work to be done. Lowder said that books published by the company in the late 1980s and early 1990s were selling "astoundingly well." A 1990 sales manual bragged that the company was "the second largest publisher of fantasy fiction in the US" and that a new TSR novel sold on average "a quarter million copies in the first year of its release." By 1990, over five million Dragonlance novels had been sold. But according to Lowder, it wasn't just books that tied into *D&D* that were selling. For example, the first novel in the Dark Horse fantasy series by Mary H. Herbert, about a woman whose clan is massacred and who then masquerades as her twin brother to get revenge, topped seventy-five thousand copies.

With novel sales exploding, Kirchoff kept giving Lowder more and more responsibilities while mentoring him as an editor. Within months of his hiring, he was editing major novels by established authors. After that, he was managing entire book lines, including properties such as the Forgotten Realms and Ravenloft.

For Kirchoff, it was a golden time. Jim Lowder was a great collaborator, but beyond that, there was the material they had to work with. The job was playing with the raw stuff of dreams, myths, and nightmares. She felt as though they'd been given "the keys to the kingdom. It was up to us to start book lines, and find authors, and make sure we maintained the integrity of our brands."

Through conversations and idea sessions, they built the Book Department up, work by work and procedure by procedure, in an attempt to turn the company into a proper publisher of fiction. According to her, the pair of them shared "a vision of transparency and fairness." Their goal was to "legitimize" the Book Department and demonstrate it was not some orphan, cast-off, or poor relation of the Games Department. Rather, Books would stand tall, and on its own two feet.

They implemented new procedures for finding authors and awarding book contracts. Previously, authors were often given contracts based largely on who they knew in the Book Department. But not anymore. Now, there would be an audition process for most projects, wherein author names were removed from proposals and multiple editors reviewed and rated each anonymous pitch. For example, Lowder had to audition for his first book contract just like every other author.

The slush pile was still an entry point to writing for the company, with Lowder serving as the first-line reviewer. Notable authors like Elaine Cunningham, Mary Herbert, Christie Golden, and of course Bob Salvatore were discovered in this way.

The slush pile was also thick with curiosities and horrors. Kirchoff said she and Jim "would chuckle over some of the things that we received that were head-scratchingly bad." One book proposal, Lowder recalled, had been "sent to us on a poorly cured animal hide scroll, which stank like week-old roadkill." Another novel proposal was made out of letters and words cut out of magazines, "like a film noir ransom note." He said, "I dutifully replied to every submission that crossed my desk. Even those."

The pair also fought to increase royalty rates for authors, getting them raised from 4 percent to 6 percent to 8 percent of the book's cover price, depending on the author's level of experience. It took lobbying and effort to convince management that it was worth giving writers a financial stake in the books they wrote. In the grand scheme of publishing, the royalty rate remained on the low side, but given the solid sales at the company in the late '80s and early '90s, it resulted in a fine payday for authors.

Another small victory came when management agreed to implement a tiered and escalating royalty system. Authors would receive an increasing royalty percentage based on the number of books sold, the number of hardcovers as opposed to mass-market paperbacks, and so on. It allowed authors whose work really took off (Bob Salvatore *cough cough*) to reap the benefits of their success. Lowder said, "The TSR contracts at the time were very lucrative and pretty decent work for hire. They offered a fair cut of translations, and the rate increases Mary and I achieved made them at least somewhat competitive with New York." If the company was looking to retain the talent they'd discovered, such moves must have helped.

An indignity the pair did not manage to remedy was that no TSR fiction writer had their name on the spine of the book while Lorraine Williams was CEO. Management was concerned about how the novels would be shelved in bookstores, so they wanted the line promoted over the writer. But for a writer not to see their name on the side of the book they'd birthed from their own blood, bone, and sinew could be wounding. Lowder said the lack of recognition was "a reminder of what management really valued—the brand, not the people creating the content."

But all the positive moves improved the lot of authors and made the department run more professionally. For all the hard work of Kirchoff, Lowder, and the editorial team in building up their division, the Book Department was moved out from under the aegis of Games to become an independent department in 1990.

These changes also helped make the Book Department a profit center for the company. By 1993, the bestselling Forgotten Realms novel sold over 327,000 copies, the bestselling Dragonlance novel sold over 847,000 copies, and in total, the company had sold over 27 million novels.

Those sales were becoming increasingly important to its bottom line, given the declining sales of RPG products and their costs. Producing RPG products was and is a phenomenally expensive proposition. Staff requirements included designers, artists, editors, and even cartographers! The

Games Department fluctuated between twenty and thirty people. A novel, meanwhile, required one writer, an editor and proofreader, and one piece of cover art. (Graphic design and typesetting were handled in-house for all departments, but even there, fiction required far fewer resources because of the relative simplicity of the books' design and layout.) Mary Kirchoff's staff consisted of three full-time editors and an assistant. Lowder said, "There was a point at which the company was making thirty million dollars a year around 1990, and the Book Department was generating about half of the company's profits with a smaller number of products."

In addition to being cheaper to make, the novels sold better. For example, the first Dark Sun novel sold 79,370 copies in 1991. That is more than all the other Dark Sun products released in 1991 *combined.*

In sum, it cost more to make RPG products than it did to make novels, and the novels sold better than RPG products. A rumor ran through the company that Lorraine Williams was considering converting the entire company into a fiction publishing house. According to *Dragon* editor Dale Donovan, one Monday morning, everyone would come into work and "all the game designers would all now be novel writers. All the game editors would now be fiction editors."

Furthermore, the rumor revealed what their fellow employees thought of the work done by Kirchoff, Lowder, et al. Their department was so successful the idea that it might absorb the entire company seemed plausible.

Despite these triumphs, neither Lowder nor Kirchoff would long remain in the cubicles and halls of the old Q-tip factory on Sheridan Springs Road.

Why?

Lowder saw a consistent disrespect of creatives at the company. For example, he ran the Book Department while Mary Kirchoff was out on maternity leave. It seemed like a dry run for a promotion that never came. This was, Lowder said, "the last straw." He developed what he described as "a bad attitude," which he was not adept at hiding. Moreover, he said, "it had become clear to me that I was not going to be respected as a creator if I stayed in-house at TSR. The corporate culture valued brand over people."

Kirchoff said that Lowder was a polarizing figure. He did not play political games, and he did not bother with diplomacy. She said, "He was no Henry

Kissinger." It was the self-possession of the righteous, the holy, the elect, the Massachusetts man, who could see the straightest way, and if others would but listen to his preaching, they would all arrive at paradise. (Even if paradise in this case was a better fantasy novel.)

One day, according to Lowder, Mary Kirchoff called him into her office to talk about his attitude. He suggested that he could improve his attitude, then quit. Kirchoff managed to keep Lowder on as a satellite employee, with reduced pay and no benefits, but he no longer had to spend every weekday at the offices on Sheridan Springs Road.

His last day as a full-time employee was January 31, 1992.

Kirchoff followed him not long after. She was tired of seeing her department constantly coming in second to Games in the eyes of management, even though the novels that her authors and editors created deserved just as much credit for generating sales. People at the company could see Kirchoff was disillusioned. The Marketing Department even offered her a position, one that she turned down because, as she put it, she "didn't want to lose the connection to art," which working on fiction provided. Finally, Kirchoff said, she decided that she "had taken the Book Department as far as my skills would allow me."

So it was that Mary Kirchoff, the woman who discovered Bob Salvatore, left the company. Her departure was not just the loss of a keen mind and manager but a great death of institutional memory.

Lowder was left to wonder if becoming a satellite employee had been a strategic error. With Kirchoff gone, he would have been the ranking officer in the Book Department. He would have been an obvious promotion. Should he have stayed?

So many of the staff responsible for making the Book Department so profitable were now gone. We return again to the great refrain: TSR failed to retain the employees it worked so hard to find and develop. Key staff left over money and over respect. Perhaps the core sickness had been diagnosed by Jim Lowder: the company valued brand above all.

The man who replaced Mary Kirchoff at the head of the Book Department was not a company man, and it certainly wasn't Jim Lowder. He was an outsider, brought in from the legitimate and tony world of New York publishing. From the point of view of a Wisconsinite, it's notable that the man who would take Kirchoff's job was not local. He was not a classmate of Ernie Gygax's. He didn't meet Gary in a bookstore. No, this man was born in New York and attended East Coast schools. He would apply his craft and élan to what had already been built in Lake Geneva and shoot the Book Department into the stratosphere.

Or so it was hoped.

The truth was, he brought discord.

THE REIGN OF BRIAN THOMSEN

The man who would fill Mary Kirchoff's shoes was Brian Thomsen. He was a New York editor of science fiction and fantasy who'd helped Warner Books start their Questar Science Fiction line. The line was such a success that in 1988, he was nominated for a Hugo Award in the category of Best Professional Editor. He'd edited the work of sci-fi luminaries like Greg Bear and Octavia Butler. *Locus* magazine described him as a "hardened New Yorker," a man so New York he didn't even know how to drive when he was hired to become executive editor of the Book Department.

Thomsen passed away in 2008 at the age of forty-nine, so his close friend and TSR veteran Jim Fallone will often speak for him in this volume. He said of Thomsen, "Brian was an editor and publisher in the true old-school sense of the words. He loved publishing most at its pulpy core. He was the Falstaff of genre books. He ate, slept, and breathed publishing. He loved the genre and was exceptionally versed in all aspects and categories. One of my fondest memories of Brian was discussing the merits of Ted Mark's erotic spy novels with [comic book icon] Julie Schwartz and expensive scotch on the patio of the Scientology Celebrity Centre at a Writers of the Future" awards ceremony.

In what would prove a sinister irony, Bob Salvatore helped Thomsen find the job at TSR. His agent was friends with Thomsen, and he put in a good word for him with Lake Geneva. He said, "I don't know if it carried any weight or not, because I was just another writer on the team, you know? But they hired him."

Jim Lowder would meet Thomsen for the first time in August of 1992. Lowder was in Milwaukee working at Gen Con. For four days, the convention filled the streets of the city with every stripe of geek, nerd, and dweeb, and it was beautiful. Barbarians clad in furs, greatswords slung over one shoulder, and backpacks full of books slung over the other, waited for the light to change on Wisconsin Avenue with lawyers, bankers, and policemen. Our sweaty, huffing, and eager tribe filled every food court, bodega, and bar within walking distance of the convention center.

The city itself seemed uncertain what to think of the sudden influx of tens of thousands of gamers. They could spend all the money they wanted in Milwaukee, sure, but in a thousand little ways, the city sent the message that the presence of Gen Con was tolerated, but not welcomed.

Thomsen met Lowder at the SafeHouse, a downtown Milwaukee landmark that was probably the coolest bar on the planet in 1966. Inspired by the James Bond craze, the bar purports to be an actual hiding spot for spies. It is riddled with secret passages and spy memorabilia.

Despite his frustration with the company, Lowder approached this first meeting with optimism. Lowder said, "I had not been particularly happy with the way in which the Book Department was treating me as an author or an editor. Brian clearly understood the problem and said he would be happy to work with me to figure out which word would go first in my hyphenated title—*writer* or *editor.*"

In addition to Lowder's problems with the company, the company had problems within the larger publishing industry, problems that Brian Thomsen was brought on board to address. Its fiction had proven phenomenally successful. This success was noticed by mainstream publishers of fantasy and science fiction. Noticed, and Lowder believed, resented. TSR writers weren't invited to fantasy and sci-fi conventions, just gaming conventions. He heard "industry chatter bemoaning the shared world and licensed lines taking shelf space away from 'real books.'" In other words, the fantasy and science fiction community looked down on the company and their publishing efforts in much the same way the literati looked down on fantasy and science fiction.

Lowder was hopeful that Thomsen would help address these issues. After all, he came from the world of New York publishing. Lowder said, "I thought all this might convince some of the industry tastemeisters that TSR was taking fiction seriously, even if we were still located in the relative wilds of Wisconsin."

At that first meeting, Thomsen had nothing but kind words for him. Lowder said, "He was very complimentary about my writing, noted several books he thought I'd done a good job on as editor, and said he was open to me settling on either author or editor as my strong suit."

Furthermore, Thomsen struck Lowder as an intelligent individual of the geeky persuasion. The pair chatted about "books, comics, film, and history." He was also very well read, as a good editor must be.

Lowder left the conversation feeling optimistic about his relationship with TSR and about the company's place in the industry of publishing. It was a promising start.

That promise, unfortunately, proved to be a lie.

From conversations with a number of people who worked with Brian Thomsen during his tenure at the company, it seemed as though he approached the management of fiction with a tribal ethos. A writer or editor was either on his team or stood against him. Those on "Team Brian" were given total trust and favored in all things. Those who opposed him would be harried without mercy.

It seemed as if that initial meeting convinced Thomsen that Lowder was on Team Brian. In short order, he told Lowder of a number of plans for changes in the Book Department.

Lowder, the Massachusetts man who descended from hardheaded Irish immigrants, would find many of these plans unprofessional and possibly unethical.

Kirchoff and Lowder fought for more money and more respect for authors, and they made progress. Yet according to Lowder, Thomsen wanted to take these hard-fought victories and scrap them. He recalled that "Brian's overall complaint was that the department and the editors treated writers too well and that the department should be harder-nosed and harder-hearted in pretty much every interaction."

This came as a surprise to Lowder. For years, he and others in the Book Department had been arguing that the company had to treat its writers better, because the New York publishing houses were. After all, Margaret Weis and Tracy Hickman left the company because a New York publisher was simply willing to pay them more to write novels than TSR was. It seemed obvious from the Book Department cubicles on Sheridan Springs Road that if the company wanted to keep the talent it had discovered, it had to treat that talent better.

Yet here was Thomsen, a blooded veteran of that very New York publishing world, preaching to the rafters in Lake Geneva that the company should treat its writers roughly. He told Lowder that he didn't like the tiered pay for different formats. He intended to rewrite the contracts using vague language that would allow the company to do what it wanted where tiered royalties were concerned. He said his revision to the contract would be so subtle that the authors would never detect the changes. (At least not until their royalty checks began to arrive, one imagines.) He would fatten the company's bottom line, and no author would even cotton on enough to complain about it until it was too late. He planned to take the very advances Lowder and Kirchoff had fought for and toss them on the dung pile.

But why was Thomsen telling Lowder all his lawful evil plans? He said, "I have no doubt about this: He was showing me and the TSR editors how clever he was."

Rather than roll over and allow Thomsen to have his way, Lowder acted. Thomsen ordered him not to discuss the details of the proposed contract changes with his writers, reminding him that he was, even as satellite staff, prohibited from disclosing company trade secrets. So he didn't tell the authors about Thomsen's plans. But he did warn them to "really, really take a close look at their next contract."

Another change instituted by Thomsen concerned the slush pile. At a departmental meeting, he placed a garbage can in the center of the room and brought in the pile of unsolicited queries and manuscripts that had been sent to the company. He said that the department was spending too much time on slush. According to Lowder, Thomsen declared the company would now adopt the "New York way to handle unsolicited submissions." He then "picked up the first submission on the slush pile, started reading the cover letter, got partway through the description of the plot, and dropped the packet into the trash. 'I've read it a thousand times before. Next.' He picked up the next submission, noted that it had the wrong-sized self-addressed stamped envelope, and tossed it into the trash. He burned through a half dozen more submissions that way, citing the wrong typeface on the cover, pink paper, a misspelled name—anything that annoyed him was a reason to reject the submission."

Lowder's reaction was one of horror. He said, "The department owed a lot of its recent success to writers who had come in over the transom."

Lowder pursued Thomsen into his office after the meeting. He "told him I disagreed strongly with the policy. We discussed the topic for a while, but he was unmoved by the list of writers I mentioned, and concluded by noting there were hungry mid-list writers who would be happy for the contracts. They'd save the editors' time currently spent on slush and teaching green writers how to write. I left TSR for the drive home glad that I was no longer in the building day to day."

Though he didn't realize it at the time, the countdown to Lowder's final departure from the company likely started that day with the slush pile demonstration.

In hindsight, it seems obvious that Thomsen should have been trying to solve the problem of talent fleeing the company. Instead, the new, aggressive style he adopted would quickly lead to conflict with one of the stars of the Book Department, Bob Salvatore. It was a battle that would drive one of them from TSR.

TSR AND TOLKIEN, OR THE GAME THAT WAS NOT

In the early 1990s, TSR had the opportunity to produce a role-playing game set in Middle-earth, the fantasy world created by J. R. R. Tolkien. Given the fish-bait strategy, this would seem like an opportunity. Tolkien and his works already had a worldwide following. Creating a game in one of his worlds might bring countless droves of Middle-earth fanatics into the *Dungeons & Dragons* community. The man in charge of this effort would be editor John Rateliff.

He discovered the works of J. R. R. Tolkien while attending Magnolia Junior High School in Magnolia, Arkansas ("Home of the Cubs!"), by methodically consuming the contents of his school library. He began his digestion of the texts by looking at all the authors whose last names started with *A*. He chose all the books that looked interesting and read them. Task complete, he moved on to *B*. This continued until he reached *T*. There, he encountered *The Hobbit,* and he fell in love. He remembered, "The thing that appeals to me most about Tolkien is I'd never met anyone who thought about trees the way I did. I think of trees as individuals, not interchangeable." He said that cutting down old trees to plant new ones never made any sense to him. "Tolkien really liked and appreciated trees, and he conveyed that," he said.

Like Bob Salvatore's, Rateliff's life was forever changed by reading the works of J. R. R. Tolkien.

Rateliff said that growing up in Magnolia, he felt like "a fish out of water" and that he didn't find people that truly shared his interests until he left Arkansas for the wide world beyond. He attended Marquette University in Milwaukee, Wisconsin, for graduate school because it was one of only two universities in America that had collections of Tolkien's documents. The university's Raynor Memorial Libraries hold "the original manuscripts and multiple working drafts" for both *The Hobbit* and *The Lord of the Rings.*

Despite this, during his time at Marquette, Rateliff was told by his faculty advisor that they didn't want to catch him working on Tolkien. Disobeying orders, he would sneak over to the archives whenever he had free time to behold the hoarded Tolkien treasures housed within. He pointed out, "Things have changed, and Marquette is very proud of having the Tolkien collection now. It fascinates me how things change over time. Like *D&D. D&D* used to be a fringe hobby, but now it's become a mainstream hobby. But *D&D* hasn't changed that much. The people in the world around it changed."

After graduation, Rateliff found work in publishing and, championed by fellow Marquette alumnus Jim Lowder, made his way to TSR. One day, he was called up to the executive suites and shown into a conference room. He'd rarely been up here before. This was the natural habitat of Lorraine Williams and her pack of vice presidents. It was all very fancy. The room had plush chairs and a large table with a glass surface and legs carved like dragons. There, he met with a representative from Tolkien Enterprises who had come to Lake Geneva to offer the company the rights to use J. R. R. Tolkien's Middle-earth in their products. Rateliff, being a renowned Tolkien scholar (his *History of the Hobbit* is possibly the most thorough commentary on Tolkien's different drafts of the novel in existence and was published with Christopher Tolkien's blessing in 2007) was made front man on this new TSR/Tolkien project.

The rights to J. R. R. Tolkien's intellectual property are a sticky web because they are possessed by two radically different entities. In 1969, Tolkien sold the film rights to his work to United Artists for £104,602. In 1976, those rights were sold to Saul Zaentz for $3 million. Zaentz started Tolkien Enterprises, now Middle-earth Enterprises, to exploit the license. Zaentz licensed the rights to make a role-playing game to Iron Crown Enterprises in 1982. Middle-earth

Enterprises would license the film rights to Peter Jackson later in the 1990s. Meanwhile, the rights to Tolkien's literary work resided with the Tolkien Estate, which was run by Tolkien's son Christopher until he stepped down from the role in 2017, at the age of ninety-three. In other words, if you wanted to make a Tolkien film, you'd talk to Saul Zaentz. If you wanted to reprint *The Hobbit*, you'd talk to the Tolkien Estate.

Which presents a number of curious questions, such as, how did the company with the film rights license a role-playing game? Apparently, by claiming the role-playing game was a film product and not based directly on Tolkien's novels. This fine distinction would get Iron Crown Enterprises into trouble when they produced *Tolkien Quest* books, interactive novels set in Middle-earth. Allen & Unwin, an imprint of the UK publisher HarperCollins, that did have the rights to publish Tolkien's literary works, sued. To appease them, Iron Crown Enterprises recalled and destroyed all copies of the *Tolkien Quest* books. This over $2 million loss, along with other problems, nearly forced Iron Crown Enterprises into bankruptcy. At one point, the company could not even make rent, and the Iron Crown staff found on its front door a notice closing the company's offices by order of the sheriff. The instability led some staff to look for greener pastures. One Iron Crown veteran, Monte Cook, would end up living in a converted church in Lake Geneva and working at TSR. And it led Tolkien Enterprises to seek a new licensee for a Middle-earth role-playing game.

TSR was certainly interested. William W. Connors was asked to start coming up with ideas for an entry-level product using Middle-earth as a setting. But the company didn't just want to make role-playing games with the property. Rateliff remembered, "Lorraine wanted all the rights to create fiction, and computer games, and calendars, and spin-offs. Everything except publishing the books themselves. You have to admit, that was vision." The company was making a lot of money with their tie-in novels. In 1992, R. A. Salvatore's *The Legacy* would be the first of the company's novels to be printed in hardcover, and it even cracked the *New York Times* bestseller list. New fiction set in Middle-earth, with a role-playing game attached, could make everyone a lot of money. Jim Lowder said Williams "was dead set on TSR publishing original fiction, both prequels and sequels, to *The Lord of the Rings*. Given the success of the Book Department at the time, the company saw this generating endless piles of cash. Inside the Book Department, we saw the financial potential, but thought it was a bad idea. TSR was already frowned upon as a publisher of fiction by significant parts of the genre publishing market, both the establishment and some readers. This could only make things worse," because the company would be seen as trampling on J. R. R. Tolkien's legacy.

But to publish the fiction that would generate those endless piles of cash and avoid the problems of the *Tolkien Quest* books at Iron Crown, TSR would need permission from the Tolkien Estate. Rateliff would be dispatched to England to negotiate the deal directly with Christopher Tolkien himself. He would even miss Gen Con for the trip by special dispensation. Tradition held that no employees were allowed to miss Gen Con, but he would miss it for this.

Rateliff managed to neatly fold a number of itineraries into this one trip to England. First, he would meet with Christopher Tolkien to discuss TSR's request to print more Middle-earth fiction. Second, 1992 was the one hundredth anniversary of J. R. R. Tolkien's birth. Oxford held a conference from August 17 to 24 in honor of the occasion. Of course, he had to attend. Third, he was recently married and would turn the trip into a honeymoon. His wife was not eager to spend a week of her ostensible honeymoon at a Tolkien conference. He recalled her saying she "didn't travel thousands of miles to sit in a room and listen to people talk about Tolkien." Married to Rateliff, "she could do that at home any day of the week." Instead of sitting in Keble College listening to speeches, "she went and saw England," visiting Blenheim Palace, Winchester Cathedral, and Stonehenge.

He recalled, "That was a memorable trip."

John Rateliff met with Christopher Tolkien in Oxford and a few days later with a representative of HarperCollins, Tolkien's publisher, in London. Rateliff laid out the company's request to create fiction set in Middle-earth. I asked him what Christopher Tolkien's reaction to the request was. He said, "I'd rather not go into that if you don't mind," but characterized Tolkien's response as "a very final no." Sequels and the like were "anathema" to the estate.

So John Rateliff flew back to America and returned to Lake Geneva.

There, in the fancy conference room with the plush chairs and the glass-topped table that had carved dragon legs, he told Lorraine Williams that TSR could not get a fiction line set in Middle-earth. A role-playing game and other products like calendars, yes, but not a single syllable of new fiction. Despite the decades, he remembered her response with perfect clarity. He said, "Her immortal words were, 'Not worth our while.'"

Rateliff felt chagrined. "It would have been fun to work on a Tolkien game," he said, but new Middle-earth fiction? He said, "I agree with the estate that Tolkien is better when it's just Tolkien, when other people don't do follow-ups. That's what fanfiction is for."

When Bill Connors heard that there wouldn't be a game using Tolkien material, he was also disappointed. He said, "I thought we were on the path to a really cool game with great market appeal. Ah well, such is life."

To this day, Rateliff has his doubts about how a beginner Middle-earth game would have done. After all, the company put out a beginner game every year in the early 1990s, and while some did better than others, none were massive hits. And a Tolkien beginner game assumes that the players have likely read Tolkien, and *The Lord of the Rings* is definitely a book for advanced readers. So an entry-level game using Tolkien does seem a mishmash of markets.

What if the company had taken the license and just produced it as a setting for *AD&D*? Rateliff believed "it would have done amazingly well." Seventy percent of *D&D* players were high school aged or above. They were old enough to have read *The Lord of the Rings* and want a role-playing game set in Middle-earth. The success of Iron Crown Enterprises with the game *Middle-earth Role Playing* suggested there was a market for it.

Those of us who were buying TSR products in the 1990s are left to gape at what might have been. Connors was one of the brilliant minds driving the Ravenloft line. What would he have given us if allowed to complete a *The Lord of the Rings* / *D&D* beginner product? It is tantalizing to imagine.

From the perspective of the twenty-first century, it is all too easy to fault Williams for passing on the rights to make a *D&D* Tolkien game. We know that Peter Jackson's movies were huge hits and won Oscars. We know that

Amazon paid $250 million just for the rights to make a TV show based on the novels. But none of that was plainly visible over the horizon in 1992. It would have been fun to have a Tolkien beginner game, yes, but there is no reason to think that it would have changed the ultimate fate of the company. The sickness was in its bones, and likely no single product would have cured it.

Part III

◆

SLAPPING A BAND-AID ON FAILURES

CAN VHS TEACH *D&D* TO EIGHT-YEAR-OLDS?

VICE PRESIDENT RICK Behling explained what *D&D* should be by holding up a copy of Parker Brothers' Monopoly. John Rateliff related that Behling said the game needed to take Monopoly as a model. It should be in the toy aisle, aimed for an audience of eight to ten years old, and have rules that could "be printed on the inside of the box top."

Simpler rules and younger players would expand the company's customer base, and it needed new customers. Yes, TSR and *Dungeons & Dragons* were the market leader in the role-playing game space and, despite problems over the years, had remained so since 1974. But by the early 1990s, other companies and their games were finding traction. FASA created *BattleTech* and *MechWarrior,* a paired miniatures game and role-playing game in which players controlled giant fighting robots (a.k.a. mechs), as well as *Shadowrun,* a game that smashed together fantasy and cyberpunk. Then White Wolf Publishing debuted *Vampire: The Masquerade.* The game was revolutionary because it allowed players to not hunt and kill vampires but rather slip into their capes and play them at the gaming table.

The rise of these extremely popular and incredibly fun games coincided with the steady drop in rule books and setting sales at TSR. It is quite possible that all these games were luring RPG players away from the company's products, resulting in falling sales for the company.

At first, the company was unbothered by all of this. Director of Sales and Marketing Jim Fallone said, "The company was, I think, happy to let those games happen because they weren't fantasy. They weren't in our backyard. They weren't perceived as being competition." In 1993, FASA published *Earthdawn,* a fantasy role-playing game aimed directly at TSR's audience. Fallone said all of this led to "the realization that more and more people were getting into the RPG category, and it was starting to get more crowded." FASA and White Wolf had book trade distribution and could be found at Waldenbooks and B. Dalton's just like TSR's products.

Seeing the success of these other companies led TSR to believe it had to innovate or fade away. TSR West was one example of the company trying to evolve into something else. Since becoming a comic book company didn't work out, perhaps it would evolve into a toy company like Hasbro. It would no longer only produce role-playing games and novels but also toys, CDs, and videos. Hence Rick Behling's elevation of Monopoly as what *D&D* should be.

Dragon Strike attempted to make that vision reality. It was a *D&D* board game intended for children as young as eight that came with a VHS tape. The game was an attempt to push TSR products into the hands of a younger audience, the logic being that if eight-year-olds became accustomed to the tropes of the game, they would have an easier time transitioning when older into *AD&D* and one of the company's game worlds, like the Forgotten Realms. It came from a management recognition of competition from other RPG companies and the realization that the company needed to change, or wither and perish. These are logical, dare I say healthy, motivations for the creation of such a product. But *Dragon Strike*'s execution, and especially management's decisions about production, reveal a number of sicknesses that proved fatal in the extreme for TSR.

Dragon Strike was a revolutionary product for its time. It was a beginner's game that simplified the rules. It came with beautiful cards, dice, and boards, and it included a video to teach children how to play. Looking back on *Dragon Strike* from our present moment, when millions of people have learned to play *D&D* by watching videos online, the idea of including the video seems brilliant.

This project would fall upon the weary but wise shoulders of Bruce

Nesmith. The same Nesmith who was hired back in the '80s for his computer skills, quit, then was rehired and created the Ravenloft setting. While management wanted the product to extend the company's reach into a younger demographic, he said that creatives were of the opinion that putting a role-playing game product in the hands of an eight-year-old wouldn't work because they simply were not developmentally ready to role-play. Nesmith said management believed twelve years old was "just too old to get them into it." Management's goal was to "introduce elements of role-playing with a game suitable for eight-year-olds."

And let us be frank here, even if we are speaking with the arrogance of retrospect. Management's request was an impossible task. A game of *D&D* requires math, storytelling, solid reading ability, and a level of social adroitness, all of which eight-year-olds lack. So while the goal was worthy, management's means to that end were seriously flawed before Nesmith wrote the first syllable of what would become *Dragon Strike*. A better strategy may have been simply to make a board game for younger kids. It would have freed Nesmith of the constraints of *D&D* during the design process. But that was not to be. Like an engineer sadistically tasked with making a flashlight for the blind, he would make *D&D* for eight-year-olds.

Nesmith began by considering what eight-year-olds could do. Developmentally, they are very concrete thinkers. Therefore, *Dragon Strike* would be a board game. However, it would introduce concepts and ideas that would prepare them for role-playing when they were older. For example, the game contained standard fantasy tropes like wizards, kings, and monsters. One player, called the Dragon Master, ran the game, just like *D&D* had a Dungeon Master who ran the game. Looking back on it in hindsight, Nesmith described the inclusion of the Dragon Master as "a mistake." It didn't work well with the age group the product was aimed at. "But we did it anyway."

Nesmith asked himself, how far could *D&D* be stripped down, simplified, and made easier for a putative eight-year-old to play? One thing he decided had to remain in the game was dice-rolling. He said it was "a key element, and one of the few tactile and audio elements of the game. You get to roll the dice. You hear them clatter. You hold them in your hand. And we figured kids would really like that."

But in both *D&D* and *AD&D* at the time, dice-rolling was where the game got complicated. To simplify things, he realized that instead of bonuses and penalties, affecting the chance of success, the die type rolled by the player should change, with higher die types of course being better. Each monster would be given an "Armor Class" (another term borrowed from *D&D*) listing how hard they were to hit, and the larger the die rolled, the better the chance a player would have to hit the monster. All other actions the characters might take would be called a "Feat," and succeeding on a Feat always required a roll of a 6 on the die. It was simple, it kept dice-rolling in the game, and it was fun.

The Dragon Master would run scenarios for their players, and Nesmith said after the basic rules were laid down, the rest of his design process was creating scenarios with Andria Hayday and finding ways to make the maps that would come with the game as reusable as possible.

The inclusion of a VHS tape with the game also sprang from the goal of reaching eight-year-olds. Nesmith said, "If you're going to teach eight-year-olds a complex subject, you're going to do much better with video than you are with a set of dry rules. That age group isn't going to read rules." He pointed out that if you open any board game created for eight-year-olds even today, the rules "are written with the assumption that an adult is going to read the rules and help them play."

Including a VHS tape meant the company was going to have to film something to go on it, and if you're filming something, you'll need actors, cameras, a crew, and so on. Better just do that in California.

Reenter stage right our old friend Flint Dille.

Nesmith described Dille as "a Hollywood guy." He would create the content of the video that would be included in the game.

Dille described becoming involved with *Dragon Strike* thusly: "I got a call from TSR, which my sister owned at that point, and they wanted to do a video, an instructional video for how to play a role-playing game."

TSR, of course, was a whale in the RPG industry, but compared to a movie studio, it was a guppy. The small amount of money the company wanted to spend meant that traditional on-set filming with actors was out of the question. At the same time, the money wasn't enough to pay animators and voice actors. Dille and his producer decided to film actors against a blue screen, remove all color from the shot, add a background, and then put the color back in. The process was responsible for the weird, low-fi, hyperreal look of the video. But it would meet the company's budgetary constraints. A large portion of the cast was found working at Universal Studios Hollywood on *The Adventures of Conan: A Sword and Sorcery Spectacular*, which explained why the actors looked like fantasy archetypes.

Despite Nesmith creating the game that the video was intended to teach players to play, he said, "the video was filmed without myself or editor Andria Hayday being there. And we only really had cursory input into the script itself." To him, it felt like the filming of the video took place "in a black box." He didn't hear questions from Dille about the game or receive updates on how casting and shooting the video was going. And Lake Geneva, Wisconsin, can feel worlds away from Hollywood, California.

The resulting video was cheesy, to be sure, but worse yet, it was boring. Hammy acting demonstrated why so much of the cast had been working at the *Conan Sword and Sorcery Spectacular* before *Dragon Strike,* and while filming on green screens today can look clean and impressive, the product of the process in 1993 looked like sub–Saturday morning cartoon fare that likely would have exhausted the attention span of any eight-year-old who watched it.

The video begins with the floating head of a middle-aged man staring out of the screen on a field of black. The man looks like he could have been cast as a cheating spouse in a romance or a mid-level criminal in a thriller. The actor is John Boyle, a man whose previous credits included the role of Prison Guard on *Cheers* and Man #3 in the 1988 Lea Thompson vehicle, *Casual Sex?* Now, Boyle is our Dragon Master, and as the music swells and he stares out of the television screen at the viewer like they owe him money, Boyle intones, "Feeling brave tonight? How brave? Brave enough to do battle with hideous monsters? Hm? Brave enough to sneak around dank castles in the dark and chance being the next victim . . . of a dragon strike!"

Writer Don Jolly asked of this moment, "Why is their 'Dragon Master' an aggressive (and sexually compelling) disembodied head?"

Flint Dille said of that decision, "So we just decided, you know what?

We're going to do him as a disembodied head . . . I don't remember exactly how we came to that."

Then, Boyle's head disappears, and a red dragon flies over a dark blue sky, fire erupting from its mouth as if, like Boyle's piercing gaze, it could shoot out of the television screen. The title then is displayed.

Next, we see a sun-spackled castle on a hill in clement weather. An unknown voice with something approaching a Brooklyn accent delivers the following line as though auditioning for a guest spot on *Seinfeld*, "All right! Your Sunstone's done! So whaddaya want me to do with it?"

Rainbow-colored bars of light—not rainbows, mind you, but rather horizontal bars of multicolored light—rise in strips from the ground and are sucked into the highest tower of the castle. What exactly these bars are meant to represent is beyond imagining, but they are clearly not good, because the rainbow bars suck up all the beautiful vegetation and leave behind a barren wilderness. They also change day to night and leave the castle in sinister darkness. Another new voice, now speaking like a B-grade, horror-flick villain, breathes, "Let darkness fall, and in the darkness, let evil grow!"

If an eight-year-old sat down to watch this in 1993, the first precious minute of her attention span spent watching this video would leave her confused, and perhaps offended that her time was being wasted watching such absurdities. Who is the scary man staring at her? He makes her feel unsafe. What is a dragon strike, and why are dank castles particularly susceptible to them? Thirdly, what is a Sunstone, and why does it make nice places nasty?

As a fifteen-year-old in 1993, I remember watching the video on a local television station early on a Sunday morning, during the hour infomercials usually hawked Ginsu knives. I watched the whole show with amazement and affection. I was just glad to see *D&D* on TV; my love for my tribe and my youth blinded me to the obvious shortcomings of the product.

The video is filled with puzzling moments. Why do sparkles cover the characters when they are attempting to break into a room? It was to cover up a technical error in postproduction. Why is there a minotaur in the video, but not one in the game? Dille was writing from an early version of the rule book, not the final draft.

This last detail is striking and explains a number of other mysteries surrounding the video. For example, the video doesn't really attempt to explain the rules of the game until the twenty-one-minute mark. Up until then, the video is much more like a pilot for a television show with a freaky, aggressive narrator. Even when it does hazard to explain how to roll dice, the explanation is hazy and vague.

Lastly, from a management perspective, considering that Dille was tasked with creating a video about how to play a role-playing game, it would be helpful to have the final draft of the rules before spending unknown sums of money making a video explaining those rules.

Dille said that the actual game content "was almost invisible to me. Frankly, I don't remember ever actually playing the game. That doesn't mean I didn't; it just means that I don't remember it."

If the target audience of the video was eight-year-olds, it appeared to miss its mark. Instead of giving a concise, clear, quick explanation of how to play, the video comes off as a bad pilot for a children's show.

Dragon Strike was playtested with eight-year-olds. Nesmith said, "We did not do a tremendous amount of playtesting with eight-year-olds," but it was done. The feedback from the playtesting was "neither highly positive nor highly negative. It didn't provide any great insights, but it didn't fall apart or fail either."

Dille did deliver Hollywood to the *Dragon Strike* launch party. The event was held in Los Angeles, in an Italian restaurant bedecked with vine-lined trellises, and both Bruce Nesmith and Andria Hayday were flown out for the event. Harry Hamlin, star of *Clash of the Titans* and *LA Law,* along with his wife, Lisa Rinna, star of *Days of Our Lives,* were in attendance. Nesmith said he actually spent a considerable amount of time talking to the pair before "they went off with Flint later in the evening to actually play *D&D.* I was not invited to participate in that, though."

At the launch party, Nesmith and Hayday got to see the video in its finished form for the first time. The pair of them were given "story by" credits, even though Nesmith said he and Hayday had little influence on the development of the script itself. He said the credit was Lorraine Williams's "acknowledgment that we had done an awful lot of work on the game and were not getting the credit we probably deserved."

Fans' reception of *Dragon Strike* was largely positive. A review of

Dragon Strike appeared in *Dragon* #200. It said of the game, "If this doesn't lure your kid brother into the hobby, it probably can't be done. Perhaps the most lavishly packaged, user-friendliest introduction to role-playing ever published, the DRAGON STRIKE game presents the basics in an innovative board-game format." It also describes the videotape that came with the game as "much touted (and unfairly criticized)."

It is very, very easy to look back on the *Dragon Strike* video and rip it to shreds. The acting, writing, special effects, and directorial choices are all often disastrously bad. But one must also consider that Dille was asked to create an instructional video for a game before a final draft of the rules existed. That one choice is a kind of original sin; it set the *Dragon Strike* video up for failure.

How can one make an instructional video for a game whose final rules don't yet exist? One can't.

One can, however, make the pilot for a children's fantasy show! Dille had an MFA from USC. A TV show with a plot he could make, and he did. Unfortunately, the video also demonstrates why RPG writing is hard.

Nesmith's memories of the game's reception are very much colored by his own impressions of it. For example, he dismissed the positive review in *Dragon* as the work of a "house organ." (*Dragon* editor Dale Donovan very much took issue with this characterization. He said, "Our reviews were independent. We generally knew what was going to be reviewed, but not the review's content. We were very proud of that.")

Nesmith said he didn't think the game accomplished what management wanted it to accomplish—namely, he didn't think it broadened the appeal of role-playing games to eight-year-olds. Furthermore, he didn't consider the game a success "either critically or commercially, but I wouldn't call it a huge failure either. But because in my opinion it didn't achieve the result we wanted it to achieve, and because it didn't fly out the door, I do not consider it a success. I consider it a wash. The money they spent they probably recouped, but they probably could have spent my time better if making money was their goal."

Flint Dille, on the other hand, described *Dragon Strike* as "a success for us at every kind of level." He cited the fact that a sequel, *WildSpace*, was ordered. "As a general rule, the real verdict on success or failure in the entertainment business is whether there is a sequel."

How can two men so intimately involved with the creation of *Dragon Strike* have such radically different views of the product's reception?

Yes, there is a difference in personality. Game designers and screenwriters are very different animals. One needs lots of sunlight, the other abhors it, and so on. One of the other likely reasons for confusion about the success of *Dragon Strike* is what management decided to do with the game after its component parts were sitting in their warehouse.

THE LITTLE DEATH OF *DRAGON STRIKE*

In the management calls that surrounded *Dragon Strike,* we can discover one of the causes of the death of the company. These decisions explain how creative geniuses can do sublime work while the company that employs them creeps toward insolvency.

According to Jim Fallone, who was director of sales and marketing at the time, *Dragon Strike* sold well initially, moving 100,000 copies with orders for another 50,000 more. Jim Ward said everyone at the company was pleased with those sales numbers.

The question was, how many copies of the game should they make in the reprinting?

Jim Ward advised upper management to reprint 50,000 copies of the game, because games usually never again matched the sales of their first printing. Therefore, printing 50,000 more copies would sate the demand of the market for *Dragon Strike.*

But according to Ward, Lorraine Williams decided to print not 50,000 but 150,000 more copies of *Dragon Strike.* Fifty thousand copies went out to fill existing orders, and the other 100,000 sat in the warehouse, waiting.

Ward said that she would often say of the copies of *Dragon Strike,* "Those'll sell."

But they did not sell. Dale Donovan remembered them. There they sat, stacked high in the warehouse's fluorescent glare, shrink-wrapped boxes of *Dragon Strike* waiting to be ordered, assembled, and then sent out to eager eight-year-olds. But the extra 100,000 orders never appeared. And so *Dragon Strike* became a long-term resident of the warehouse, piled high and waiting. Donovan said of the sight, "It was kind of impressive, in a sad way."

Dragon Strike may be another example of Lorraine Williams and speedboat thinking. The wise old salt Jim Ward told her that games do not usually ever match their first printing sales. But since this was her company, which she owned, who could stop her from revving up the engines and printing another 150,000 copies of the game? No one. She was the captain, and the slow would suck her wake.

Management acting on hope or whim—or for all I know, astrology instead of market forces—is one of the core reasons for the company's fall. But the *Dragon Strike* episode reveals that the rot at the company went even deeper than that.

THE POISONED APPLE IN THE RANDOM HOUSE CONTRACT

Tens of thousands of copies of *Dragon Strike* sat in the warehouse, waiting for orders likely never to come.

Then Jim Fallone was ordered to double-ship Random House a massive number of *Dragon Strike* copies. Why? The game wasn't selling. He thought the number had to be an error, so he stopped the shipment.

A week later, his boss, vice president of marketing Rick Behling, discovered the games hadn't shipped. He came to see Fallone.

Fallone remembered, "Rick Behling stormed into my office while I was on the phone with my counterpart at Random House and screamed at me at the top of his lungs and stormed out. After a second, my buddy from Random House said, 'Did you just get fired?' All I could say was I wasn't sure. I showed up the next day, and nothing was said of it again, but the product got shipped before the close of the quarter."

Why would the company ship those units to Random House? It was bonkers. They wouldn't, and didn't, sell. So why in the name of Arneson's beard would the company ship that large a number of unwanted games to Random House?

There was a reason. It had to do with contracts stretching back to 1979 and decisions made by Gary Gygax himself. It had to do with the peculiarities of the company's relationship with its distributor to the book trade, Random House.

It was an email in 2017 that convinced me that while I thought I knew everything about how TSR collapsed and was sold to Wizards of the Coast, I in fact knew nothing. That email was written by Jim Fallone. He proved a vital source for this book, because as director of sales, he was deeply knowledgeable about the business side of the company. Sales, expenses, profits, losses, and returns were his daily bread at the company, and he was willing to talk about all of it. Given TSR's penchant for secrecy, this was incredibly helpful.

Fallone was born in Pennsylvania, north of Pittsburgh, but before he could walk, his family moved to Rockville, Maryland. His father was an English teacher, and Rockville was a community that compensated its teachers very well. He grew up a geek and loved comic books. His father, of course, had an impressive library that seasoned him with the best works of fantasy and science fiction.

Fallone initially attended New York University's film school, but said, "Like all good graduates, I dropped out." He'd been working at Waldenbooks, a bookstore chain that seemed to be in every mall in America in the 1980s. Eventually, he was promoted to their corporate headquarters. Fallone said he "got into gaming from a corporate standpoint." He was in charge of buying TSR's products for Waldenbooks. From there, he "saw the scale and scope of" the company's titanic success. "I really got to understand the background of how gaming works in the marketplace and see it explode across the country," he said. Sales of the game's rule books were akin to *New York Times* bestsellers. Then the fiction line got rolling and also started putting up huge sales numbers. The sales of the company's novels showed him "that there was a world underneath everything that people wanted to know more about without the game mechanics."

Despite its success, Fallone thought that TSR was leaving money on the table. The company was only publishing fiction in paperback. If they moved to hardcover, it would make more money because while hardcover books sell for significantly more than paperbacks, they do not cost significantly more to produce and are therefore more profitable. He arranged a meeting in Wisconsin to explain all of this to Lorraine Williams. (He loved visiting Wisconsin because it meant he got to visit the Elkhart Lake racetrack, and he was a huge race fan.) He said that eventually, she agreed to begin publishing the company's fiction in hardcover. But publishing hardcover books was easier said than done. The company would need an infusion of experienced staff in both editing and sales. Williams called Fallone and offered him a job. He said, "I told her I could not move to Milwaukee for less than twice what I was making. The following day, she called and made me an offer for twice what I was making. Sadly, and I say this in retrospect, I accepted before I told my wife." The increased pay, and seeing what that kind of money could do in Wisconsin as opposed to Connecticut, brought her quickly on board. The pair and their two children moved to Delavan, Wisconsin, a town twenty minutes down Highway 50 from Lake Geneva. He became fast friends with Brian Thomsen, another East Coast émigré new to the company.

In that 2017 email, Fallone explained to me that TSR's deal with Random House was the root of many of the problems at the company.

The 1979 contract between TSR and Random House was my white whale while writing this book. Jim Fallone told me about it, and other alumni confirmed its existence and the surprising relationship it created between the two companies. But I had not seen the actual contract and had little hope that I would.

Then I got lucky.

In the fall of 2019, I was contacted by historian and researcher Michael Calleia. He had discovered the contract I was looking for. Calleia emailed it to me, an act of generosity for which I cannot thank him enough.

The contract itself is a hard read. The document is dotted with black patches like a piece of paper photocopied too many times, and it's written in legalese, but the bones of the matter are plain enough.

Ordinarily, the publisher-distributor relationship worked thusly: Publishers sent books to distributors. Distributors then sold books to bookstores and sent a check for the books sold to the publisher. Payments to publishers are linked directly to sales, upholding the law of supply and demand as is right and good.

This is not the arrangement that the 1979 contract established between TSR and Random House.

TSR received payment from Random House *not* when its products were sold by Random House. Rather, it received payment from Random House after products were received by the distributor *whether the product sold or not.* (Technically, these monies were loans against future sales.) In other words, the money that flowed into TSR's coffers was not dependent on sales. All the company had to do was create, print, and ship products, and cash would flow like the mighty Mississippi back to Lake Geneva. The printing of products was essentially the printing of money. The company had broken free of supply and demand. (Perhaps this is why the company kept making settings even though almost every new iteration sold less than the last one?) Employees in the know began to refer to their distributor as "El Banco de Random House."

The legalese of the contract put it thus:

> Upon completion of a discrete delivery to Random's Distribution Center of copies of said works . . . Random will lend within seven days of written notice of a loan request by [TSR], a sum of money up to 27.3 percent of [TSR]'s suggested retail list price of the copies of the Works in that discrete delivery. The unpaid principal balance of each such loan will bear interest until repaid at the Chase Manhattan Bank N.V. prime rate in effect on the date the loan is made. Publisher may repay all or any part of such loans at any time or times without penalty.

That 27.3 percent represented an advance, minus interest, on the sale of whatever product TSR was shipping to Random House. (The distributor, Random House, would then tack on about 30 percent, and the retailer would add about another 30 percent to make up the full sticker price of a product.)

But what if the books didn't sell? There was a clause for that too. TSR's products "shall be returnable by Random to the Publisher . . . without affecting Publisher's repayment obligations." In other words, TSR would still have to repay Random House for the money owed, plus the interest. Initially, this wasn't a problem. Jim Fallone said, "When you're chasing sales and momentum is strong, there is little in the way of returns."

To my eyes, this setup seemed bizarre. Why would Random House agree to pay TSR money before its products sold? It seemed like it was exposing Random House to unnecessary risks. What if Gygax took the money loaned to the company and used it to buy gold-plated d20s or something, and then

Random House returned a hundred pallets of product? Random House appeared to be trusting Lake Geneva without an upside for them.

But Jim Fallone thinks he knows where to find the upside.

I provided him a copy of the contract, and after looking it over, he had some thoughts. The Random House contract appeared to be structured to solve a number of problems for TSR. Fallone pointed out that publishing lengthy hardcover books with gorgeous covers was not cheap. Each product printed and shipped represented a significant investment of capital, an investment that might be made back only over years if sales were slow, meaning it would take the company some time to make back the money it invested in those books. The loans allowed the company to recoup their investment immediately and start making more products.

And if those beautiful hardcover rule books were selling well, that also presented the company with a challenge. Reprinting them was still expensive, and TSR had a publishing schedule. If the *Player's Handbook* sold out and had to be reprinted, that cost money, and the company might have to choose between a product on the schedule and reprinting a rule book. Fallone said, "From the very beginning, *D&D* was a bit of lightning in a bottle in the book trade. As the product line grew, we still were chasing reprints of the rule books." If both a rule book and a hot product were on the docket at the same time, he said the company faced "the difficult decision of paying for new product which you budgeted for and delaying reprinting and breaking the momentum of product you have already published."

When facing that decision, Fallone said, "our success was our problem."

The Random House loans would have been a way to overcome the hurdles printing and reprinting gorgeous rule books presented. The loans from Random House "would have been intended to address the inability of TSR to resupply Random House in a timely manner to meet demand. It was in Random House's interest to front the funds to ensure demand could be met," he said. In other words, if the *Player's Handbook* needed to be reprinted, and a new Forgotten Realms product was slated for release, the company could print both, knowing that while the *Player's Handbook* might take longer to sell, the company would receive payment for it when Random House received it.

Fallone said that using the loans to finance the company worked fine, so long as only about 20 percent of products were returned. He said that because the company "knew the size of our audience almost to a T, we had a relatively modest return rate." But a number of initiatives undertaken by the company in the 1990s, along with slower sales, increased the number of returned products to around 30 percent.

First, there were all the new game worlds introduced by the company. Fallone said that the company had dedicated shelf space in 1,200 Waldenbooks nationwide that "we could pretty much fill as we wished." For rule books, this was wonderful, and he said the company could "project sales increasingly accurately" for them. The problem arose with new game worlds, like Dark Sun and Birthright. He said that because these "new items didn't have an established audience, we had to guess a little. Birthright might only appeal to fifty percent of the fan base, but we might have initially placed it on one hundred percent of Waldenbooks' shelves. What sat on the shelves for a few months unsold got returned to make way for newer titles." He said bookstores had to "maximize revenue out of each square foot of shelf space," so they couldn't leave a product lying around gathering dust for a year and waiting for it to sell. It had to sell, and fast.

Second, TSR began overprinting products. *Dragon Strike* comes to mind. It was a successful product that management insisted on overproducing. This was likely done for two reasons. First, a genuine belief that the game would sell. Second, to have product to ship to Random House to generate loans. Fallone said that the company chose to "abuse the loan aspect of the contract by shipping product to Random House that there was no actual sales demand for just to generate the advance payment." The practice was pouring gasoline on the fire of the company's financial situation. He remembered the over-shipment, and Behling's reaction to it, as "the first sign of a crack" in the company.

Because of the contract with Random House, TSR received payment for the overshipped copies of *Dragon Strike.* But Jim Ward was right. They did not sell. Eventually, the games would be returned, and Random House would demand repayment. Jim Ward believed they ended up getting rid of the 100,000 copies of the game by selling them for a buck each.

The company needed money, yes, and shipping *Dragon Strike* got them paid. But there were consequences to just shipping product without thinking about consumer demand. Dale Donovan said that "forcing *Dragon Strike* down the supply channel soured it for the sequel." Donovan said of these overprinting blunders, "TSR managed to snatch defeat from the jaws of victory again and again."

These management decisions can also explain Dille's and Nesmith's different assessments of the success of *Dragon Strike.* Selling 150,000 copies of a game is a major accomplishment, and if that is all Dille remembered, it could be considered a success. If Nesmith simply heard that the sales weren't what management hoped, without the context that the game sold 150,000 copies but management decided to print 250,000 copies, he could certainly remember the game's success differently.

Also, Fallone said that a "bubble" of TSR debt began to build at Random House.

Over twenty-five years after the publication of *Dragon Strike,* I explained the company's overprinting debacle to Bruce Nesmith. He said of that decision, "There was a lot of hubris in the management team."

If speedboat thinking, treating the company like a personal plaything, and ignoring the market was the first cause of the company's failure, El Banco de Random House was the second, compounding the errors of the first. Shipping product to generate loans allowed the company to paper over many of its problems, but a pile of debt began to stack at Random House, a pile that would heap higher and higher until it threatened to bury TSR.

Despite all of this, the very next year, Bruce Nesmith was again assigned a beginner game. Within the company, he had become the employee who specialized in creating introductory material. In 1994, Nesmith, Zeb Cook, and Rich Baker created *First Quest,* an introductory product that came with a CD. The audio was very slickly produced, with sound effects and mood music, but also included the table talk of new players learning how to play. In *Dragon* #210, a review cooed over the product: "This may be the birthday present of the year."

The video for *Dragon Strike,* while impressive, and perhaps even so bad it's good, seemed at best a mediocre tool for teaching the game. *First Quest*'s

CD, on the other hand, seems much more effective. It quickly gets down to the business of explaining role-playing, while remaining engaging to the listener. Furthermore, two of the four adventures in *First Quest* use the CD, enhancing play and making life easier for the first-time DM.

Still, it is worth asking why the company was making yet another beginner's product in 1994. In 1991, they put out a revision of the *D&D* rules for beginners in a large black box with a beautiful red dragon on the front. In 1992, the company released another introductory product, *Dragon Quest.* Then 1993 brought the world *Dragon Strike,* and in 1994, *First Quest.* In 1995 and 1996, rather than releasing new introductory products, the company repackaged and renamed *First Quest* under the names *Introduction to the Advanced Dungeons & Dragons Game,* and then *Advanced Dungeons & Dragons: The Complete Starter Set.*

As historian Shannon Appelcline wrote of this in *Designers & Dragons*:

> Astonishingly, this means that TSR put out a new introduction to *D&D* every year from 1991 to 1996, which sounds like an inefficient use of resources and might be an early foreshadowing of problems in the time period. It also suggests that TSR was growing increasingly desperate to bring new role-players into the hobby.

The answer comes back to Monopoly. Bruce Nesmith explained the company's constant lunging into the beginner market by saying, "At the time, mass-market board games were the holy grail. That's where all the money was being made. Parker Brothers and Milton Bradley ruled the roost. TSR wanted to be them. They wanted that prestige. They wanted that money. They wanted that name recognition. They wanted that penetration into the American home and the American psyche. So TSR kept trying to create things that would push them into that realm."

Jim Ward agreed with this interpretation. He said that at the time, Lorraine Williams "wanted TSR to sell more stuff to the mass market as opposed to the hobby market."

Nesmith and others in the Games Department did everything they could to create fun, beautiful games. But management decisions were injuring the company. The decision to continue producing new settings injured the company. The decision to produce so many beginner products injured the company. The decision to overship products to generate payments from Random House injured the company.

How long could this go on before TSR was injured unto death?

Nesmith himself would not be there to see the company's final days. He said he "cajoled, bludgeoned, and bribed" his way into a promotion in the mid-1990s, a promotion that directly led to his departure. He observed that while editors were often promoted, game designer was a dead-end position with no opportunity for advancement. He went to Jim Ward with these concerns and was eventually promoted to creative director, a title usually only given to editors. This promotion, however, put him in frequent meetings with Lorraine Williams, and in one of these meetings, he said that she "said something that was offensive to me professionally." He was clear that what she said wasn't personally insulting or socially insensitive, and for the life of him, he can't remember what it was, but he can remember his visceral reaction to it. He said she was "in the habit of saying things that would offend people, on a fairly regular basis. She was not someone I would have gotten along with." He said she came off as though she thought she was of higher quality than her employees. The comment made him realize he had to leave. He found a job at Bethesda Softworks, makers of the *Fallout* and *Elder Scrolls* series of games. To say that he was successful there is to damn with faint praise. He was lead designer on *Elder Scrolls V: Skyrim*, which grossed $450 million in its first week of release, more than ten times what TSR made in its best year. He also just released a novel, *Mischief Maker,* which is an urban fantasy story about Loki and Norse mythology.

Again, a brilliant creative mind was alienated and driven from TSR.

In 2020, a computer archivist found a copy of *Dragon*, the video game Nesmith created that one summer back at Beloit College on an HP 3000. Using an emulator, Nesmith booted it up and saw his name on the loading screen. Despite the decades and the leaps tech has taken in that time, the game still ran fine.

"It was," he said, "a real trip."

DEPARTURES

TSR PROVED NO more adept at keeping artists than it did writers, editors, and game designers. Two issues that would be repeated sticking points among the artists were the company's freelancing policy and their policy on who kept the originals of the paintings produced by the staff artists. Jeff Easley said that both policies changed dramatically over the life of the company.

Regarding freelancing, when Easley arrived, artists had free rein to freelance as much as they wanted. Then, there was a period where no freelancing at all was allowed by artists.

Brom pointed out that this policy, from the point of view of the company, made perfect sense. He said that one of the things the company was paying their artists for was "an exclusive branding of their product. If Jeff Easley is the look of TSR's house dragons and then he paints his red dragon for another game company, I can see where that is a problem."

But the inability to produce work for other markets proved deeply frustrating for the staff artists. Brom said that TSR was a very "narrow market." They were painting full-time, but their work was only being seen by gamers. Even though Brom had his nose in fantasy art his whole life, he hadn't heard of Larry Elmore, Keith Parkinson, or Jeff Easley until he arrived in Lake Geneva. Furthermore, he said that doing covers for fantasy novels and *Heavy Metal* magazine "felt more prestigious and higher profile" than creating covers for TSR products. He added, "In hindsight, I can see this wasn't necessarily true, but at the time, all the top artists in the genre were painting covers for novels, so it was easy to feel you were being left out of something."

In the late 1980s, the freelancing policy was altered to allow artists to work for other companies, but only with the okay of management. Even this policy would trip up artists. For example, Jeff Easley was contacted by video game producer Accolade. The company was working on a video game featuring Elvira, the horror-comedy character who was as well-endowed as she was revealingly dressed, created by actress Cassandra Peterson. And Accolade wanted him to do cover art for the game.

Easley said, "I really wanted to paint Elvira."

Unfortunately, as Easley remembered it, the entire management team was gone when Accolade's offer came in. Although, he added, "I might be being too kind to myself." But because management was gone, he was unable to ask them for their permission, so he accepted the offer from Accolade.

To cover his tracks, Easley decided not to sign the painting using his own name. Instead, he signed the painting "Bill Connors." Connors, of course, worked in the Games Department and was a huge Elvira fan.

Easley believed that he was "under the radar" and that "no one will ever see this thing."

Time passed.

Then one day, Easley was summoned downstairs. When he walked into the room, Lorraine Williams was sitting at the table, along with "a pair of the main hoptey-doos" of management.

There, lying on the table, was a copy of *Elvira: Mistress of the Dark*, a video game with Jeff Easley's work on the cover.

He said, "I can just imagine what my face looked like when I saw that. The blood drained right into my feet."

One of them asked, "What's this?"

Easley said he responded, "Uhhh . . . that's a freelance job." He said that he wanted to get management's approval, but they were all gone, so he signed the painting using Bill Connors's signature. And he thought nobody would see it.

At that point, one of the two "hoptey-doos" produced a promotional flyer for the game from Accolade, which read at the top, "Featuring art by *Dungeons & Dragons* artist Jeff Easley!"

He thought, *Oh crap.*

The next words out of Williams's mouth should come as no surprise to anyone at this point. It was a threat of a lawsuit. According to Easley, she said that TSR had already entered into a contractual agreement regarding the production of video games with another company and that his work may have violated that agreement. Therefore, he had opened himself up to the possiblity of a lawsuit with his work on *Elvira: Mistress of the Dark.*

Easley said he left the meeting feeling like he "was going to be thrown in prison for doing this cover." He said that he was "naive" about such threats at the time, but the more he thought about it, the less sense it made. If management was actually cut to the bone by his decision to do outside work without permission, they could and would have fired him. But they didn't. The entire meeting was just a scare job.

Another issue that reared its head was the possession of the original paintings done by the artists.

When an artist at a company produced a work in the 1930s and 1940s, they would turn the original of the painting in to the publisher. Jeff Easley said that many of these publications, after using the paintings, would simply throw these original works of art away. He said, "It kinda curdles my blood just to think about it."

When Easley arrived at the company, the policy was that when an artist had completed a work, they would also take the original away from them. The artist was paid to make the painting. They painted at the company on a canvas paid for by the company with company paint. It was, therefore, company property. (TSR, however, didn't make a habit of tossing original paintings in the trash.)

Easley said he was so glad to have a job painting full-time that he thought nothing of the practice when he first arrived at the company. He was so pleased to be painting for pay that management "could have lopped a toe off every now and then, and I wouldn't have complained."

Soon after Easley's arrival, however, the policy changed. Artists would be allowed to retain their original works of art. They could sell them, keep them, or give them away.

This would prove a significant source of secondary income for artists. According to Brom, an original painting at that time would fetch anywhere between $2,000 and $8,000 on the art market. To put those numbers in some perspective with the time and place, Brom said that his first house in Lake Geneva cost $46,000. Clearly, the ability of artists to own and then sell their original works was extremely lucrative.

But in the early 1990s, the company decided to again keep ownership of all the paintings. Because this did mean a functional cut in pay for the artists, they did all receive raises. Easley described the raise as "a good size," but said that "the artists were not too happy about it anyway."

Brom said, "If they had hired me and said TSR gets to keep the originals, it would have been easier. But when they hire you and say you get to keep the originals, it's an area of contention." He said that in addition to the raise, artists were allowed to keep two favorite pieces per year.

Despite all of this, Brom believed that all the disagreements he had with receiving direction from management and the possession of original art were, at heart, "minor." He said, "I had incredible freedom at TSR. I mean really, there was very, very little interference from management compared to other companies I've worked with since, though I didn't realize that at the time."

But Brom would end up leaving the company.

Why?

Brom said his "number one" reason for leaving the company was he wanted ownership of his own work. He said during his time in the Art Department, "the company owned everything you created for them." They owned the painting, the image, the character, and the world. Every speck of vitality he poured into his paintings was no longer his. It belonged to the company.

Brom was clear that he did not in any way believe this to be unethical or wrong. The deal the company gave him was totally fair. He had accepted pay to do the work they asked of him, and the work was theirs at the end of the day. He said he wasn't mad, and that he left "to make artwork that I owned if I could make a living doing it. It was a business decision."

Thwarted ambition also played a role.

Brom's work was being seen, but it was not being seen by as many people as he would have liked. He admitted, "I wanted to get my artwork in publications that I thought were more prestigious." After four years at the company, he felt like he had to go freelance in order to continue growing creatively.

So Gerald Brom left to make his way in the world.

Jeff Easley remained. He would be at the company for the dark times and go on to work for Wizards of the Coast.

What happened in the Book Department was also occurring in the Art Department. The company discovered, groomed, and nurtured talent. As the talent came into full bloom, they decided they could do just as well or better without TSR.

Brom's work since leaving proved he is a virtuoso in the field of fantasy art. Yet when he arrived at the company, he didn't even know how to gesso a canvas. The company clearly helped make him into the artist he is today. And yet due to its policies, which he goes out of his way to point out he felt were legal, ethical, and fair, he left.

Brom's lack of acrimony or bitterness is notable. In his telling, it is not that management was maleficent, dastardly, or backhanded. Rather, they were doing what they thought was best for the company, while driving homegrown talent away.

As happened before and would happen again, genius creators were leaving TSR.

DRIVING OUT BOB SALVATORE

Book Department head Brian Thomsen wanted Drizzt creator Bob Salvatore to write more books for TSR.

This should have been an achievable goal, no harder than parking a car. After all, his Drizzt books were a towering success. The company's first hardcover novel, *The Legacy,* by Salvatore and featuring Drizzt, debuted on the *New York Times* list of bestsellers at the number nine slot on September 27, 1992, just behind *The Bridges of Madison County.*

(They only gave him six weeks to write the novel!)

Given that Salvatore was a proven hitmaker, of course Brian Thomsen wanted more novels from him. In 1994, Salvatore signed a three-book deal with Warner Books and hoped to sign another three-book deal with TSR. They had a good thing going. Why mess with it?

Then came the rub. Thomsen wanted Salvatore to write *six more books.* He was already one tired writer, having written fourteen books in the prior six years, a feat of literary endurance that calls to mind most immediately Tolstoy's production of *War & Peace.* With his already existing Warner deal, agreeing to six books would contractually obligate him to write a total of nine novels, each likely 100,000 words long. To put that in perspective, the King James version of the Bible is 783,137 words. Thomsen was asking him to produce a volume of words in excess of that after already having written his fingers to the bone.

Salvatore, to say the least, was not enthusiastic about the proposition. He'd have to write three (three!) books a year to meet his obligations. It would reduce him to a quivering pool of jelly. When he raised these concerns with Thomsen, he said the response he received was, "I don't care, this is what we [TSR] need." Thomsen offered to find a ghostwriter, Salvatore said he'd never do such a thing to his readers, and the negotiations became contentious.

So contentious that Thomsen actually threatened Salvatore, the writer who'd created the most iconic character in the *D&D* canon. The writer who was producing *New York Times* bestsellers. He decided that the best way to bend that writer to his will was to threaten him.

But what weapon could be brought to bear on Salvatore? He was not an employee. He'd never even been to the company's headquarters in Lake Geneva. (Why not offer him more money? Money seems to be an excellent way to get people to do what you want.)

Thomsen told Salvatore that if he did not agree to write six books, he would find someone else to write Drizzt Do'Urden.

Again, the idea that it was the brand that was important, not the creator, raised its misbegotten head. If Dragonlance could continue without Weis and Hickman, Drizzt could go on without Salvatore.

Salvatore felt bullied by the very company his creative energies had enriched. It was galling, maddening, and frustrating. So he replied with a threat of his own. He told Thomsen that if he found someone else to write Drizzt, Salvatore would never write the character again. He said Drizzt "will have died in the last book I wrote as far as I'm concerned." The man was an electric success when writing that character. To deny TSR his talents there was to forever turn off a stream of revenue that might bring untold but likely vast sums of cash flowing to Lake Geneva.

Thomsen didn't budge. But Salvatore did.

Salvatore recalled that it was on a Friday that he contacted Lake Geneva to say he would sign the contract and write nine books. He had a new house, a mortgage, and no day job to pay for insurance for his three small children. With all of that hanging over his head, he said, "I felt like I didn't have a choice. I was going to kill myself basically, but I really didn't want to do it."

That Friday night, Salvatore went to bed, but he didn't sleep. The man couldn't sleep Saturday either. Something gnawed at him.

First thing Monday morning, Salvatore called Thomsen and told him, "I can't do this. I'm not signing this contract."

Thomsen replied with his prior threat to find someone else to write Drizzt.

Salvatore told him, "You know my deal on that. I can't do this. I can't in good conscience do this because there's no way I could write three books a year, and I don't like the tactics being used on me."

So it was that *New York Times* bestselling author Bob Salvatore left TSR. Salvatore, who was discovered and nurtured by Mary Kirchoff, was out.

Salvatore said that his Friday-to-Monday flip probably made Thomsen look like a fool, and he "felt really bad about that." But he didn't want to write all of those books, and he sure as hell didn't like being threatened. After all, Salvatore was a Massachusetts man. Rightness had meaning. Rectitude was important. And these values were worth living.

Later, Book Department editor Peter Archer found "an acidic note" from Thomsen to Salvatore's agent "in which he accused Bob of not having any integrity." He does not know if the note was ever answered.

With decades of vantage on this moment, it cannot be viewed as anything less than an unmitigated disaster for TSR. The company could have had three books from Salvatore. It wanted six, but would get none.

Salvatore certainly wasn't looking at this as any great victory either. The change from success story to outcast happened so fast that he was "shell-shocked. Things had been going better than we ever could have anticipated." And then it was all over. He soon found consolation in a three-book deal with Del Rey.

Jim Lowder theorized that corporate ego was at play in this fracas. He explained, "If you make a star, you are beholden to that person. The fans recognize that person's input into what is your IP." This recognition by the fans brought power to such stars. According to him, that power was often interpreted by management as a threat to their control over the company's intellectual property. In other words, taking Drizzt away from Salvatore may have been viewed as a win by management because it cut off the creator from his creation.

Jim Fallone, Thomsen's close friend, remembered hearing about this incident. He said, "That's a two-sided story. We were in negotiations to get a new series from Salvatore, and at the last minute, after making a verbal agreement to sign with us, he ended up signing with Random House Del Rey."

Furthermore, as Fallone remembered it, the order of events and circumstances were significantly different. Specifically, the deal with Del Rey that Salvatore was considering would have been exclusive, meaning he would not have been able to write for TSR. Fallone said, "Bob did create one of the most iconic fantasy characters in novels, just like Wolverine or Harley Quinn, but to ask TSR not to release a Drizzt novel for a significant period of time was not going to receive a favorable response from any publisher."

In this version of history, Thomsen made a reasonable decision about moving forward with an intellectual property. After all, Salvatore could write for whatever company he wanted, but if he chose not to write for TSR, of course the company was well within its legal rights to find someone else to write Drizzt.

Fallone added, "Brian Thomsen's job wasn't to make Jim Lowder or Bob Salvatore's life perfect. It was to get them to create the best product they could for TSR. Some of that was keeping them happy, and a lot was keeping Lorraine, Random House, and Barnes & Noble happy. No Drizzt books would not make any of them happy." Fallone continued, "He felt betrayed. It made him very, very bitter. One thing about Brian Thomsen, he was one of my best friends at the company, but he was a very Machiavellian man who did not let go of a grudge." So he was left sitting in the offices on Sheridan Springs Road in Lake Geneva holding the most popular character in the *D&D* universe, but Drizzt was dead in his hands without a writer to write him.

What about Jim Lowder?

Lowder described this notion as a brilliant but evil stratagem on the part of Thomsen because it solved two problems at once. First, it would put a talented writer back on Drizzt. Second, it muzzled Salvatore. Thomsen knew that Lowder and Salvatore were friends (they were both from Massachusetts after all, and Lowder had previously edited Salvatore's work), and a friend couldn't trash another friend's book in public.

Furthermore, writing Drizzt might change Lowder's life. It would have meant more money, no small thing now that he was a satellite employee, and it would have immeasurably advanced his career. Given the past performance of Drizzt novels, it was a likely *New York Times* bestseller, and being a *New York Times* bestselling author alters a writer's life forever. Perhaps the money and the fame would finally be enough to lure him onto Team Brian . . .

Lowder's answer?

"I told Brian to get stuffed."

To write Salvatore's character after it was taken away from him would be an intimate betrayal. Furthermore, to take Thomsen up on his offer would be to validate his strong-arm tactics. And Lowder was no fan of the way he treated his writers. He said no even though it meant turning down more money, a career boost, and possibly even a different life path. That is what friendship meant to Jim Lowder.

After that, Lowder was not long for TSR. His final fight at the company concerned a novel he'd been contracted to write during Mary Kirchoff's reign, *The Screaming Tower.* Once it was written, Thomsen refused to greenlight it for publication, but also refused to cancel it, trapping Lowder and the book in a loop of endless edits. Between this authorial nightmare, continuing conflicts over the direction of the Book Department, and sudden changes to his employment agreement, he resigned effective July 1, 1994.

Even after his opponent's departure from the field, Thomsen pursued him. When Lowder attempted to publish *The Screaming Tower* elsewhere, Thomsen claimed the novel was the company's property, kicking off a yearslong legal dispute.

With Lowder out of the running, the company approached Mark Anthony, an author who'd written a number of novels set in the Forgotten Realms, to complete the next Drizzt book. He accepted. Peter Archer said this was "an effort to rub Bob's nose in things."

Obviously, I did not interview the late Brian Thomsen for this book, as he passed away in 2008. Recollections of Thomsen, as well as motivations imputed to him, all come from the women and men who worked with him at the time. The image their words weave of him is, in the main, not kind.

This troubled me deeply. His role at TSR, especially in driving away Salvatore, seemed vital in the negative. But he had passed, and I could not interview him so he could defend himself. I did not want to print a hit job on a dead man.

I decided the only responsible thing to do was to find his friends and those who worked with him most closely and to interview them in an effort to find his side of the story. No one lives their life thinking they are a villain. I believed Thomsen would have had reasonable explanations for a lot of the unflattering stories about him.

And I did find some people willing to speak up for him. Author Jean Rabe, for example, sang Thomsen's praises. Jim Fallone explained his fraught relationships this way: "Brian was a bit of an outsider because he came from book publishing. He was an editor at Warner Books. He'd been hired to help the company's publishing program grow into a legit publishing program. And under him, we expanded significantly how many books we were publishing, creating more content to try to get interest in film properties, et cetera. He was not a gamer and didn't really associate on that level. That's where there was also some of that resentment. He wasn't coming from the gaming community, and he was considered equal to Jim Ward because ratio-wise, he was producing fairly significant portions of profitability for the company." It is worth recalling that one of the critiques of Lorraine Williams was that she was not a gamer. Being on the receiving end of that criticism, as Thomsen was, apparently was not easy.

Fallone added that another reason for the man's unpopularity was that he distributed freelance book contracts. He said, "Many of the authors that we had that were writing for us were in-house game designers. There was aggressive freelancing going on within the company. So that also is a factor where if Brian turned down your book and you wanted to buy new living room furniture on your royalties and now you don't have it. He was a gatekeeper for the paycheck of freelance novels." It makes sense that people who were refused the chance to write novels, and make money doing it, would have some harsh words for Thomsen. One must also wonder then why he ended the blind audition process instituted by Mary Kirchoff and Jim Lowder.

Furthermore, Fallone pointed out that while there were many great writers working for TSR, the company's shared worlds gave them all a leg up in the market. He said that Bob Salvatore, Jim Lowder, Margaret Weis, and Tracy Hickman "are talented writers, but the worlds they were allowed to create in were already built and seeded with existing geography, monsters, and history for them to use." He continued, "A major part, arguably *the* major part, of their success was due to the Forgotten Realms or Dragonlance logo over the title."

But this is a chicken-and-egg argument. Yes, the brands gave writers a leg up, but the brands were created by writers and game designers. Margaret Weis and Tracy Hickman were two of the creators of Dragonlance. Ed Greenwood and Jeff Grubb created the Forgotten Realms. Bob Salvatore created Drizzt.

We live in a unique historical moment where corporations have unparalleled control over popular culture. But the line where genius creators meet management is one of the rough edges of that control, where there is often chafing and bleeding. Thomsen was supposed to take the Book Department to the next level. Instead, he added to the bleeding by weaponizing the company's ownership of Salvatore's creation, using it against him, and driving him into the wilderness.

In the wake of all of this, Brian Thomsen was promoted.

Perhaps if Salvatore had stayed, TSR would have survived. But that seems unlikely, as in the early to mid-1990s, it seemed that no matter how good a product was, no matter how excellently written or cleverly designed, its sales struggled.

Perhaps no product exemplified that superb work failed to sell more than the *Planescape Campaign Setting.*

TSR'S GREATEST SETTING CAN'T STOP SALES SLIDE

THE MOST EXTRAORDINARY setting boxed set to be produced at TSR in its decades of life was the *Planescape Campaign Setting* by Zeb Cook with art by Dana Knutson and Tony DiTerlizzi. It featured Sigil, City of Doors, which sits in the center of the multiverse. From Sigil, adventurers could set out to explore any of the many different planes of existence that had been laid out in 1987's *Manual of the Planes.* The setting's art was lush and evocative, and its writing transported the reader to Sigil just like a good work of fiction. It is the pinnacle work of second edition *AD&D* designer Zeb Cook's legendary career at the company. Perhaps such a product, a birth in cardboard and paper of a visionary world conceived by writers, designers, and artists all working at the height of their powers, could turn TSR around.

How did Cook come to write *Planescape*? "Madness," he said.

Jeff Grubb's *Manual of the Planes* was a towering work of cosmology. The volume detailed a universe where planes of existence nestled one within another, among them Gehenna, the Happy Hunting Grounds, Pandemonium, Elysium, the Abyss, Hades, Acheron, Arcadia, the Nine Hells, and one plane each for earth, air, fire, and water. Even ash, dust, vacuum, and salt got their own quasi-planes of existence in the *D&D* universe. The book also described how combat and magic changed on each plane. It opened a cosmos, literally, to the play of gaming groups.

But the work was not without its faults. The book's mythology and cosmology were stunning, but how playable was it? As Dori Hein, who would go on to be project manager for *Planescape,* observed in *Dragon* #208, "I remember eagerly purchasing the *Manual* back when I played the 1st Edition game and longing to bring my gamers into the planes. The book was fascinating reading, for I loved mythology and the grand majesty of all the planes, but, try as I might, I couldn't create an adventure without killing all my players' PCs. So, regretfully, I put the book aside."

Why were the planes so deadly? Consider the Elemental Plane of Fire. It's temperature is "equivalent to that encountered in a stroll through a volcano." There, metal melted, ice boiled, and characters had to make an immediate roll or explode in flames before burning to ash and cinders. A difficult location to write an adventure for, to say the least.

Furthermore, the *Manual* came out in 1987, and in 1989, the second edition of *AD&D* was released, and no updating of the material in the *Manual* had been attempted.

Once a year, pitches for new products were generated by the designers in the Games Department. Cook said that designer Dale "Slade" Henson pitched doing a guide to the planes that would be an enormous multiyear, multivolume series describing each plane, from the Nine Hells to the Seven Heavens, with one book per plane. He said that no matter how whiz-bang cool it would be to do a book on every plane in the game's cosmology, the consensus was that it would be "impossible. Who's going to buy *The Guide to the Lawful Good Plane*?"

But the idea was intriguing. It wouldn't die. Project manager Dori Hein, Jeff Grubb, and Slade Henson worked on what Hein described as "a proposal for an entire game line" based on the idea. Due to the vagaries of scheduling, when the time came to actually take the proposal forward into a product, the job fell to Zeb Cook instead of Jeff Grubb or Slade Henson.

This was about the time the Spelljammer line of products was ending. Spelljammer was the company's space fantasy setting, where ships that would look at home in the Venetian navy of 1452 plied the "phlogiston" between worlds. The setting allowed characters in the Forgotten Realms a way to visit Krynn or Athas or one of the other *D&D* worlds without breaking the fiction. Cook described Spelljammer as "fun," but said the line "ran into problems because people were not using it as a campaign. We couldn't really sell much Spelljammer secondary material because most people viewed it as a cool adventure system to get from here to there." In other words, gamers would use the ships provided in the supplement to move between already existing settings more than running adventures in space.

Cook said that Spelljammer's lack of a central setting was a problem that would have to be resolved in the planar product he was working on. Thus was born Sigil, City of Doors. It was a single location from which adventuring parties could set out to any of the many planes of existence to loot, plunder, and do good if so aligned.

In addition to past products, Cook said that the company's competition also influenced the creation of Planescape. In the 1990s, White Wolf Publishing was the griddle-hot gaming company of the moment. Filled with young blood and spiked leather, the White Wolf crew published games such as *Vampire: The Masquerade* and *Werewolf: The Apocalypse,* which allowed players to portray traditional villains. Their games' aesthetics were all roses and fangs, the opulence of the full moon over a squalid alley, and grimy night clubs where terror and wonder simmered in equal measure. They attracted a new crowd to role-playing, theater geeks, goths, and larger numbers of women. There was nothing more eye-catching to wear to high school in 1993 than a *Vampire: The Masquerade* T-shirt. The shirts sported Tim Bradstreet's iconic art for the game—images that were prurient, decadent, and above all, cool enough to freeze beer.

White Wolf games also featured factions. You weren't just a vampire, you were a vampire of Clan Brujah, and you were desperately interested in taking down your enemies in Clan Ventrue. These factions gave players and their characters special abilities, worldviews, goals, and a preset opinion of others in the fiction. Factions, in short, brought characters to life at the gaming table.

There was nothing like factions anywhere in *D&D.* In the beginning, it was assumed that all characters wanted to kill the monsters and loot the dungeon, full stop. Your character might have a reason for sacking Bargle the Bandit's caves, such as revenge, greed, or do-goodery, or your character might not. Finding that motivation was up to the player.

The White Wolf family of games was cool and sold well. Cook said that TSR saw the success of White Wolf, and that the thought around the office at the time was, "We need something like those factions, all of those vampire clans. We need something like that." Sigil, then, would have fifteen factions for characters to join.

Incredibly, when Cook first set out to do *Planescape,* those were about the only instructions he was given. Do the planes. Have a base location as a setting. And do factions. He agreed to the project, but said that he "had no real idea what he was supposed to work up." The vagueness gave him license. He could do almost anything and play anywhere in the *D&D* cosmos.

Cook also looked at the wide world for inspiration. At the time, his literary diet consisted of experimental novels. For example, he read *Dictionary of the Khazars,* a Serbian novel by Milorad Pavić, though calling it a novel may be a generous description. It is a series of lexicons describing the Khazars, a Turkic people that purportedly converted to Judaism in the eighth or ninth century. The book had no conventional plot and was issued in "male" and "female" editions, in which seventeen lines of text were different. He also read Italo Calvino's *Invisible Cities,* a novel in which Marco Polo regales Emperor Kublai Khan with tales of a kaleidoscope of mind-bending metropoles. Polo describes cities of "high bastions," with "aluminum towers," where "steps make up the streets rising like stairways." There are cities of "concentric canals" and kites, and "streets thick with signboards." But, Polo says, telling Kublai Khan all of that "would be the same as telling you nothing."

Echoes of Calvino are heard in the description of Sigil in *Planescape*: "Get it right out front: Sigil's an impossible place . . . A city built on the inside of a tire that hovers over the top of a gods-know-how-tall spike, which rises from a universe shaped like a giant pancake . . . It happens all the time, right?" In Sigil, for example, there is no proper up and down. Anywhere one stands, if one looks up, one sees buildings.

The language of *Planescape* also made the product stand out. Cook invented the distinctive slang of Sigil, where a mouth is a *bone-box* and a *berk* is a fool, by smashing together Elizabethan slang and some Dickens.

Cook also looked at existing cosmology. When he examined the *Manual of the Planes,* he realized, "Wow, this is really a messed-up place." He leaned into that. He said that when producing *Planescape,* "I would get a bad idea in my head, and off we go."

One of those "bad ideas" was the Lady of Pain. But her origin lay in the hand of an artist.

Dana Knutson was a company artist who, according to Cook, was "between projects for about a month." Having seen the success of incorporating artists into the design process with Dark Sun, Knutson was assigned to *Planescape* for concept work. Visually, Cook said that he wanted Knutson to make *Planescape* look like a product TSR wouldn't publish. He wanted a clean break from sunny heroes slaying red dragons in dark dungeons. Knutson started by working on the line's logo, which was a stern and beautiful woman's face wreathed in naked blades.

This was the Lady of Pain, and Knutson's work was so compelling that it helped to sell executives on the project. The Lady of Pain is not human, and she is powerful. She has no house, and she has no temple, as those who worship her have their skin flayed off. Sometimes she's seen in the streets, and anyone she looks at erupts "in horrid gashes at just the touch of her gaze." She also keeps hostile forces, such as gods, out of Sigil. While she doesn't give a whit about murder in a back alley or simple thievery, she frowns upon efforts that imperil the city of Sigil. In another of Cook's bad ideas, those who threaten the city are imprisoned by the Lady in "mazes." A maze is exactly what it sounds like, a labyrinth in the Deep Ethereal Plane. Because she is cruel, every maze has a way out, a portal back to Sigil. Finding it is another matter. This faint hope is another cruelty from the Lady.

The presence of the Lady of Pain provides a modicum of order in Sigil. This allowed Cook to fill Sigil with fifteen factions, none of whom can simply murder their rivals out of existence. *Planescape* describes these factions as "philosophers with clubs," and the description is apt. The Doomguard, for example, believes that entropy and decay are the goals of the universe, and it is their job to hurry these forces along. The Bleak Cabal preaches, "Once a sod believes it all means nothing, everything starts to make sense." But it is the Lady who keeps the philosophers with clubs from switching to bloody bastard swords. For Cook, creating the factions was one of his favorite parts of the design process.

As this barest glimpse shows, the design of *Planescape* was imaginative, elegant, and grandly succeeded in inspiring DMs to run it. Its art was also revolutionary. In addition to Dana Knutson's Lady of Pain and completing symbols to represent the factions of Sigil, Cook said his art "helped inspire the tone and the writing."

"Then," Cook said, "we got super lucky."

Tony DiTerlizzi had submitted a few sketches for the *Monstrous Manual* the year before, and his work was so popular that he was brought on to be the interior artist for *Planescape*.

The only interior artist. For the entire boxed set.

Cook said that the art manager at the time wanted the product to have a consistent interior look, and so DiTerlizzi would do all the interior art.

And staggering art it was. He drew Sigil as a nightmare city, portraying its inhabitants as Renaissance-punk refugees. Buildings brooded. Hallways darkened. Menace, peril, and threat loomed from every wall and window.

But being the only interior artist for the project was an immeasurable amount of labor. Cook said DiTerlizzi was young when he agreed to do this and "didn't know what he was committing to. But he got himself a ton of work."

Of DiTerlizzi's contribution to the setting, Cook said he "added the final bit that really pulled everything together visually."

Looking back on *Planescape,* Cook confessed that he wasn't sure the game was "completely playable" but it certainly was "fun."

Despite Cook's doubts, reviews at the time responded enthusiastically to the product. In *Pyramid* #8, TSR West alumnus Scott Haring wrote that *Planescape* was "the finest game world ever produced for *Advanced Dungeons & Dragons*. Period." Posterity and history's verdict has been similar. I of course agree it is the greatest setting product produced by the company and believe it is the second-greatest work of any kind ever produced at TSR, topped only by the original *D&D*.

The year 1994 marked Zeb Cook's fifteenth anniversary at the company, and *Planescape* sent him out on a high note. He said, "I wasn't looking to leave, but I got a call from Lawrence Schick, who hired me into TSR back in

'79." Schick himself had left in the '80s to move into computer games. Schick was calling because he was "setting up a video game division" for a company outside of Washington, D.C., "that wanted to get into the game." Was Cook interested? It was more money and a fresh challenge.

Furthermore, Cook couldn't help but notice that as of 1994, "role-playing games were noticeably dwindling." Sales were down, and *Magic: The Gathering* was selling like gangbusters. He said, "It didn't seem like there was going to be a long-term future" in role-playing games. He had a wife and a son. And there was always retirement to think about. Would TSR be there in ten years? In five? Who knew?

And so, Zeb Cook left.

While reviewers and historians have been kind to *Planescape,* sales were another matter. Director of sales and marketing John Danovich observed, "We had a lot of products that were very good at the time, but they were failures." Released in April 1994, the boxed set sold 40,418 copies that year, and a mere 20,889 over the next four years. Those numbers are of course low from a historical perspective, continuing the trend of settings not selling like they did in the early '80s, irrespective of the quality of the product.

PRODUCTS AND PROFITS, OR LACK THEREOF

With sales down, how was TSR to survive?

Produce more products. Fewer sales of more things could be a course forward. So a flood of products surged forth from the offices on Sheridan Springs Road.

Some examples: In the 1980s, TSR went years without introducing a new setting to its fan base. But in 1994, it released two new settings (Planescape and the Council of Wyrms), in addition to reintroducing old settings with second edition rules in *Karameikos: Kingdom of Adventure* and *Red Steel.* (The company now had fourteen setting lines!) Individually, all had unspectacular sales. But between those new releases and the back catalog, the company did have a lot of products out there, and they sold 179,318 copies that year. By comparison, in 1984 the company released one setting, *The World of Greyhawk,* which sold 122,097 copies.

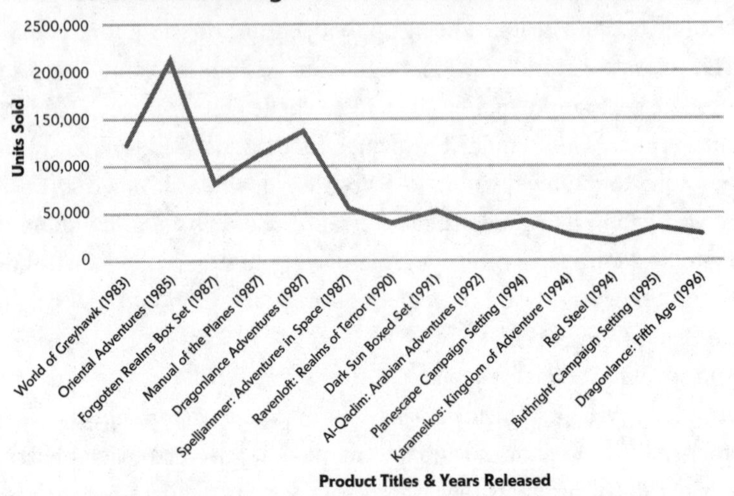

Something similar was happening in the Book Department. Novel sales were down. The bestselling Dragonlance novel sold over 847,000 copies, but the bestselling Forgotten Realms novel sold only 327,000 copies. Therefore, TSR published more novels. It produced one novel in 1984, and three in 1985, but churned out twenty in 1994.

One cannot escape the feeling of a company flinging product out the door, but it seems to have been effective, at least in the short run. Making more products kept gross sales about flat for years.

Which raises a question about the fish-bait strategy. The production of new settings was supposed to be introducing the game to new fans. If that was occurring, shouldn't gross sales have been rising as every new setting brought thousands more people into the fold? It turned out there was a huge problem with the fish-bait strategy, one that would not be discovered until after TSR was sold off to Wizards of the Coast.

Furthermore, the decision to produce all of those novels and settings and adventures had a fatal flaw: Many of those products were not profitable. Because the company made many gorgeous products that were expensive to produce, if it didn't carefully monitor costs and price point, these items would not make money even if they sold well.

One example of this was the *Encyclopedia Magica* line of books. Released between 1994 and 1995, the line promised to "cover every magic item published between 1974 and 1994. Yes, EVERY ONE[!]" It would be a great resource for DMs who no longer had to scour through their *D&D* library searching for a magic item if they could not remember where they read it. And the books looked like something a wizard might keep beside their crystal ball. They were thick, with leatherette covers and shiny ribbons to be used as bookmarks. The first three volumes put up decent sales numbers for a supplement of the time, selling over two hundred thousand copies from 1994 through 1996. Despite this, the company made almost no money on them because the production costs of these beautiful books were so damnably high. Director of sales and marketing John Danovich said that the year the *Encyclopedia* debuted, despite its strong sales, "it wasn't even in our top ten sellers, profit-wise, for that year." When Wizards of the Coast reprinted *Encyclopedia Magica* years later, they were just plain old paperbacks, a decision that shows what Wizards thought about the profitability of the initial product.

Furthermore, this was not uncommon. Danovich's fellow marketing director, Jim Fallone said, "It seems like that happened quite a bit." He mentioned *Dragon Strike* as a product that likely made no money. He suspected that the expense of producing the video was not included in the final cost of the product, because if it were, the game would have been so expensive it would not have sold.

Worse yet, many of these stunning products *actually lost the company money* with every copy sold. One example of this was the first Dark Sun adventure. TSR experimented with including flip books in these releases. These colorful, spiral-bound volumes featured maps, stories, and the adventure itself. They were cool, easy to use, and lay flat on the table. Problem was, they were expensive, so much so that the company ended up losing money on each flip-book adventure they made. Fallone said, "At the end of the day, I believe we were losing about a buck per adventure." Between their respective release dates and 1999, the four flip-book Dark Sun adventures sold, in total, 85,980 copies. That's a lot of design, thought, creativity, and sales to lose money. It's also worth mentioning that the company released four of those adventures in just under a year before ceasing production of the profit-killing flip books. In other words, this wasn't just one product in the line that sneaked out the door to lose money for the company. They produced four before someone realized that given the cost of the components and price point, each item sold actually lost money.

Fallone said, "Our profitability of products sometimes did not become apparent until after the fact."

TSR WAS NOW trapped in a doom loop of prodigious errors. Sales were down, so the company produced more products. Making more products increased costs, which reduced profits. Furthermore, many products were either not profitable or actually lost the company money with every sale. Like some sort of demonic punishment meted out to lackadaisical CEOs in hell, the company was literally doing more work to make less money. Therefore, it abused the Random House contract by overshipping units to their distributor to generate loans that would keep the company afloat.

Those cursed, damnable loans! They heaped one on top of another for years; their sinister shadow cast TSR's future into doubt for all who knew of them. But the number in the know was, of course, small. Lorraine Williams seemed to have a passion for secrecy and did not keep creatives informed of these matters. Of the dozens of writers and designers and editors I interviewed for this book, precisely zero of them knew of the Random House contract and its abuse until I told them about it.

And Arneson forfend Random House should ever request payment on those wretched loans in full. Such an event might kill the company!

John Rateliff summarized by saying, "You can only make so many bad decisions before they overwhelm you."

RANDOM HOUSE WANTS ITS MONEY BACK

December 19, 1995

Lake Geneva, WI—TSR, Inc., the producers of ADVANCED DUNGEONS & DRAGONS® games, announces yet another year of tremendous sales! "TSR's financial outlook is extremely positive," says Willard Martens, the company's Chief Operating Officer. "Our role-playing game revenue increased 20 percent in 1995—as it has annually for the last six years." In addition, he said the figure does not include increases from the company's card game or magazine business. The company's disclosure comes as its fiscal year is about to end—and in response to a recent inaccurate comment made on the internet by Wizards of the Coasts's president, Peter Adkison. In response to a question about the role-playing game industry, Adkison said the industry's and TSR's role-playing game sales have been on a steady decline. "It is unfortunate that Mr. Adkison painted with such a broad brush . . . his statement in regard to TSR is completely inaccurate," said Lorraine Williams, TSR President and CEO. She added, "We wish Wizards of the Coast well as they divest role-playing and

> *other products from their company, however, their inability to produce successful RPG lines does not necessarily reflect the state of the industry—and certainly not TSR!"*
>
> *"Consumers are going to see some extremely exciting changes in our products and marketing in 1996," said Williams.*
>
> —TSR PRESS RELEASE

EIGHTEEN MONTHS AFTER that press release, Wizards of the Coast president Peter Adkison would purchase a dead TSR.

The press release painted a picture of a company flourishing and thriving. It shouted that TSR was still the indispensable RPG company, eternal and central as the sun.

But it was all marketing flimflam. The truth of what was happening on Sheridan Springs Road in Lake Geneva was far different and more troubling.

TSR would be overwhelmed.

The company was no longer able to keep its head above water in managing its loans from Random House. As of June 10, 1995, TSR owed $11,822,180 to Random House. The distributor wanted its money. The two companies worked out a repayment plan. TSR would reduce the debt to $8.2 million by December 31, 1995, and have it down to a mere $1 million a year later. If TSR missed a payment deadline, it would have to pay off its debt immediately in one lump sum instead of over time. Such an event would push the company into crisis, if not bankruptcy.

HOW TO PAY OFF RANDOM HOUSE?

Random House's demand that TSR reduce its debt set off alarm bells in the executive offices on Sheridan Springs Road. At the time, Jim Fallone didn't know the details, but he knew that their distributor "began to put pressure on TSR to pay down the debt." He said there was talk about garnishing a percentage of the monies paid to TSR and applying it to outstanding loans.

That could not be allowed to happen. Fallone said the company "was built on a business model like the old Hollywood movie studios. There was a lot of overhead for a game company with writers, designers, and artists all on the payroll full-time with health benefits, unlike much of our competition. This put TSR in a position where there was not a lot of room for big cash flow fluctuations." Furthermore, he said that because of the money the company was spending on innovative products such as *Dragon Strike* and the *Advanced Dungeons & Dragons CD-ROM Core Rules,* "our overhead had increased to a point where there was no room to lower our cash flow."

Something needed to be done about the debt. And fast.

The company was short on money and long on creative genius, so it picked up its artists and writers and threw them at the problem. Creatives were ordered to pitch Random House a proposal for a joint young adult book series and game line. Fallone described it as a "mash-up of Percy Jackson and the Teen Titans if the Teen Titans were international Olympic athletes." He added, "The concept had a strong tie to the Olympics so we could take advantage of the promotional media frenzy leading to summer of 1996." It was to be called AmeriForce. He said this would give the company "breathing room" because the money from the creative work would then be applied to the debt.

In the fall of 1995, TSR staff, including Jim Fallone and Lorraine Williams, drove down to the O'Hare airport Hilton for a high-stakes meeting, with the future of the company on the line. The goal: to sell Random House on the AmeriForce idea. At the hotel, the TSR folk met with Random House executive vice president Jerry Harrison to explain the concept. Despite the importance of this meeting, or perhaps because of it, Fallone recalled that Williams pressured Harrison for a financial commitment to the project a mere fifteen minutes into the meeting. Harrison said he could not promise any money without running it by Random House president Alberto Vitale. When this became clear, Fallone recalled, "Lorraine said, 'I guess we are done,' and got up, and we all walked out."

The fact that Random House was not willing to make a deal without authorization from the very top and that Williams appeared desperate for a deal indicated to Fallone that "things were much more serious than we thought. Rather than go back to what was sure to be a tense executive wing in Lake Geneva, we went to a bar for the rest of the day."

Given that things with Random House were going so badly, perhaps TSR could find a different distributor to put their products in malls?

THE COURTSHIP OF MACMILLAN

Jim Fallone said that relations with Random House were "strained" given the state of the debt between the two companies, and the oh-so-brief O'Hare Hilton meeting. TSR began to flirt with other distribution partners, hoping that their distributor might forgive some of the company's debt in order to keep them as a customer. He said the company began discussions with "Macmillan to make Random House jealous but also to see if Macmillan would buy us out of our Random House deal and our debt."

To drive home that the company was on the prowl for a new distributor, a dramatic plan was hatched. In spring and fall of every year, Random House held a sales conference with all their publishers. TSR of course attended every one, and at a sales conference after the O'Hare Hilton incident, the company was scheduled to deliver a presentation.

In an (ironic) attempt to improve their position, TSR ditched the Random House sales conference and instead flew to New Jersey for the Macmillan sales conference. But not so much as the edge of a word was to slip out about the impending snub. Fallone said, "I was told under no uncertain terms I could not tell Random House we weren't coming. Our rooms at the hotel remained booked, and our presentation slot stayed on their schedule."

Williams took Jim Fallone and David Wise along to the Macmillan sales conference. Wise was there to run demos for East Coast executives who didn't know whether *D&D* was an acronym for an obscure government agency or some new disease. Upon arrival, it was demonstrably clear that Macmillan was taking matters seriously. Waiting in the room of every TSR attendee was a fruit platter with a chocolate centerpiece in the shape of the company logo.

The next morning, it fell to Jim Fallone to call Random House and tell them that TSR would not be attending their conference a mere hour before they were scheduled to address their sales force. He said, "It was an awkward call." On the other end of the phone line, he heard only "a resigned silence. My Random House counterpart and I knew this was out of our hands."

Random House, however, was unmoved. No offer to decrease the debt to keep the company as a customer appeared from New York. And after all the bother and drama, TSR didn't manage to sign with Macmillan either.

Later, Wise remembered hanging out at an empty bar with Jim Fallone. Given that the company was now in extreme distress and the New Jersey trip was a bust, the pair began discussing philosophy. Wise said that employment at TSR had become "grimness." Worse yet, Wise had no idea of the specific problems facing the company. He, like the vast majority of the staff, didn't know about the 1979 distribution agreement with Random House. He didn't know the tremendous size of the outstanding debt. The way management kept staff imprisoned in a labyrinth of ignorance only increased the terror of their situation.

Life at TSR was a realm of uncertainty.

For Wise, that bar with Fallone was a "twilight zone" where they "waited for something, probably bad, to happen and not knowing what it was."

These attempts to use stratagems, ruses, and aggressive negotiation tactics to deal with the pile of money owed to Random House all failed.

Twelve days before its first repayment deadline, on December 19, 1995, the company put out the above press release gloating about its financial vitality and sticking a finger firmly in the eye of Wizards CEO Peter Adkison. "Financial outlook extremely positive," it said; "Role-playing game revenue increased 20 percent in 1995," it said; "We wish Wizards well as they divest from the RPG field," it said.

Perhaps there was some truth to the swagger and swank of the press release. While I've been sent a lot of internal documents from this time, I don't have access to all the company's records. I've seen a lot of sales data, but not everything. For example, I only have anecdotal evidence about how card games sold.

But the numbers I do have suggest that the main ingredient in that press release was marketing bullshit. For example, TSR grossed $36.5 million in

1994 and $38.4 million in 1995. That's a 5 percent increase in sales, which is fine but far from rosy. Even that $38.4 million number doesn't tell the whole story. For example, in November and December of 1995, the company shipped Random House enough product to generate $1.3 million in loans. Borrowing money and calling the loans gross income is a wonderful way to make a company look good on paper.

And if the company's future was so bright, if all the smarm in that press release was warranted, if what COO Willard Martens said was true, one would imagine that it would meet its obligation to Random House to pay down its debt to $8.2 million by December 31, 1995. A company seeing a 20 percent increase in revenue over six years when faced with an apocalyptic payment deadline will surely meet it, right?

Yet it didn't. The company only reduced its debt to $9.5 million instead of the required $8.2 million.

In consequence, Random House sued TSR in April of 1996 in an effort to recover the money owed. The lawsuit was delivered to the offices on Sheridan Springs Road and signed for by lawyer Connie Lindman. Random House sought the remaining $9.5 million it was owed forthwith.

TSR was on a perilous perch and in danger of a great fall, though management kept that from the rank and file. Therefore, employees created tales to explain the curious things that happened at a company supposedly in the flush of health.

THE VIZIER WITH TEN GOLD BARS

Jim Ward remembered TSR grossing $40 million. (Probably this was 1995, when records show the company grossed $38.4 million.) It was more money than the company had ever brought in before. He credited his brilliant designers, editors, and sales force with the feat. But in meetings with Lorraine Williams, Ward said he didn't get praise. Rather, he was told that he and his team "had to do lots better." From the experience, he constructed a myth that goes like this, with some embellishment from your humble author.

Jim Ward imagined himself as a poor but virtuous vizier in the royal court. The vizier was loyal, and wise, and knowledgeable in the ways of magic. He knew his queen, like all monarchs, needed ready money, and so he pored over the books and tomes of his library until he found a spell for hewing purest gold from the thoughts of the wise.

Without hesitation, he began the ritual. He imagined fantastic new lands, outlandish monstrosities ranging over the wilderness, and abominations burrowing deep into the raw stone below. Lastly, he imagined the heroes who would hold the horrors back.

And the vizier cut these imaginings from his mind, and where they touched the naked air, they burned, and out of the pure flames flowed a stream of gold. When all that he imagined had burned in the air, he was left with eight solid bars of unalloyed gold.

The gold bars shone like the sunrise, and in their bright sides, the vizier was able to see himself as clearly as in a mirror.

Proud, he brought the gold bars before the queen. Ward said, "The queen sniffed at the effort and said she expected nine bars."

The vizier returned to his chambers and imagined things even more extraordinary than before. A city with doors that led to any place in the universe. A world of blasted sands and magical depredations. And more. The vizier cut these imaginings from his mind, they burst into flame in the naked air, and from them, he made ten bars of purest gold.

Again proud, he brought the gold before his queen. Ward said, "The queen looked at the effort and said she wanted twelve bars."

Then, Ward said, "The vizier left the royal court knowing there wasn't enough gold in the kingdom to suit his queen."

The myth is an effort by Ward to make sense of the fact that even though TSR brought in a lot of money, it wasn't profitable. Thing was, Williams kept these problems from her staff, which is why Jim Ward created a story about how greedy she was. Yet what bosses do in businesses is to try to increase sales, and she knew that the company was sailing deep waters with a leaky hull. If the company didn't bring in more money, it would sink.

Like all good myths, it explained the mysteries of the world in a satisfying way and therefore found purchase among the staff. For example, Bruce Nesmith found the tale of the vizier and his gold bars so affecting that "Where's my *other* bar of gold?" became a thing he often found himself saying throughout his career in games.

From the perspective of Jim Ward and Bruce Nesmith, Williams was avaricious and interested in only the almighty dollar. There is, however, one thing missing from the myth. The queen had taken out loans. And those creditors needed to be paid back, lest the kingdom fall into the hands of bankers and moneylenders, who had no idea what made the kingdom so special.

The problem was that given the company's debts and obligations, even $40 million was not enough to right the ship.

Compounding matters, TSR used curious financial instruments in the hobby trade that also put it in a financial and strategic bind, making it slow in the face of fleeter competition.

THE GIANT WITH FEET OF LEAD

The Random House contract complicated TSR's relationship to the book trade. In its sales to hobby stores, the company used another arcane technique of finance in an attempt to improve its situation, but one that would again prove disastrous to the company.

The man in charge of sales to the hobby trade was John Danovich. Danovich was Jim Fallone's counterpart as a director of sales and marketing. From that perch, he saw the company hem and haw about producing products that were profitable, and engage in financial practices that made it strategically sluggish, transforming the company into the lead-footed giant of the RPG market.

John Danovich worked for TSR twice. First, between 1982 and 1984, then again between 1994 and 1996. He was hired by the Sales Department in 1982. He met his wife at the company. (She worked in accounting, and they've been together ever since.) But he was fired in 1984, during one of the purges that plagued the era.

From TSR, he moved on to New Infinities, the company Gary Gygax founded to make new role-playing games after his expulsion from the company. Danovich said of his time at the company, "They still owe me money." (Lawsuits in the Walworth County courthouse show that Saint Gary was not particularly diligent about paying the people who worked for him at New Infinities.)

After a disillusioning stint in the comic book industry, he got a phone call from Jim Ward. A few interviews later, he was the director of sales and marketing. He was responsible for selling the company's products to the hobby trade; every revised *Player's Handbook* and every copy of *Planescape* that was purchased in a game store got there because of Danovich. Unlike the book trade, where the company dealt only with Random House, in the hobby trade, he was selling products to a number of different distributors, who then sold those books to game stores and hobby shops.

For a company that made hobby games, Danovich said that the higher-ups in the company didn't seem to like the hobby trade. He said, "Upper management definitely favored the book trade. The hobby trade was always the rubes, the younger stepchild, the one we didn't really care for." This attitude persisted, even though the hobby trade was "the core of the role-playing game industry for us and the core of our sales. But it was not the direction that management wanted to go." According to him, the hobby trade was perceived as bumpkin town. TSR deigned to make products for this market.

There was some sales data to back up that preconception. For example, Danovich said that the company sold more units through the book trade than the hobby trade. But the reason for that was, primarily, novels. He said, "If we sold one hundred thousand copies of a novel through the book trade, we might be lucky to sell five thousand copies through the hobby trade." That's because people at the game store didn't go there to buy novels; they went there to buy games. Hence, almost all the amazing sales of the Book Department were channeled through the book trade. Because the book trade moved more units of highly profitable novels, it also made more money than the hobby trade.

Despite that, the hobby trade was still crucial to TSR's financial health. The book trade brought in more money, yes, but only slightly more money because the company's game products were more expensive than their novels. A boxed set might cost twenty or thirty dollars, which is why the book trade might have sold more units but only grossed a little bit more money for the company. Danovich described the difference in money brought in by the book trade as compared to the hobby trade as "minimal, pretty much fifty-fifty."

In short, while the book trade may have been the air TSR breathed, the hobby trade was its food and drink. Both were needed for the company to stay alive. Its ability to generate loans from Random House almost at will polluted the book trade channel as it racked up significant amounts of debt with their distributor. Management put together a similarly clever arrangement with the hobby trade that would also in the long term prove disastrous for the company.

It worked like this: TSR would plan out its releases for the year. For example, May 1995 would see the release of the revised second edition *Player's Handbook;* in June, the company would release *The History of Dragonlance;* in July, the *Birthright Boxed Set* would come out; and David Wise's sourcebook, *Van Richten's Guide to the Vistani,* would be released in August, and so on. In January, Danovich would then take this product schedule and use it to generate preorders. He said, "All of the sales that were done through the hobby trade were predicated on a preorder system that was triggered in January. We tried to get every single unit we could sold in January. All new releases, all prerelease, any back sales, it was all predicated off of January sales."

To encourage distributors to commit to making purchases on products that they had not yet seen, the company sold these products in January at a discounted rate. Perhaps the sweetest part of the deal from the buyer's point of view was that they didn't actually have to pay for these products until the product was published and shipped to them. They got a discounted price for just signing a contract agreeing to make the purchase at a later date.

TSR then took these contracts and sold them to investment banks. From the banks' point of view, purchasing these contracts was a solid investment. The company had an exceptional history of hitting deadlines for products. The distributors had already signed contracts agreeing to the price. The bank, of course, also wanted a percentage. Danovich said that after the discount to the buyers and the bank's cut, TSR was left with "eighty-two percent of what you would have gotten if you sold it later on." When the promised product was created and shipped, the buyers would then pay the agreed-upon price to the investment bank, not TSR.

Why would the company go through such a bother just to end up making 18 percent less money on every sale? Because "you get it all in January," Danovich said.

This was called *factoring*. He said, "Lorraine Williams was a big proponent of factoring." TSR benefited from this arrangement because it permitted the company to receive a large sum of cash early in the year, allowing it to budget for costs and expenses with certainty about money on hand.

There were two significant downsides in factoring. First, there was the 18 percent it lost on every sale it made. Second, it meant that the company lost flexibility. It could not respond with any degree of speed to changes in the market because of the commitments it made to the investment banks and its distributors in the beginning of the year. If a new setting bombed in June, the company could not stop production of an adventure for that setting in September, because it had already received money for that sale from the investment banks. If another company put out a hot new product in February, TSR could not cancel or delay other products to fund a competing product, because it had already received money for those products in January.

Over the long term, factoring would have an insidious effect on the company's financial health. One example of this involves the *Advanced Dungeons & Dragons CD-ROM Core Rules* and Babbage's, a computer software store.

In the 1990s, it was obvious that the internet was going to be a huge deal, but no one knew what that meant or how it would play out in the marketplace. On the one hand, TSR spent a large amount of time contacting gamers on the internet with cease-and-desist orders. RPG historian Shannon Appelcline, for example, was told by the company to stop posting material about *Dungeons & Dragons* online, even though he was only putting up files about *Ars Magica*. A more positive attempt by the company to advance into the world of the internet came in June of 1995, when the company uploaded *Ivid the Undying*, a two-hundred-page Greyhawk supplement, on TSR Online.

But perhaps TSR's bravest attempt to sally forth into the nascent realms of the internet came in 1996, with the release of the *Advanced Dungeons & Dragons CD-ROM Core Rules*. The company funded a tech start-up named Evermore Entertainment to make the supplement. Jim Fallone said, "Costs of the development quickly exceeded the initial estimates and continued to expand." At one point, the start-up needed more computers, and who had to pay for it?

TSR. Despite the expense, Evermore Entertainment did produce the desired product. The CD-ROM rule set allowed buyers to view the second edition rule books on their computers. The books had hyperlinks and a character generator. The product was bold. Nothing quite like it had ever been done before, and from the point of view of today, putting out a digital rule book in 1996 seems revolutionary, visionary, and perhaps even ahead of its time. After all, what RPG gamer doesn't have a gaggle of RPG PDFs on their computer today? It was an attempt by the company to meet the challenge of the digital future and was therefore worth the expense.

But as with so many other TSR endeavors, a quality product would end up costing the company money due to management decisions.

Babbage's was a computer store in seemingly every mall in America in the 1980s and 1990s. According to Danovich, Babbage's committed to ordering approximately thirty thousand copies of the *Advanced Dungeons & Dragons CD-ROM Core Rules.* (He later added that it might only have been ten thousand copies.)

Then Babbage's went bankrupt.

He knew what would happen if those thousands of CD-ROMs shipped to Babbage's. They would immediately be sold at a major discount. That would destroy the market for the entire product field of digital *D&D* rules, because thousands of people who wanted to buy the rules could go buy them for cheap at Babbage's instead of picking them up at their local game store or another retail outlet. As a result, sales of the product would be poor at those other locations, souring them on buying any future digital rules products from the company. Danovich set up a meeting with Williams where he told her, "We can't send this product out." He said it would be sold at a discount and ruin that product and possible follow-up products.

According to Danovich, she looked him right in the face and said, "You have to send it out." Because of factoring, TSR had already received money from an investment bank for the sale of those CD-ROMs. If the company did not send the product out, it would be breaching that prior agreement. (Now, it could have attempted to pay back the bank for the money it had already received, but one of the themes of the 1990s was there was no money available for anything like that.)

The units shipped to Babbage's. Danovich said, "They immediately hit the market as liquidation. Every single one of them. It literally killed that marketplace for that product and subsequent products in that line because we had zero credibility for those product lines in the book and hobby trade at that point. We'd sold a dud product out into a product category that we were trying to break into."

Jim Fallone remarked dryly that TSR's expenses were "not recouped" on the CD-ROM rule set.

Like *Dragon Strike* before it and TSR West before that, the company put significant monies into a project in an attempt to enter a new market space and, due to management decisions, failed in the attempt. I don't have any data on how much money the company spent funding Evermore Entertainment, but software development is not cheap. Instead of the CD-ROM rules making TSR the leader in a new field of gaming, the company was left with a mess of red ink on its balance sheet.

Again.

How many mistakes could TSR make before it broke the company?

Factoring also left creatives out in the cold. It even contributed to Jeff Grubb finally leaving the company.

Recall that the company split the trunk of *Dungeons & Dragons* in two, creating *Advanced Dungeons & Dragons,* which attempted to throw a net around the world with its rules, and *Dungeons & Dragons,* which was simplified and left room for Dungeon Masters to make rulings on the fly. Grubb said that by the time the 1990s rolled around, TSR was looking to end the *D&D* line, and bring its default setting, Mystara, or "the Known World," into *AD&D* second edition. Since he had already shepherded the Forgotten Realms into *AD&D,* he seemed an obvious choice to do the same for Mystara.

Grubb loved Mystara. He was eager to adapt the material, already planning character class kits that would mesh the setting and second edition rules. The product as planned would cover the entire Known World. It was to be a massive overview, and he set to work.

Then, over the span of a weekend, management entirely changed the nature of the product. Grubb said that Jim Ward appeared in the office, "looking kind of beaten up, saying, 'This is what we're going to do, and don't get mad.'"

First, the boxed set would no longer introduce the entire wide world of Mystara to a second edition audience. Rather it would focus on only one realm in the Known World, that of Karameikos. Second, the new product would include a CD. Grubb said that at that point, no one had any idea what would be on the CD. But a CD there would be.

Oh, and even though the content of the product had changed and an entirely new element was being added to the work, none of the production schedule deadlines changed.

Factoring was why scheduled dates for the product couldn't be changed. Just like the company had to ship those CD-ROMs to Babbage's, it had to produce a Known World boxed set.

Despite all of this, the final product, *Karameikos: Kingdom of Adventure,* was produced on time and was well reviewed. I myself walked to a nearby game store and purchased it when it came out. The boxed set was beautiful, and the CD was exciting. I got caught in a rainstorm walking back from purchasing it and went on to run the adventure in the set for my friends on forty-five minutes' notice that afternoon.

After that, Grubb said he was "pretty much done." He didn't like having to "scramble to account for managerial decisions." He was "tired" and "frustrated." He put out a few more products, such as *Neither Man nor Beast* for Ravenloft, and then resigned. He said, "There were no hard feelings. I packed up my stuff. I went out the door. Everybody waved goodbye. Then they went back upstairs and looted my office, because I had all sorts of old stuff up there."

Factoring played a role in driving genius Jeff Grubb from the company. It would also hurt the company again in its response to the tectonic release of *Magic: The Gathering.*

MAGIC COMPETITION

Wizards of the Coast, the tiny Renton, Wash., company that makes Magic, *has put out 50 million cards since it released the game six months ago. The cards are selling from coast to coast. They come in basic packs of 60 and booster packs of 15; some players have collected hundreds. By May, the company expects to have 150 million cards in play.*

—"IT'S MAGIC," *THE NEW YORK TIMES*, MARCH 20, 1994

JIM WARD SAW *Magic: The Gathering* at Gen Con in 1993 in Milwaukee, Wisconsin. The game sold out and opened up an entirely new game genre, the collectible card game. Soon, Wizards would be shipping one hundred million cards per month. Ward knew TSR needed to get in on this.

According to Ward, Lorraine Williams was skeptical. She would say, "Oh, those Wizards guys. They're only going to last six months. They haven't got a chance in the world. They're a one-trick pony."

Still, Ward insisted that the company had to move into this new market, and fast. He got the green light and was given a mere ten weeks to develop the rules. John Danovich said the designers did a "bang-up" job of getting the rules out in almost no time. Lake Geneva's response to *Magic,* the *Spellfire* collectible card game, would be the second CCG on the market.

The development and production of the game was consistently hampered by factoring. For example, because the game was developed late in the year, there was zero budget for art. As a result, the company recycled previously used art on the game cards. This art was stunning, but tired. It hadn't only been used before. It had been used multiple times before. It had even appeared on cards before. The result, according to Danovich, was "grumbling in the marketplace." Ward recalled the complaint and said he found the objection "ridiculous. Our art was magnificent. Why knock us for using it a second time?"

Danovich said, "If I was a consumer, I would have loved to have seen new art, but it just wasn't feasible with how TSR could operate at the time. There was just no budget for new art because of the way we were doing business."

While the art was lackluster, sales were not. *Spellfire* sold well. Despite that, Williams did not want to produce the game. Danovich said, "Every single release was a fight. Lorraine hated the product and hated that she had to do the product and had to use money she didn't have to pay for it."

The first piece of evidence management would cite when trying to kill the game was *Spellfire*'s returns from the book trade. When it was returned from bookstores, the product came back in individual packs of cards, while it was sold to the hobby trade in boxes. This meant the product returned from the book trade could not be sold into the hobby trade, where the game was doing well. Danovich said that the company took "a huge write-off" on those returns, which was a big "negative" in the eyes of upper management. Because of this, he said, *Spellfire* "became a product line that had no more support at the top, even though the sales were bringing in more money than almost any other product line at the time." (It's worth pointing out that this sales data is from his memory, not from any documentation.)

He continued, "I was generating millions of dollars' worth of sales in *Spellfire.* But it got to the point where Lorraine hated the concept of the game. First of all because it wasn't a TSR-driven idea; it was something that another company did out there and was doing better, and it was not supported by the book trade." Perhaps that management prejudice against the hobby trade came into play here? Or perhaps it is the company not listening to the market again?

The development team put in for several releases of *Spellfire* for 1996. All were denied. This was frustrating for Danovich. He said that Williams would often come into his office and lay out how much money she needed him to generate in the hobby trade. According to him, she would say, "We need three million, we need two million, whatever many millions" that he needed to produce. ("Where's my other bar of gold?" demanded the queen who was being sued by Random House for failure to pay down her debts.) Generating those sales was no easy matter. It seemed like every buyer for hobby game distribution companies had once been in military intelligence with a high-level security clearance. They were a shrewd and difficult market to sell in, to be sure, and management was denying him a product he knew they'd buy.

He could not let that stand. He went to accounting and COO Willard Martens. He argued that the company was "leaving millions of dollars on the table" by not creating more *Spellfire.* According to Danovich, Martens then went to see Williams and persuaded her to produce more of the game.

Danovich said going to Martens was "not something you did to Lorraine. You didn't go behind or around or to the side of her to get things done, which is something that I would do frequently because it needed to be done. It was in the best interest of the company. I was going around her to make sure that things were running efficiently and the way they should be running for the hobby trade to succeed."

As a consequence, Williams would give Danovich what he wanted and then some. Even though he was in sales, he would be in charge of creating this new *Spellfire* product. And he would have to create it with a budget of zero. Skimping on the game seemed to be a management tradition by this point.

Again, TSR seemed hell-bent on *not* making what its customers wanted.

And in the past, the company muddled through such errors. But in 1996, all margin for error disappeared. While *Spellfire* was selling, practically nothing else was. That year saw TSR's gross sales plunge to $32.6 million, a plummet of 15 percent. This was the abyss opening its maw to swallow the company. Sales could no longer cover its basic financial obligations. Ugly things would have to be done.

So the company stopped paying freelance authors the royalties owed them.

NO PAYMENTS, MORE LAWSUITS

Soon, Massachusetts men Bob Salvatore and Jim Lowder were both experiencing the same problem with TSR: It wasn't paying them their royalties. Given that the company didn't have money to spend on vital new products like *Spellfire,* it is not surprising that it found other ill-advised places to skimp.

In April of 1996, the very month that the company was sued by Random House, it missed royalty payments to a large number of its authors. So many, in fact, that Lorraine Williams wrote a form letter with the late royalty payments sent out in June saying TSR's "largest customer has not paid us for the last several months thus causing a very difficult situation for us." She also wrote, "I cannot help but express our gratitude for the good humor and patience with which all of you have dealt with this very unfortunate and hopefully never to be repeated situation."

The situation repeated immediately.

Jim Lowder received no further royalty payments in 1996. It was so bad, he remembered, "by the middle of 1996, authors couldn't even get replies to queries about the missing payments."

Bob Salvatore, despite cutting ties with TSR, had his last novel with the company come out in 1996. He had not seen a dime of the royalties owed on that book, which (shock of shocks!) had gone on to be a *New York Times* bestseller.

This failure to pay money owed was a betrayal of the most basic agreements undergirding management and labor. In response, Salvatore sued the company in an attempt to recoup money owed.

Neither Lowder nor Salvatore succeeded in getting any royalties while Lorraine Williams was still CEO. It is tempting to say that the company had no money to give, but Salvatore's books were selling. He was still bringing money home to the company. But someone, somewhere, at the company decided to put that money to another use, neglecting the legal and ethical obligation the company had to Salvatore. Unless we take Williams's words in her June 1996 letter to authors literally. She wrote, TSR's "largest customer has not paid us."

Had Random House stopped sending the company money and simply started applying all payments to its outstanding debts?

Was TSR dying?

ALWAYS PAY YOUR PRINTER

> *In 1996, [TSR] sold JB Kenehan its existing facility to provide debt relief for previous unpaid invoices, and entered into a long-term exclusive contract with Kenehan for production of its products and a rental lease for its offices.*
>
> —NOTES FROM FIVE RINGS PUBLISHING GROUP PERFORMING DUE DILIGENCE ON TSR, SPRING 1997

TSR also stopped paying its printer, J. B. Kenehan.

Debt swelled. By the time all was said and done, TSR would owe them $6 million.

To placate their printer, TSR gave them their offices on Sheridan Springs Road. A meeting was called with the entire staff to make the announcement. Dale Donovan said that Williams presented the move as one that would "allow us to move forward. All business-speak and marketing rah-rah."

Donovan said that in retrospect, that should have been a warning sign. After all, it meant that the company owed such a large amount of money to their printer that they had to give away real estate to make a move toward settling it.

The sale turned TSR's printer into its landlord.

The company also entered into an exclusivity agreement with their printer. TSR was now legally and contractually obligated to print their products with J. B. Kenehan and no one else. Like the sale of the offices, Dale Donovan recalled management "touted [the exclusive printing agreement] as a great thing, but it was because TSR already owed the printer so much money, [Kenehan] forced the agreement on TSR as a form of insurance."

If relations soured between the company and its new printer/landlord, it could not go somewhere else to publish its products.

TSR had given J. B. Kenehan vast amounts of power over its future as a company.

The stage of the disaster was now set. The company's penultimate act would start with the departure of one of its longest-serving employees.

THE WARDEN DEPARTS

Jim Ward quit TSR in October of 1996 after decades with the company.

Ward quit because he'd been ordered to fire over twenty employees. At the time, Ward was the vice president of product. The twenty people he was ordered to fire were artists, writers, and game designers. In short, the people who made up the muscle and sinews of the company. Ward described them as the "geese that laid the golden eggs. They were the people making products and bringing in sales." He said, "I couldn't fire those people. It just seems so stupid to me that management would want to do that when those people had been responsible for bringing the money into the company."

Rather than fire the people who created the games whose sales kept the company alive, Ward quit.

When I first heard that story, from Ward himself, I thought it was too good to be true. He walked away in a gesture of self-sacrifice, a sacrifice that won him nothing? The tale was both noble and a little bit mad. I thought it must be fabricated or at the very least shaded to make him look more the shining knight. I wildly speculated that perhaps, just perhaps, the story existed to cover up the real reason Ward was let go, though I had no idea what that real reason might be. After all, who would quit a job as an executive at the company that made *Dungeons & Dragons*? The job granted you alpha nerd status, and firing people, even if they were your friends, came with that position on the food chain. Furthermore, he left the company over twenty years ago, and the man is one of the deans of the role-playing game field. Who could call him to account?

Jim Ward was also one of the first people I interviewed for this book. So I fact-checked his story with everyone I could over the next two years. Everyone in a position to know backed up Jim Ward's story, often vociferously. As Zeb Cook said, "Jim liked to protect us hobbits from upper management," in which case, quitting was his last act in defense of the Shire.

Thus exited Jim Ward.

Ward finds the memory of his departure so painful that over twenty years later, he refused to discuss his last day at the company. He would not even look into his memory to tell me what time of year he had quit. (It was October, a detail provided by his lieutenant, David Wise.)

Regrettably, Ward's departure did nothing to halt what was about to happen. Instead, list-making duties would fall to Wise.

David Wise was born in Kansas City, but grew up in Detroit. He said, "Dad was a YMCA guy, and they moved YMCA guys around the country." In 1968, his family moved to Milwaukee, where he spent his adolescence and young adulthood. He graduated from the University of Wisconsin–Milwaukee with a master's degree in creative writing, and a professor suggested he go into publishing for a while, write a few books, and then migrate back to academia if he wanted to teach college.

When he mentioned this plan to his *D&D* group, Anne Brown, an editor at TSR, suggested he look for a job in Lake Geneva. In 1990, he was granted freelance editing work, of which Wise said, "I got the job done ahead of schedule, and it was correct, so they brought me in-house."

Wise thought of himself as different from the other writers and editors at the company. *D&D* wasn't just a game to them, nor was TSR just a job. These sisters and brothers in Lake Geneva were devoted to the holy chore of game creation for publication, hewing new worlds out of words and rules, and gifting them to the reverent faithful.

That wasn't Wise. He'd played *D&D* and liked it just fine, but he said, "I didn't have this burning desire to be a game-maker. I was just out of college and trying to figure out what to do with my life, and it sounded like fun working for a game company, so I did."

Wise's ability to turn in excellent edits early led to his promotion to creative director. Essentially, he became the product line supervisor of Dragonlance, Planescape, Ravenloft, and the Forgotten Realms. That led to further promotions, and in 1996, he was the director of creative services, working directly under Jim Ward.

So it was that when Jim Ward quit, his job fell to David Wise. Laughing to think about it now, he said, "I didn't get the promotion, and I didn't get the pay, but I did get the direct line to Lorraine."

The task of choosing who would be fired also fell to Wise. He said, "Lorraine came to me and said, 'All right, Jim wouldn't do it, so now you have to do it. I need a list of eight staff members to lay off.' It was a horrible thing to have to face."

Ward had quit rather than do such a thing. Should Wise do the same? These were his coworkers and friends, and now he had to select those who would suffer the little death of leaving the company.

Guilt racked Wise.

But if he didn't do it, who would? Williams? With Ward gone, he was the highest-ranking creative. Williams didn't know the staff and their assignments the way he did. These firings were major surgery, and at least Wise knew the anatomy. If she decided who stayed and left, vital staff might be shown the door. It could kill the company. He said, "I wanted to make sure that the people who deserved to stay did stay."

Furthermore, Wise wasn't ready to follow Ward out the door. TSR was not a gaming club. It was a business, and in business, "these things happened," he said. It was a butcher's job, yes, but it had to be done, so somebody had to do it.

Wise gave Williams her eight names. He said, "I gave her an honest assessment and said, 'If you have to lay off eight people, this is the list that I would use.'"

According to Wise, she looked at the list and said, "Good, now go back and give me seven more." He did, and after providing them to her, she asked for more names. He said, "She kept on sending me back over and over to go through these terrible exercises of deciding who was going to lose their job and who wasn't."

A mass firing on the scale of those from the 1980s approached.

THE BILL COMES DUE

Whispers began creeping through the halls and cubicles of TSR headquarters, past the bathrooms, through the games library, and at last into the ears of the staff. The company, the whispers said, was in peril. Menace and hazard filled the future. Monies were owed, in significant amounts, and in many places. The cancer of debt was so thick and deep within the company that not only might layoffs be in the works, but the company might not survive.

Game designer and future third edition *D&D* cocreator Monte Cook remembered that there were people who took the rumors seriously and people who didn't, but either way, what could a game designer or editor do about it, other than make certain that they did their best at the job that they had?

The wooded hills of Lake Geneva faded into orange and red as if putting on their best to celebrate the passing of the year. The leaves could also have been the funeral decorations of TSR, for it would never again see the season.

In the autumn of 1996, six semitruck loads of material returned from Random House rumbled into the parking lot to be unloaded into the company's warehouse. (Or rather, the warehouse they now rented from J. B. Kenehan.) It was millions of dollars' worth of product.

Yet for employees, it was just a regular day. No one in the executive suites gnashed their teeth and rent their clothes. The news that a deadly amount of returns had just been delivered was not whispered over cubicle dividers or hinted at in the games library. Alarm fires were not set on the roof to signal to all of Lake Geneva that the company was in peril.

Except for the warehouse staff who had to unload all the trucks, it was just another day. Management stayed in their suites like spiders in their webs. Everyone else went about their business. There had been large returns before. *Dragon Strike*, for example. The company already owed Random House millions of dollars and was unable to pay it off. The company had likely already received payment from Random House for the returned materials, in which case they would already have been factored into the debt owed.

But this return was different. What each one of those returns represented was a sale in a mall denied to TSR. A book sitting in the warehouse could not be sold to help lessen the company's outstanding debt. Between 1995 and 1997, Random House returned approximately $14 million of product.

The reason for the Random House returns are unknown, though theories abound. Some said it was an attempt to push TSR into bankruptcy, perhaps with the intention of being purchased by Random House. Perhaps it was an attempt to demonstrate the power Random House possessed. There was an RPG bust in the mid-1990s. Perhaps the demand for RPGs in 1996 had crashed so far that the returns were simply justified by waning demand.

But what is certain is the effect that the returns had on sales numbers. Many books and games had their numbers pushed into the negative, with more copies returned than sold in 1996 and 1997.

It was, of course, dire disaster for a company already in debt up to the rafters.

Although she did not speak to me for this book, I imagine that it was about now that Williams began contemplating the sale of TSR, as most of the actions she will take in the coming months of this crisis make the most sense if considered in light of selling the company.

THE CHRISTMAS AXE

Drowning in debt, awash with returned product, and seeing sinking sales, TSR's staff would need to be trimmed to its very bones. The firings would happen on December 20, 1996, the Friday before Christmas.

David Wise went into the office early that day. He had Christmas cards to hand out and wanted to get them on people's desks before they got there. He stopped by the executive suites to put a card on Carol Hubbard's desk. In some ways, putting that card on her desk was a natural foreshadowing of the events that would transpire that awful Friday, because while Carol Hubbard wore the outward form of a sweet little old lady, her true shape was that of the HR angel of death. She swooped around the company on black wings, her passage an occasion of dread, because she was in charge of firing people.

As Wise laid a card on her desk, he noticed that the conference room was full of managers and executives, even though it was 7:15 in the morning.

He immediately thought, *Uh-oh.* He should have been at that early-morning meeting, but he didn't even know it was scheduled.

Wise knew he would be fired.

Double time, he sprinted around the building, trying to deliver all his Christmas cards before he was let go. Done, he returned to his office. Williams entered bearing a manila envelope. According to Wise, she said, "This is your last day at TSR. We're letting you go. Here's your severance package. You have to leave the building now. Take it home, read it, sign it, and then you can bring it back and collect your personal belongings."

He said, "The line I'll never forget is, 'We've made some mistakes, and now we're going to have to pay for them.'" He thought, *You mean you've made mistakes, and now* I'm *going to have to pay for them.*

With that, he was escorted out of the building.

David Wise went home, got his chocolate Labrador retriever, Hershey, and took to the hills. He got away from the phone and from people and wandered the drumlins, tumps, and trails of the Kettle Moraine State Forest beneath slate-gray clouds that promised snow but brought none. He said he felt a mixture of anger and relief as he ranged the forest with Hershey. His professional life had been painful ever since Jim Ward left. He said, "It was a terrible time to be in charge," because he'd spent his days watching the company inch toward its grave, every day a loss of ground toward what seemed the inevitable end. But now it was all over, apparently forever.

And Wise found that he was happy. It was, he said, "a wave of happiness that had been lost to me seemingly forever."

Later, he learned that the people fired that day didn't even match the list of names he had torturously constructed for Williams. He felt like a traitor to his own staff for recommending people to be fired, and she didn't even fire those he had recommended! "That was the kicker for me," he said. "I fully understood why Jim Ward had resigned. I ultimately felt lucky to be terminated before it could go on any longer."

John Rateliff went to work that day wearing a fedora and bearing candy canes. It was his Christmas custom to give a candy cane to every single person in the building. He would grab a handful and distribute them with a "Merry Christmas," his voice soft and sweet, with just a hint of Arkansas around the edges.

As 1996 headed for the door, Rateliff thought it would take the company's darkest days with it. Things seemed to be looking up. Recently, the company had held a charity auction, staff bid on items, and the proceeds went to a good cause. He won an original piece of Dave Sutherland art. The executive suites were in the middle of being remodeled, and that had to cost money. It seemed the crisis had passed.

It turned out to be the deep breath before the plunge.

Dale Donovan remembered Friday, December 20, 1996. John Rateliff came by to give him a candy cane. Dawn Murin and Dana Knutson were holding their annual Christmas fête that night. Monte Cook and Sue Weinlein were throwing a party too. So when Donovan sat down at his desk that morning, he wasn't thinking about layoffs.

Dale rose to go to the men's room and walked past Steve Miller's cube. There, he saw Miller packing his belongings into a cardboard box, tears welling up in the man's eyes.

Donovan said, "I was not prepared to see that. I gave him a half smile and kept walking."

What do you do, what do you say, when someone is fired from TSR? What would their next job be? Teacher? Journalist? Marketing? Whatever it was, you wouldn't be working on *Dungeons & Dragons.* You wouldn't be paid to think about bugbears, beholders, or bladesingers. For some, leaving the company wasn't just losing a job, it was leaving a life. And the ill-starred exiles escorted out the front entrance were marched right past the executive suites as they were being remodeled, salt in the raw, open wounds of those banished that Friday in 1996.

Donovan returned to his cube and heard rumors that it wasn't just Steve Miller. Executives were firing employee after employee after employee. It was sheer murder. Donovan couldn't just sit at his desk and wait for his turn, but he couldn't leave either. He began to pace in his cubicle.

What happened to game designer Ed Stark that Friday seems like something from an overly sentimental screenplay written by an undergraduate.

Fate played him a shocking twist, one that, if you saw it in a movie, would make you say, “Things like that don’t really happen.”

Stark knew that the company was in trouble, but he had this gut feeling that if he just made it through the holidays, everything would be all right. But here it was, the week before Christmas, and heads were rolling. He knew a number of senior staff had been pulled into a meeting and that he was not one of them. Therefore, there was a chance he was going to be fired. He had a personal laptop in his cubicle. Better go get it just in case . . .

A senior staffer saw him picking it up and entered his cube looking crest-fallen. The staffer said, “Oh, you’ve heard?”

Stark certainly had not heard. He said, “No, what?”

The senior staffer’s face drained of blood, turning white as an egg. He had said what he shouldn’t have.

The horrifying moment ended when an HR minion appeared and asked Stark to come with her. He was led to Lorraine Williams and Carol Hubbard. The pair told him he was being let go. It was just as he’d feared. He would be cut away, expelled from the creative life of the company. He said, “They were as nice as they could be under the circumstances.” He could come back later to get his things, but for now, he had to go, so it was a good thing he’d grabbed his laptop when he did. Departing, Stark said he felt “shock. I was very productive and the lead designer in the Worlds group. I didn’t think I was untouchable, but it didn’t make a lot of sense to me.” But he had a good résumé. He’d be able to find some freelance writing work, surely. And he sure as hell wasn’t going to let this ruin Christmas.

Once at home, he called his wife to give her the bad news. She worked in childcare and didn’t have time to talk. He gave her the basics, and she promised she’d call back as soon as she could.

Stark waited at the phone, feeling “antsy.” He wanted to call unemployment and get the paperwork going, but couldn’t because his wife was going to call back. So beside the phone he waited.

The phone rang on game designer Bill Slavicsek’s desk, which was weird. His phone never rang. He picked up. It was Lorraine Williams, which was even weirder. She never called him. She said, “Bill, I need you to come to the conference room.”

He said, "All right."

Not knowing that people were being fired, he assumed this had something to do with *Alternity*, the sci-fi RPG he was working on. When he arrived, he saw seven or eight other employees in the room, and Williams. She told them to take a seat and relax. "We want you to be in here while things happen," she said.

In the lore of company alumni, this gathering has come to be known as the Passover meeting. Carol Hubbard, the dire and terrible HR angel of death, at that moment stalked the office, ending careers while they remained safe. It was like when God loosed the angel of death upon Egypt, but the angel passed over the houses of the Hebrews.

Unfortunately, the conference room wherein the Passover meeting took place overlooked the parking lot. The safe and saved watched as the fired below shambled to their cars.

Monte Cook remembered, "We were all told to stay in our cubicles because you might be getting a phone call. We didn't know, but many of us guessed" that a phone call meant you had to go see HR to be fired. He remembered huddling in his wife Sue Weinlein's cubicle with a klatch of other nervous employees. Weinlein, an editor in the Games Department, remembered that once it became clear what was going on, people didn't even attempt to work. Other employees drifted into her cubicle, trying to talk each other through the stress of the day. She said, "People were trying not to think about the call that might be coming for them."

Her cubicle was the perfect spot to hang out that Friday because it was at the crossroads of the office. She was situated "right at the base of the stairs to the second floor, across from the bulletin board, and at the corner of the aisle that would take you either to marketing/executive land or deeper into designer/editor territory. It was a location where you could hear much of what was going on on two different floors."

But the clustering and the talking in Weinlein's cubicle meant that many people were not in their cubicles, and calling cubicles was how management was reaching those employees selected to be laid off. A phone would ring, and everyone would perk up. *Whose phone is ringing? Is it mine?*

Monte Cook made it through the day. So did Sue Weinlein. "But the guy in the cubicle next to me didn't," she said. "It was harrowing." The experience stayed with her in the years since. She said, "It has come to mind every time I'm in a layoff situation since" as one of the most emotionally fraught ways of informing someone that they'd been fired.

Weinlein and Cook wondered if they should still have the Christmas party they'd scheduled. The pair lived in a church that had been converted into a living space, and they rented the basement apartment to fellow employee and longtime friend Bruce Cordell. Being a converted church, the house took to the Christmas season in grand style. Decorations were hung, and candles burning in the windows sent light and shadow dancing on the high ceilings. But throwing a party after the day's slaughter, wouldn't it be in poor taste? Somewhat like dancing on the graves of the laid off?

But whenever Weinlein voiced these concerns, the answer she got from her fellows was, "No! No! You have to have the party! In fact, buy more booze."

Come lunchtime, Dale Donovan decided he couldn't stay in the building. He and a couple of other friends who'd survived went out for lunch. They met in a common area near the stairs that led up to the second floor. Donovan stood there, shell-shocked from the morning.

He saw John Rateliff climbing the stairs, a fedora filled with candy canes in hand. Donovan thought to himself, *Oh, John's still here! That's good.*

"Hi, John!" said Dale.

"Hi!" John returned.

The only reason Rateliff was still in the building was because when an executive called his cubicle to fire him, he had been out delivering candy canes.

And it was at that moment, before Donovan's very eyes, that a company higher-up stepped out from the hallway that led to the front of the building and saw Rateliff. They said, "Oh, John! Could you come with me, please?"

Donovan saw his head drop. He descended the stairs.

The sight of John Rateliff marching to his termination was so grating, so unpleasant, that Donovan left the area rather than watch the scene unfold.

Very weirdly, Monte Cook has another story about being with John Rateliff when he was fired that day in 1996. He said Rateliff huddled with the klatch of employees in Sue Weinlein's cubicle. The group was talking about who had been laid off so far when a phone rang. Rateliff stood up and said, "Is that my phone?" and ran off to answer it. Cook remembered that after he left the cubicle, the rest of them looked at each other, dread and sadness mingling in their eyes.

Rateliff himself doesn't remember either incident but knows he was fired by COO Willard Martens. He recalled Martens saying, "Sorry, we're letting people go, and you're one of them." The first thought that went through his head was that he regretted spending any money on that Dave Sutherland art at the charity auction. Rateliff left the building, the last person to be fired that day.

Once the layoffs were complete, the employees in the Passover meeting were released. Bill Slavicsek was promoted to creative director because the previous creative director had been fired. However, Harold Johnson did not get up to leave the room. Williams asked him if he was all right. He said, "I know you're trying to save the company, but if you told me I could only keep two people on my staff, you just let those two people go." One of the two people he had wanted to keep was Ed Stark.

She said, "Oh, I'm sorry."

He said, "Lorraine, I'll go and we'll deal with this and we'll figure this out."

About an hour later, with a rustle of black wings, grandmotherly Carol Hubbard appeared before Johnson in all her dread magnificence, the stench of charnel fires wafting behind her. She spoke the sinister words that no employee wanted to hear that Friday: "Lorraine wants to see you."

He said, "What?"

She repeated that baleful sentence and asked him to come down to the office.

He thought, *Okay, now it's my turn.* He had said too much, damn it! Williams preferred yes-men, and he spoke his mind. Now he'd pay for it. Johnson pessimistically trudged to her office, dreading that he'd soon be joining Stark at home because he'd stuck up for him.

There, Williams said, "Harold, I made a mistake. I should have asked you. I should have known you'd have the best interests of the company at heart." And she told him one employee from his team could come back. He should pretend it was all some sort of mistake, a horrendous bureaucratic error.

Ed Stark was waiting for his wife to call back, but when the phone rang and he picked up, it was Harold Johnson. He said he'd gone to Williams and told her that if she wanted his team to produce any product, he needed him back. Stark was surprised that Johnson stepped up for him. "Not because Harold wasn't that sort of boss," he said, "but because it worked."

Flabbergasted, Stark said, "When do you want me to come back?"

"Now," Johnson replied.

After telling his wife the news, Stark returned. He said, "Lorraine was there to greet me, along with Harold, and she apologized."

The offices he returned to were a ghost town. Empty cubicles, empty chairs, empty desks, empty halls. The company had been hollowed out. It all left him feeling "pretty numb." He said the remaining staff were obviously in shock.

That night, Dawn Murin and Dana Knutson's party went on. Donovan said, "Apparently, there was a lot of drinking involved."

Attendance at the Weinlein-Cook Christmas party was sky-high. Weinlein said, "That was the biggest turnout for any party we ever had. We got people who hadn't worked for TSR in ten years to come to that party because we all needed to be together and experience our shock together."

John Rateliff didn't want to go to the party. To cheer him up, his wife, Janice, drove him to Mayfair Mall, a good hour away from Lake Geneva, and bought him a ring with his name on it in hieroglyphics. She reminded him that he liked the people he worked with and that he wouldn't be seeing them every day anymore. He went and enjoyed the festivities. "There was a lot of camaraderie between the people who stayed and the people who left," he said.

Ed Stark was there too, and it was awkward. Everyone who kept their jobs knew that he had been hired back, but everyone who was fired thought he had been let go as well. He had to explain that Harold Johnson went to the wall for him with Williams, and he still had his job. He said explaining that to those who were laid off was "tough." He said, "I'll never forget the various feelings that went with it."

One can only imagine the thoughts of the newly unemployed when they heard Stark's tale. *What is so special about him? Why was Johnson willing to go so far to get him back?* Perhaps even, *Am I such a useless lump that I got fired and no one even cares?*

Then the crowded house and candles in the windows came together.

John Rateliff smelled something burning. He turned and saw that the recently fired Steve Miller was now literally aflame. His thick sweater was smoking and frizzling. Rateliff and a few others patted the flames out.

Weinlein remembered that she was in the kitchen when a voice rang out, "Steve Miller's on fire!" She saw the aftermath. The sweater must have been made of acrylic because the candle, she said, had left "a melty hole."

The moment brought Rateliff to reflect philosophically about the events of the day. He thought, *There are worse things than being laid off from your job. You might find yourself on fire.*

Terrible and ham-handed as they were, the layoffs were at least an attempt to right the company ship and get it sailing again.

Sadly, it was a move that came too late.

EXISTENTIAL ABSURDITY IN 1997

The impression [is] that TSR is going away for good.

—DISTRIBUTOR EMAIL, MAY 13, 1997

MORE BAD NEWS followed with the new year. J. B. Kenehan could no longer be held at bay. Because of the money TSR owed them, they refused to print any further products until they'd received payment for prior work. Given that the company had signed an exclusivity contract with Kenehan that forbade it from printing work anywhere else, it was now imprisoned in a hole of its own digging. TSR was a publisher that couldn't publish, with significant monies owed to its distributor, printer, and freelance creatives. Without the ability to publish new products, there appeared to be no way to generate enough revenue to keep the company alive. If all the debts were added together, they totaled approximately $30 million.

The company's problems could no longer be hidden. Signs of the sickness were everywhere in the winter of 1997. It stopped restocking supplies, and soon employees were bringing their own toilet paper to work. The plants that dotted the hallways and offices disappeared to save money on their care. It was a plague of disappearances. People, plants, and finally new products.

It was the absence of new products that was the clearest sign of the company's impending death. No products would again be published by the company during the reign of Lorraine Williams. Products were certainly finished during that time. But none would be published.

Instead, in the front of the building, where management dwelled in their suites, near the office of vice president Mike Martin, there was a room. It was empty and windowless, but otherwise unremarkable. It was here that designers and writers put their finished work in the form of ziplock bags full of printouts and floppy disks. The bags, which would normally be sent to the printer, were crammed to the zips with the wildest imaginings of the staff. If one could have seen unaided what lurked in those bags, the room would have been filled with necromancers and barbarians waiting for something to do. If the denizens of those bags could have somehow made themselves real and escaped, they would have razed Lake Geneva to the ground, resurrected the dead as servants, and established a kingdom black and foul among the green hills of southern Wisconsin.

But the denizens of those bags could not be seen, and they could not escape. At least not without being published by J. B. Kenehan, and the printer refused to do exactly that. So these marvels and monstrosities had to sit in this empty, lonely office and wait.

But Dale Donovan remembered. "I saw the room. I saw those bags. After six months, there were a lot of ziplock bags," he said. The sight of them was depressing.

The bags sitting in the office, brooding, were a physical manifestation of the sickness running through the company and a warning of doom. Bags represented products that had gone unprinted. Unprinted products could not be sold, and if they were not sold, the company made no money, and if the company made no money, how could they pay anyone to paint dragons or write about wizards?

And the number of bags in the room kept growing.

A publisher that wasn't publishing was a fish that didn't swim. They are called dead fish and float to the surface to stink and swelter in the sun. Would TSR die to float and bob on the waves of capitalism?

The company failed to perform the act that defined its existence. Sue Weinlein said of that time, "That's when things really started to feel different.

After months of that, you begin to wonder, what is it even for? What are we playacting at?"

What was TSR?

Instruction on the matter was not forthcoming from management. Consequently, gossip and innuendo filled the gap where work once had been. She reported, "Mastering the rumor mill was at least a half-time job. We didn't have email, so you just kinda had to check out what everybody had heard. Is anyone making any offers for the company? Is Hasbro going to buy us? What's this about Five Rings Publishing? Are we going under?"

The uncertainty was at such a height that come Friday, many employees would cash their checks right at the bank rather than depositing them, for fear the checks would bounce. For all the missing people and products and plants, they never did. Williams saw to it that everyone on the payroll still got paid.

Employees took the company's ill health into everyday decisions. Brian Thomsen had brought Margaret Weis and Tracy Hickman back to write for the company. During this troubled time, Weis completed a novel, *The Soulforge,* and called Thomsen to tell him the good news. She would bring it to the offices on Sheridan Springs Road for him to edit.

His response was, "No, don't do that!" Instead, he offered to meet her for lunch and receive the novel from her then and there. She agreed.

At lunch, Thomsen told Weis that he was not going to take the manuscript of her novel into the office. She had completed the novel, and he would of course see to it that she was paid, but he was not going to take the manuscript into the building.

Why?

Thomsen had heard rumors and was deeply concerned that if the company was forced into bankruptcy and her novel was on-site, it might be seized as an asset. Who knew where the novel might end up in a bankruptcy? To avoid such an end, he kept the manuscript of *The Soulforge* in the trunk of his car, and Weis said, "Brian edited it, carrying it around in the trunk of his car."

Jim Lowder, though outside the company at the time, heard about the black mood infecting the staff. He said people "came into work every day wondering if the building was going to be shut down." Employees went to lunch, and when they returned and were able to reenter the office using their swipe cards, Lowder said they thought, *Well, I got back from lunch today and I still got in the building. We're not closed today.*

The competition began to consume the company's market share. Distributors reported that RPGs like *Shadowrun* increased sales by 20 percent that season. Others said that Palladium Books' RPGs were also seeing better sales.

TSR and its staff awaited the abyss. Problems and mistakes had cascaded one into another, gaining speed over the years until they became unstoppable: the company's inability to keep literal geniuses on its payroll; management's habit of using the company to make what it wanted instead of what the market demanded; its inability to successfully innovate and evolve, even when it attempted to do so with initiatives like TSR West and products like *Dragon Strike*; the use of Random House as a bank to paper over these failures and keep the lights on, allowing unsustainable debt to accrue; and finally, its inability to respond with any dispatch to changes in the market because factoring locked its production schedule in stone every January.

Here, in this ultimate moment, almost nothing could be hidden at a company where management secrecy was a custom of great antiquity. How were sales? Obviously abominable, since product in vast amounts had been returned. How did the future look? Dim as starless space seeing as how the company had fired staff and couldn't publish new products.

But one secret remained.

Filings at the U.S. Copyright Office show that in June of 1996, TSR gave notice that it was using the copyrights of dozens of its works as collateral to guarantee promissory notes with Random House and State Street Bank. Though I didn't see the note and no one I spoke with knew of its existence, here's what I'm guessing occurred.

In April 1996, Random House sued to recover all $9.5 million that TSR owed. Obviously, the company didn't have that kind of money lying around. So the promissory note was likely a new schedule of repayment. Perhaps State Street Bank provided the cash? This would also explain why Random House's lawsuit was dismissed on June 28.

While this arrangement likely helped to keep the lights on a little longer on Sheridan Springs Road, it did so by taking an awful risk: the institution of *Dungeons & Dragons* itself was now in danger. Those dozens of copyrights used as collateral included the *Player's Handbook, Dungeon Master's Guide, Monster Manual,* the Ravenloft, Planescape, Dark Sun, Dragonlance, and Forgotten Realms settings, as well as dozens of novels. If the company went under, as now seemed increasingly likely, all of those copyrights would go on the auction block.

What would happen if the *Player's Handbook* copyright and the *Dungeon Master's Guide* copyright were acquired by different individuals? What if the Dragonlance setting and the Dragonlance novels likewise had their ownership split? In these strange circumstances, who could be said to own the game? It would become a fraught question that could only be resolved by lawyers and judges. This might be a gamer's apocalypse, an event cataclysmic enough to shatter an already fragile property and decimate the hobby.

The future of the company, its staff, and the game itself hung in the balance in the winter of 1997, a future that looked increasingly dreadful.

I wish I could ask Lorraine Williams about this moment, though I imagine avoiding answering that question is itself a reason not to talk to me. Fundamentally, of course, the question is one of failure and responsibility. But I would also want to know how she felt going into work every day as CEO of an impotent publisher. What did she do with her time? Read? Brainstorm? Listen to the radio? If she was actively seeking a buyer, no one mentioned it. If she had a plan beyond keeping the lights on one more day, no one I spoke to heard of it. Did she simply continue going through the motions, presales in January, hearing about new releases, and so on? Perhaps she did, because I know the company had a booth at the American International Toy Fair in February of 1997, and she was in attendance. Perhaps pretending everything was fine was another way to get through the day.

I would guess she was embarrassed. As CEO, the firing of employees and the failure of the company was all on her, and everybody knew it. We all would keep our mistakes to ourselves if we could, and hers were now distressingly public.

But I do have some evidence to suggest one thing Lorraine Williams wanted in that dark, white winter of 1997: for all of this to be over soon.

THE TOMB

I will show you fear in a handful of dust.

—T. S. ELIOT, *THE WASTE LAND*

THERE WAS NO escaping the fact that TSR was dead in 1997.

Game designer Monte Cook had a vivid memory from those ghostly, twilight days. Harold Johnson, who had been at the company since time immemorial, marched into his office. He said, "I need your help. It's really important, but it's going to take your afternoon."

Cook replied, "Okay."

The pair of them got in Johnson's pickup truck and drove off. On the way, he told Cook that they were heading to a storage facility in Racine, Wisconsin, rented by the company.

Cook said, "TSR hadn't been paying its rent. So that afternoon, at the end of the business day, the facility managers were going to literally throw everything away in the storage unit." Cook and Johnson were to go to the unit and put anything of value in his truck to save it from the dump. Neither of them had any idea what was actually in the storage unit, but they had the long drive from Lake Geneva to Racine to think about it. When they finally arrived at the storage facility, signs informed the pair that they had only one hour before closing.

Cook described the sight that greeted him upon entering the storage facility as surreal. The rental unit was the size of a four-car garage and packed to the ceiling with splendors. There were dioramas of dungeons, graveyards, caves, villages, and fields. He discovered a floating castle, probably from Dragonlance. He also found box after box after box of miniatures.

Cook realized what the storage unit contained. "All the stuff that TSR had been utilizing at Gen Con for the last twenty years, that had been stored there," he said.

For years at Gen Con, the company built a castle in the center of the exhibit hall. In the nooks and crannies of the castle, there would be *D&D* demo zones. Players could try out Ravenloft or Forgotten Realms and then wander over to buy products. But the centerpiece of each of these demo zones was a lovingly detailed landscape for playing with miniatures.

These dioramas were straight-up works of art, exhibiting a level of technical mastery on par with what one might find in some pharaoh's tomb. (Egyptian funeral goods were often miniature representations of things the dead would need in the next world: cows, warriors, etc.) In the dioramas, tiny torches the length of the nail on your pinkie finger were properly painted brown, with flames of orange and yellow. The stonework of castles was slate gray with white mortar between them. The mortar must have been painted with the thinnest of brushes and the steadiest of hands, making a white line no thicker than a thread. A single diorama represented hours and hours and hours of work by a devoted artist and often cost thousands of dollars.

There was a spaceship shaped like a nautilus. Eleven two-by-two-foot blocks made up a titanic desert diorama, over which rose a mountain. The top of the mountain came off to reveal layers of dungeon beneath. There was an asteroid with a dragon's lair within. Its creator was so dedicated to making fantasy real in his work that he inserted piles of dragon droppings festooned with tiny human skeletons, doubtless the remains of the last group of adventurers that attempted to kill the dragon and loot its lair.

Cook saw so many of the dioramas in that space that he couldn't even count them.

Then there were the boxes of miniatures. Most of the figures were shorter than one of the joints of your thumb and again mind-numbingly detailed by an artist's brush. Faces the size of a lentil with eyes the width of a grain of rice peered up at Cook. How long had it taken to paint those faces and eyes?

The storage locker contained diminutive universes, and whole armies of warriors, wizards, and monsters that could be measured in millimeters.

Cook and Johnson had an hour to save what they could, filling his pickup truck.

It fell to Cook to close the door on the storage unit for the last time. They hadn't taken a fraction of what it contained. He said, "Knowing that all this beautiful stuff was going to go to a landfill somewhere in southern Wisconsin was just heartbreaking. But that's what happened. They're all gone."

Reflecting on the fate of those treasures appalls me. It reminds me of the feeling I get when I think of bone saws or dental drills and what they can do to the human body. There is a mental tense and cringe. Is it akin to the emotions of a devout believer imagining heretical hands destroying holy relics?

TSR was dead. Cook closed and sealed the company's tomb. There is no heaven for dead companies, and though I have no definitive proof of their fate, like as not the dioramas and miniatures were crushed in a landfill.

Part IV

◆

THE PREACHER'S SON PERFORMS A RESURRECTION

PETER ADKISON

PETER ADKISON HAS a superpower, one that he used to change the world. If you present him with ideas for games, he can pick out the one that will generate billions of dollars in sales. The next era of the history of *Dungeons & Dragons* must begin with him.

Adkison was born into Seventh Day Adventism, and every Saturday, he would hear his father preach the word of God. ("The Seventh Day Adventists are like Christian Jews," he said of the Saturday sabbath.) His family also had a camper, the kind you could hitch to your car and take out to have a bit of comfort in the wild places of the west. But the family never went camping; instead, they played war games in it. There his father introduced him to the war games of Avalon Hill and SPI.

Adkison attended Walla Walla College in College Place, Washington. Like countless undergrads in the '70s and '80s, he started a *D&D* campaign set in a world of his own creation, Chaldea. He would gather a clutch of men and women to heap high the bodies of monsters and raid dungeons for treasure.

But Walla Walla College was a Seventh Day Adventist institution, and the satanic panic was at its zenith of froth and fury. Adkison was identified as the ringleader of *D&D* activity at Walla Walla College and was dragged into the principal's office to be informed that since *D&D* was a satanic devil game, it was now banned from college premises.

So his game moved to his mother's basement. Her house was three blocks from campus, and though she was also religious, she wasn't concerned about *D&D.* His parents had divorced, and his father was serving in Korea, leaving his mother to raise Peter and his sister. He said, "She had bigger, more reasonable, more traditional fears" about what teen boys with access to cars and girls might do on a Saturday night in College Place.

After graduating, he landed a job at Boeing as a systems analyst. He moved to Seattle, got married, and found himself working in a cavernous engineering bay. Row after row of cubicles and desks were packed with engineers, each one seemingly sucking on a cigarette and heaving gouts of smoke and ash into the air. The haze and stench of tobacco pervaded the place. Adkison shared his cubicle with a retired air force colonel who stuck out because in the afternoon, he lit a cigar.

For three years, he went to work in the fuggy murk of that room with the horde of his fellow engineers. For three years, he watched the retired colonel huff down his cigar after lunch. He thought, *This is what my life is going to be like until I die.*

In 1990, seeking something more, he decided to start a role-playing game company and named it Wizards of the Coast after a magic guild from a friend's campaign. The nascent company's first release would be *The Primal Order*, an RPG supplement about deities and the religions they spawn. Adkison would pen the volume. After he wrote a first draft and showed it to people, a problem became apparent. He said, "It turned out I'm not really that good of a writer." He described the first draft of the book as "really fucking boring. Really dry."

It is worth pausing to consider Peter Adkison's assessment of his own writing ability here. It is honest to the point of brutality. To what degree did his ability to see his flaws as they truly were contribute to his later success? Hard to say, but his take on his limitations as a writer is one of the most savage things anyone I interviewed for this book said about themselves. Yet he is obviously one of the most successful people I interviewed. The juxtaposition stands out.

While *The Primal Order* was being revised, Wizards found its first full-time employee, Lisa Stevens. Acquiring Stevens was akin to signing a young Michael Jordan. She already had a résumé thick with incredible work. In 1987, she joined Lion Rampant, an RPG company founded by two college compatriots, Jonathan Tweet and Mark Rein-Hagen. Their first product was *Ars Magica,* an RPG that took wizards and made them the central actors of the game. In 1990, Lion Rampant merged with White Wolf. There, Stevens was made vice president and also helped write *Vampire: The Masquerade,* which was a titanic hit for the company. From her perch at Wizards, she flew off in 2002 to become the most successful female CEO in the history of tabletop role-playing, building her own RPG empire at Paizo, publisher of the incredibly popular *Pathfinder* RPG. As of this writing, she is probably the most powerful woman in role-playing games, a rank held by Lorraine Williams for more than a decade.

When hired by Adkison, she suggested that Wizards acquire an already-existing RPG line, which it did, licensing the rights to the 1987 fantasy game *Talislanta.*

For the first three years of its existence, the only offices Wizards of the Coast had were Adkison's home, specifically the basement, echoing how during its infancy TSR operated out of the dungeon beneath House Gygax. At one point, seventeen employees hustled in shifts down there.

Adkison himself worked like a locomotive. He kept his full-time job at Boeing. He did pass after pass on *The Primal Order* with editors, involving so many people so intensely that the final work listed eight authors and five editors. While doing all of that, he also sought out and pitched people willing to invest in Wizards of the Coast.

On April 1, 1992, copies of *The Primal Order* finally arrived at his home. He described seeing those books stacked high in the garage as "perhaps the greatest day in my life other than my wedding day. To hold that book in my hands and see thousands of copies in boxes, after working on it for over a year and a half, was just incredible." It was also positively reviewed. *Pyramid* magazine said it was "probably the single most useful book a GM can buy regarding the proper and effective use of gods and religion in a campaign." Unfortunately, the volume's notes on how to use it with the *Palladium Fantasy Role-Playing Game* prompted a trademark lawsuit from the game's publisher, Palladium Books.

The lawsuit sapped company resources and time. Come Christmas 1992, Adkison told staff that their current paychecks would likely be their last for several months.

By spring, an out-of-court settlement was negotiated thanks to the intervention of Game Manufacturers Association president Mike Pondsmith. Wizards paid Palladium an unspecified amount of cash, and promised to never mention Palladium in any further products.

According to Adkison, *The Primal Order* was the product that taught Wizards how to be a company. It learned that iterative design, attacking a project again and again, revising and revising, could result in a great product. He also learned that RPG products were a hard sell. The genre was in a slump. Maybe a decline.

Perhaps there was something else Wizards could sell to keep its head above water . . .

PRESENT AT THE BIRTH OF A NEW GAME GENRE

The nerd universe would change for all time after the meeting of Peter Adkison and genius game designer Richard Garfield. Imagine walking outside one night and seeing a second moon overhead. That is the caliber of change the pair wrought and the sense of wonder their creation awoke in fans.

Garfield visited Adkison while on the West Coast to see his parents and pitched him a game called *RoboRally.* Adkison thought the game was brilliant and wanted to publish it in a year or two, once the company found its footing.

Garfield then made a fateful offer. If Adkison wanted, he could give Garfield an idea for a game, and Garfield would design it for him.

Adkison said, "Well, I had always thought it would be really cool to have a fantasy-oriented card game that was quick to play, easy to carry (playing cards *only*), fairly easy to learn, that could be marketed through the convention circuit. I had noticed that people spend a lot of time at conventions hanging out in lobbies, standing in lines, et cetera, and I think having a game like this could sell very well in that market."

Garfield said, "Okay."

A week later, Garfield returned to pitch Adkison on the game. Parked in a garage outside the Seattle Center, Garfield laid out the idea that would go on to become one of the most profitable non-digital games in all of recorded history.

He described a card game of dueling wizards, spells fueled by mana, and perhaps most significantly, cards that would be sold in randomized booster packs. Like baseball cards, you never knew what you might get in a given pack, and some cards would be rarer than others. So even though this was a game, it was also collectible. This last innovation was what made this idea, which would grow up to be *Magic: The Gathering*, not just a brilliant game but an economic force that would reshape the geek marketplace. Seeking out new cards for the game was so compelling, so addictive, that *Magic* cards at my high school were nicknamed "crack in a pack." It was the birth of an entirely new game genre, that of the collectible card game.

Writing for a newsgroup in January of 1993, eight months before the official release of the game that would make him a millionaire, Adkison wrote of that moment:

> This game was the single most awesome gaming idea I had heard of since 1978, when I heard of roleplaying. I started whooping and hollering and yelling because I knew at that moment that we had an idea that would add a whole new dimension to gaming, and if executed properly, would make us millions. This wasn't just a new game, it was a new gaming *form*.

It is worth noting the date of the above account, January 1993. *Magic: The Gathering* would not be released until August of that year. When Adkison said *Magic* was "the single most awesome gaming idea I had heard of since 1978," he used nothing to assess it but the tools he had inside himself. He knew the seed of *Magic* would grow into a whole forest.

Of course, everyone who starts a company featuring a new product thinks they will go on to make millions. The wrecks of almost all of those companies litter the ocean floor of capitalism. Yet he predicted that *Magic* would make him millions, and he was goddamn right.

This is Adkison's superpower, his ability to recognize an idea that would go on to make billions of dollars. It is akin to Mary Kirchoff's ability to pick bestselling novelists out of the slush pile, and in a world that relentlessly lauds creators, it is worth pausing for a moment to praise those who can recognize genius in others when they see it.

But to dissect this superpower with more granularity, perhaps it is simply that Adkison can see things as they truly are. He could see he was no writer after just the first draft of *The Primal Order.* He saw that *Magic* was a stunning idea for a game while it was still just a concept in Richard Garfield's head. Pairing his true sight with work ethic may have been what ultimately made Wizards of the Coast phenomenally successful.

Two months later after that parking lot pitch, twenty decks of cards handmade at Kinko's arrived at Adkison's house. He distributed them to the Wizards crew, and they had an immediate effect.

"Productivity stopped," he said.

People did not write, edit, plan, or market. Rather, "nobody did anything but play *Magic: The Gathering.*"

It was a historic moment of playtest bliss, a slice of game nerd heaven transported here to Earth, and it went on and on, day after day, for two weeks.

That was the first evidence Adkison had that his initial euphoria was correct. Wizards needed to get *Magic* to market, because it would be a hit.

And it was.

Magic: The Gathering detonated, and everything everywhere in gaming changed forever. Money undreamed of flooded into the coffers of Wizards of the Coast. This wasn't good for gaming money or a hit at TSR-level money. No, this was akin to the money that would be generated by a Hollywood film studio.

What does one do with all of that money? Go out and buy properties to make even more money, raise the flood until greenbacks are spitting out the chimneys. TSR, and with it *Dungeons & Dragons,* would have been an immensely valuable addition to Wizards of the Coast. Adkison arranged to meet with Lorraine Williams and Willard Martens at Gen Con. In a meeting so brief he doesn't even remember sitting down, he told the pair, "I'm under pressure from my board and investors to look for good opportunities to grow this company through acquisition." He said if they ever wanted to sell the business, he would be an interested buyer. The pair were "gracious" and thanked him for his interest, but said they weren't looking for a buyer at that time.

Given how bad things were at the company, it was a shocking refusal.

THE DEAL THAT SAVED *D&D*

TSR, ITS STAFF, and the institution of *Dungeons & Dragons* itself was in fearful peril. Peter Adkison offered Lorraine Williams a way forward, and she did not take it. I can only guess why, and based on what I've been told, I would suppose it was because she disliked Wizards, she disliked *Magic,* and she disliked Adkison.

But we know, obviously, that in the end she did sell to Wizards. She agreed to the very deal she'd just turned down. How did that come about? What bridged the gap?

To understand the events that followed, we must come to know another man with a business superpower, Bob Abramowitz, and the company he ran, Five Rings Publishing. Abramowitz was a former TSR employee who worked at the company in the early 1980s, when *D&D* was selling like hot dogs at a ballpark and the satanic panic boiled and raved. The man is a raconteur gifted with a million-dollar tongue. The story of his accomplishments shows that he has a Jedi-like, nigh-irresistible ability to convince people to do as he wishes.

Five Rings Publishing was a gaming company in Seattle that produced a collectible card game called *Legend of the Five Rings.* It was set in a medieval fantasy Asia, with mechanics significantly different from those of *Magic: The Gathering.* The first printing of the game cost $163,000. The company tried to raise the money to print the game for most of 1995, but failed. To cover the costs, one partner put in $100,000 of his own money, and another's parents mortgaged their house to put in the rest. Now, Five Rings wanted to publish an expansion, *Shadowlands,* and more money was required.

It was a friend at the golf course that brought Five Rings Publishing to Bob Abramowitz's attention. *Magic* was selling in nigh-biblical amounts, and Five Rings had a product that promised entry into that market. Intrigued, he agreed to become its CEO and went forth to raise money for the company. He recruited Scott Oki, a multimillionaire who had previously been a vice president at Microsoft, to join the board of directors, and Abramowitz raised $750,000 from investors. These funds allowed the company to begin licensing already existing properties. For example, the company created a *Star Trek* dice game and a *Dune* collectible card game. Sales grew, burgeoning from hundreds of thousands of dollars per year to millions, but it was still an insect compared to the industry leader, Wizards of the Coast.

Despite the increased fundraising and increased revenue, Five Rings still needed more money. Vice president of product development Ryan Dancey said, "We ran the company as a high-growth, high-risk vehicle. That was what we promised the investors when we started it, and that was what Bob was there to do. We put every penny into developing new games and printing the existing games that we had. Our goal was to flood the market and then expand. That was all expensive."

Things were so tight that Abramowitz had personally guaranteed a $400,000 line of credit from the bank, and it was maxed out. "It was the one and only time I would ever do that," he said. "We were getting close to the edge."

By the fall of 1996, Five Rings didn't have enough money to print new products. Furthermore, the company was spending more money than it was bringing in. Another round of fundraising was planned, this time to raise $10 million. The company hoped to use that money to become so large that it would begin to threaten Wizards of the Coast, prompting them to purchase Five Rings, or to become so successful that Five Rings was financially viable, independent of infusions of cash from investors.

Other than threatening their market share, was there anything else Five Rings Publishing could do to make Wizards of the Coast interested in purchasing them?

Simultaneously, rumors began to fly around the industry that TSR, the old dragon of Lake Geneva, was not well. The company missed publishing deadlines for the first time in years, and gamers gossiped about it. TSR's fraught position represented an opportunity, and Bob Abramowitz acted on it. At the American International Toy Fair in February of 1997, he sought out the company's booth, and there finagled a meeting with Lorraine Williams. Abramowitz had heard her company was going bankrupt. Could Five Rings swing a deal to buy it and *Dungeons & Dragons*?

He put that question to Williams in their first meeting together. Gnomically, she asked him to return the following day to discuss the question again.

The next day, in a ninety-minute meeting, Abramowitz laid out his case. He said that she didn't need to confirm or deny it, but he'd heard that "the financial strength of TSR is not as good as it should be." He said, "I'd really like to come to Lake Geneva and do some due diligence on the company and look to see if it's the right acquisition for Five Rings. I've got plenty of access to capital, and I'm intimate with your staff." In other words, he knew the company and had the money to buy it. (Something not strictly true at the time, but what the hell?) Why not sell to Five Rings, and then Williams could walk away from all the problems and headaches of running the company?

She agreed to let him and a team come to Lake Geneva and begin due diligence for a possible sale. However, she did ask that when he and his team arrived, they should keep a low profile. How would it look if word got out that another company was looking to buy TSR? What would she say if an employee asked about it? A low profile was crucial to mission success.

In the teeth of the Wisconsin winter, Abramowitz, Dancey, and Richard von Riesen, a financial advisor to one of the investors in Five Rings Publishing, traveled to cold and lonely Lake Geneva. They checked into a hotel downtown and ordered pizza. While waiting for it to bake, they wandered the empty downtown. What was the only store open in Lake Geneva on that desolate and frigid night? The Game Guild, a game store opened by Margaret Weis. Abramowitz and Von Riesen ducked inside.

There they found Ernie Gygax and Jeff Easley. The pair instantly recognized Bob Abramowitz. They chatted for ten minutes before returning to get their pizza. Abramowitz knew that Williams would hear that they had been sighted in downtown Lake Geneva. They were supposed to keep a low profile, and their first night in town they ran into a TSR employee *and* the son of *D&D*'s cocreator. Was that it? Was the deal blown before they'd even walked in the front door?

The next morning, the team began their due diligence. Ryan Dancey later wrote, "I found myself standing in the snow outside of 201 Sheridan Springs Road staring at a building bearing a sign that said 'TSR, Incorporated.'" Williams gave the Five Rings delegation a tour of the company headquarters. (Did she already know they'd been sighted at the Game Guild?) To anyone who asked, she said that Abramowitz and the rest of the team were there exploring the possibility of another *D&D* collectible card game.

Dancey wrote of the mood there, "In the halls that had produced the stuff of my childhood fantasies, and had fired my imagination and become unalterably intertwined with my own sense of self, I found echoes, empty desks, and the terrible depression of lost purpose."

The Five Rings team was given a swath of materials to explore the company's guts. Dancey began to go through the documents, gazing on papers no one outside of TSR may have ever seen before. He saw the corporate logbook, its "first page penned in haste by Gary Gygax." He saw the "smudged photocopies" wherein the idea for Dragonlance, a fantasy world explored in both novels and game products, was expounded. He saw "euphoric copyright filings for the books of [his] lost summers." He saw Gary Gygax's severance papers. He saw the Ed Greenwood contract for the sale of the Forgotten Realms. He saw the Random House distribution agreement. Clearly, they weren't holding anything back. But what would all of this reveal about the health of the company?

That night, Abramowitz got a phone call. He was told that Ryan Dancey had posted on the internet that he was in Lake Geneva doing due diligence on TSR. This was not a slipup while waiting for a pizza. This was the cat crawling out of the bag to defecate on the kitchen table.

Abramowitz went and woke Dancey up to ask him, "What the blank do you think you are doing?" He knew Williams would hear about this and that she would not be pleased. Had it ruined the whole deal?

When asked about the incident, Ryan Dancey said that while he could not recall it, it was "plausible."

Abramowitz said he knew "something was going to hit the fan the next day. Which it did. Lorraine was a little pissed off." To cover for the snafu, Abramowitz suggested that they put out that Five Rings was considering making an investment in TSR, not that they were considering buying the company outright. The deal was allowed to continue.

Due diligence complete, the Five Rings team returned to Seattle. On the plane back, Dancey pulled out a legal pad and began consolidating his notes about the current state of TSR. He wrote that the company owed $500,000 to authors. He wrote that the company had lost $4.3 million so far that year, and they were only a few months into 1997. He wrote that its debts totaled approximately $30 million, owed to Random House, various printers, vendors, and banks. He wrote, "Random House returned $14 million [of product] in two years." In short, the company was in terrible shape. If it had been a person, they would be near death from blood loss, their only hope being a transfusion.

Despite the massive amount of debt and the fact that Five Rings Publishing would have to assume those debts with the deal, Abramowitz agreed to pay approximately $25 million for TSR. This was formalized in a letter of intent.

The acquisition would give Five Rings Publishing a new IP to exploit and likely make it the industry leader in the creation of RPGs. However, with the company line of credit already maxed out at $400,000, how would Five Rings be able to find the $25 million it would take to finish the deal? Abramowitz believed it would take him months to raise that kind of capital. Dancey was uncertain that Five Rings could have ever found that kind of money.

Furthermore, Wizards of the Coast was still looming over all with their domination of the collectible card game market. Why not sell TSR to Wizards, as long as they were also willing to buy Five Rings along with it? Merging with the competition was one way to eliminate competition, wasn't it? And Wizards was clearly sitting on fat stacks of cash. Bringing them in on the deal would solve the problem of finding $25 million.

As Bob Abramowitz tells the story, at 7:30 on a Friday morning, he met Peter Adkison for breakfast at a diner. In a folder, Abramowitz had the letter of intent to buy TSR. It was printed on stationery with the company letterhead and signed by Lorraine Williams. He chatted a bit about the *Dune* collectible card game before getting down to the real reason he'd called Adkison for this meeting. He said, "Peter, I know there's a company you've always wanted to buy, and you can't seem to buy it. But I'm going to buy it."

Adkison said, "What are you talking about?"

Abramowitz replied, "I'm going to show you the letterhead, and I'm going to show you the signature on this letter, and you're going to have to trust me that the rest of what I'm about to tell you is true. I signed a letter of intent to buy TSR." And he showed him the letterhead, and Williams's signature. He said, "The rest of the letter describes the timing and the price."

Adkison said, "So how do I get involved?"

Abramowitz said, "You're going to write me a check for a million dollars. It's going to be a loan. And if we don't complete the deal, we'll pay you back. But if you want to buy TSR, you're also going to buy Five Rings." He remembered asking "six to eight million dollars" for Five Rings. (Ryan Dancey vividly recalled that Five Rings sold for $3.85 million.)

Breakfast finished, Abramowitz returned to the Five Rings offices. There, his wife, who was working in customer service at the time, asked him how the meeting with Adkison went. He said, "It was interesting. I expect he'll get back to me sometime in the next week," and he sat down to work.

He'd been at his desk less than five minutes when the phone rang. His wife answered it and told him it was Peter Adkison. Assuming he had some follow-up questions, he picked up the line and said, "Hi, Peter."

Adkison replied, "Bob, how do we write you a check?"

The following morning, Abramowitz and his attorney both had bar mitzvahs to attend, so they scheduled the negotiation for two o'clock Saturday afternoon.

At the appointed hour, Adkison, Abramowitz, and attorneys met to negotiate the deal. If Wizards purchased TSR, they would have to purchase Five

Rings as well, and the million dollars would be part of the purchase price. If the purchase fell through, the million dollars would be a loan, and Five Rings would have twenty-four months to pay it back. The deal made Five Rings the only gateway for Wizards to purchase TSR, and Abramowitz showed Adkison the entirety of the letter of intent.

The two parties agreed to the terms discussed, and a cool million dollars flowed into the coffers of Five Rings Publishing. The company paid off its $400,000 line of credit and put $600,000 in the bank. According to Abramowitz, that money gave him a "runway" to keep Five Rings afloat while the deal was negotiated to its finality.

Peter Adkison and Ryan Dancey remember the story differently. They recall Abramowitz calling Adkison and telling him that he was going to send him a fax, and after that, he would loan Five Rings Publishing $1 million. Adkison scoffed, but awaited the fax. Abramowitz then sent the letter of intent. Adkison called back, asking where he could send the check.

However the deal came about, Adkison said he was "elated" to have the opportunity to buy TSR. It was, he said, "a dream come true." He was so excited about the purchase that he worried his emotions would cloud his decision-making and lead him to acquire the company and damn the consequences instead of doing what was right for Wizards of the Coast.

Ryan Dancey said of his involvement in the deal, "I feel like it's the second or third most important thing I've done in my life, and it's going to be difficult to ever do anything that's as meaningful ever again."

The Wizards board of directors had two major concerns about the possible purchase: management and price. TSR was $30 million in debt. Buy the company and yes, Wizards would get *D&D*, but they would also be purchasing every cent of that debt. Which begged an obvious question: Why not just let it go bankrupt and then buy it?

Adkison countered by saying, "We want to buy TSR now before we lose momentum, before employees start leaving, [and] before intellectual property starts walking out the door." And given that the choicest cuts of the company's intellectual property had already been used as collateral, a bankruptcy would have been full of peril.

The other concern was that Wizards of the Coast lacked management depth. Vince Caluori, Adkison's mentor from his time working at Boeing, was brought on to help.

With Wizards on board and the future of Five Rings secure, Abramowitz and his lawyer had to fly back to Lake Geneva to tell Lorraine Williams he'd negotiated a deal to sell TSR to Wizards, a company she purportedly loathed.

Abramowitz went to her office alone. He left his lawyer outside and made sure that no one else was present for the meeting. Whatever happened, Abramowitz didn't want to cost Williams any face by having this conversation with even the smallest of audiences. He recalled saying, "Lorraine, we want to live up to this deal. But some things have changed. You're not going to like what I'm going to say, but I want you to hear me out, because I think it's the best solution for all three of us."

She said, "Three of us?"

Abramowitz explained that Wizards of the Coast, and with it, Peter Adkison, was taking over the deal to purchase TSR.

Williams reminded him that she did not like Adkison. According to Abramowitz, she "didn't like what he had done to the industry."

He reminded her that this decision shouldn't be personal. Adkison had built a fine company around an amazing product. He said that Wizards "had the wherewithal to put *Dungeons & Dragons* back in the space it belonged." He also reminded her that she had employees depending on the company for their livelihoods. (Monte Cook and Sue Weinlein had recently bought a house!) If the company perished, what would happen to the artists, writers, and editors who made it go? Wizards had the resources to keep those who wanted to remain.

Finally, he reminded her that back in 1985, she'd saved TSR—and with it, *D&D*—from bankruptcy. The company had been lying in a shallow grave waiting to be buried when she bought it. She kept it on its feet, producing epic content for another twelve years. Abramowitz said, "Lorraine took on a very weak company that had a significant product line. She saved *D&D*. It was her legacy. Problem was, she wasn't growing the business, and they were bleeding. And she didn't have the ability to grow the business. It was time for her to move on."

After an hour and a half in her office with Abramowitz, Williams came around. He said that she was "not happy," but she did ask if the deal could be completed in the next fifty days. He told her that if the lawyers could crack and slap the contracts with all due speed, they could close the deal in thirty days.

Toward the end of the conversation, Williams asked if there was anything else she needed to know. He told her he wanted the ten-key calculator off her desk as part of the deal, and she agreed. (He said he's still waiting for the calculator.)

After negotiating with Williams about purchasing her company for millions of dollars and then informing her that he would be passing that deal on to a man she detested, Abramowitz said of the experience that "Lorraine was great. She was a very proud person with a huge family history. Personally, I enjoyed my time with her. Very professional, very smart, very proper."

The decision to sell to Wizards was another moment where Williams made a choice that has benefited the nation of geeks for decades to come. For example, a rumor going around TSR in early 1997 was that the company would be sold to Random House. If *D&D* had passed into the hands of a large New York publishing house with little fluency in role-playing games, who knows what the brand would look like today? Because she chose to sell to Wizards, which was populated with *D&D* fanatics, the geek faithful would receive an amazing third edition of the game designed by a cabal of design geniuses—namely, Jonathan Tweet, Skip Williams, and Monte Cook, as well as the Open Gaming License (OGL). The OGL allows anyone to make adventures, settings, and rules for *D&D* without having to pay for the rights. Imagine Disney saying anyone can make *Star Wars* movies, novels, comics, and the like *without* paying Disney any money, and that's what the OGL is to role-playing. Even you, dear reader, could finish reading this book, then create a TSR setting for *D&D*, publish it, and profit from it without paying Wizards a dime. (And I'd love to see the character sheets for Gary Gygax and Lorraine Williams!)

While her decisions as CEO were the reason TSR was in the dire place it was, she must also receive the credit for selling it to an organization that knew how to take the *D&D* brand to new heights, despite personal animus on her part.

The next day, Abramowitz flew back to Seattle, and Adkison and his team took control of the deal. Now he had to negotiate a new letter of intent with Williams. "And as is often the case," he recalled, "letters of intent can take on a life of their own." Both he and she had things they wanted, and the letter began to look more like a draft of a deal to buy the company.

Williams insisted that Adkison take care of her employees. She wanted as many of them as possible hired by Wizards, and those that couldn't make the transition be given a good severance. Lisa Stevens, who was helping Adkison during the sale, described Williams as having a maternal attitude toward her employees. "I always liked that about her," she said.

In negotiations, Adkison described Williams as focused on "decorum and process, which I tried my best to respect." He said there were tense discussions, but he doesn't remember them being "particularly pleasant or particularly unpleasant."

One day during the negotiations, Adkison entered the office, and a receptionist greeted him with a pall upon her face. She said, "Ms. Williams needs to talk to you right away."

He thought, *Uh-oh, something's up.*

He was ushered into Williams's office and sat down. There, she gazed at him with an expression full of seriousness and cut right to the chase. "Peter," she said. "I hope this doesn't kill the deal. But I cannot include Buck Rogers in the sale."

Buck Rogers? Buck Rogers? Adkison had no interest in Buck Rogers. Almost nobody did. The company had been putting out Buck material for years, and it always sold abysmally. If Williams's family hadn't owned the IP, it is difficult to imagine TSR would have ever sought out such a moldy, age-worn property. Telling him he didn't have to buy Buck Rogers was like telling him he wouldn't have to eat a worm. But he didn't let that show. He kept his business negotiation face on. ("I feel like that was one of my best poker face moments," he said later.)

He replied to her, "Well, of course that's going to affect the price."

She nodded.

"And I think we got half a million bucks knocked off the price because Buck Rogers wasn't part of it," he said.

Working closely with Adkison may have changed Williams's opinion of the man. At one point, she hosted a dinner party at her home where Adkison was the guest of honor.

The due diligence period was a somewhat awkward time for Adkison. He was in the offices for several days at a time, and people knew he was there and knew who he was. But he couldn't tell the staff that he was working on buying the company and becoming their new boss. And even though these people were his nerd heroes, it wouldn't have been appropriate to go hang out with the staff after work.

Instead, Peter Adkison spent several evenings with Gary Gygax. The pair sat on his porch playing classic war games like *Overlord* and *Battle of the Bulge*. They didn't talk TSR. He didn't ask Gygax what he thought should be done with a possible third edition. Instead, they just hung out and played games. "It was a delight," he said of those nights.

On Thursday, April 10, 1997, Wizards of the Coast and TSR signed a letter of intent. That day, *Wired* ran an article titled "Disaffected Fans Cheer D&D Buyout." In it, one employee admitted to feeling "relief" upon hearing of the deal and predicted, "They'll probably take TSR properties and use them more effectively."

Now, Adkison could begin to really know the company he was buying. His favorite memories of that time were meeting the staff. These were the women and men who had discovered unknown worlds of delight, from the sands of Athas to the mists of Ravenloft. He was not just a CEO acquiring a new company. He was also a *D&D* fan gaining control over the game.

One Saturday, he went down to the Sheridan Springs Road offices. He didn't have any particular work to do. Instead, he wanted to see who else might have been at the office. It was a way for him to measure the company. Did some people come in to do work on the weekends?

He wandered the twisting corridors of the building. Above the warehouse, beside mail order, through a pair of white-framed doors with glass panels, he discovered two men working. They hunched over drawing tables, the skylight illuminating their work. Pens in hand, the pair labored over maps, but these were not maps of interstate highways or local municipalities. No, these were spartan, stark, and mesmerizing maps of places that existed only in the imagination until the pair drew them into existence.

He asked them, "Who are you guys?"

They said, "We're Rob and Dennis."

"What do you do here?"

"We're cartographers. We make maps." They were there on Saturday because another cartographer had gone AWOL, and now they were stuck catching up on the other guy's work.

Adkison replied, "Cartographers? I love maps, man. I'm Peter." He sat down, and the pair began to show him their work. It was stunning. He remarked that he wished he could make such beautiful maps.

The pair replied, "You can! We'll teach you how to do it!"

"What? Seriously?"

"Yeah! Sit down!"

Adkison spent that entire Saturday learning cartography from Rob Lazzaretti and Dennis Kauth, a pair of master mapmakers. While they worked, they gave him assignments. They showed him different ways to draw mountains, told him to try out different pens, but then to be certain he took notes on what different pens he used and the lines they drew.

"The funniest part," he said, "was that they had no idea who I was. I was just some guy that wandered into their room on a Saturday."

Later, when Lazzaretti realized his new boss was so nerdy he'd spend an entire Saturday learning cartography, he said, "Previously, most of the people who managed our department at TSR did not have a clue about working with creatives, or even the RPG industry. It was such a great feeling of overwhelming relief to realize things were going to get better."

Adkison said that after all the negotiation, and minusing Buck Rogers, the final price of TSR "was over $30 million, including the debt. The shareholders didn't get much." Again, according to the Five Rings Publishing due diligence documents, the company was in about $30 million of debt. He also said that Wizards had very little success negotiating down any of those debts.

With that selling price, did Lorraine Williams make any money in the sale? In October of 1985, she bought all of the Blume family's stock and exercised an option to buy fifty more shares for $300, allowing her to take control of TSR for $591,800. By the end of the year, Gary Gygax also sold her all his stock. Even with such a modest investment of her own capital in the company, it appears she lost money on the purchase. Her salary, and the payments made to use Buck Rogers, could have pushed her time there into the black, but all the evidence indicates that running the company was no great windfall for her.

The purchase of TSR didn't even stretch Wizards' bank account. Adkison said, "We had a lot of cash, so we did not have to take on financing to pay for these costs. We paid for everything out of cash flow."

On Monday, June 2, 1997, the final documents were signed. Wizards' lawyer actually handled the paperwork with Williams, leaving Lisa Stevens and Peter Adkison free to gleefully wander the halls of the company they were about to own. She said, "We were in awe. This place was our mecca." She was so excited she kept hitting Adkison in the arm, as if to be certain this wasn't all a dream.

That joy juxtaposed with what Stevens remembered of the TSR staff that day. Downcast eyes. Dejection. Fear of the future. It reminded her of the fall of a besieged city. When the victorious army marched through the ruined streets and their defeated enemies, now their new subjects, bowed before their conquerors, this is what their faces must have looked like. She said, "It was a weird dichotomy of the victor and the vanquished." That said, what Wizards had in mind for the TSR staff was not humiliation but restoration. She said, "We turned that attitude around pretty quick."

By the occult power of legally binding contracts, pieces of TSR moved invisibly from one owner to another. The stocks of the current shareholders were transferred to Wizards of the Coast. If reality were arranged to reflect the importance of events in the high spheres of nerd culture, strange lights would have been seen in the sky. Hikers might have glimpsed a long-necked monstrosity cutting through the waves on Geneva Lake. That afternoon, perhaps it would have rained frogs. Night shrieks, or maybe hosts of angelic choirs, would have disturbed the sleep of the locals, announcing that tomorrow things would not be like they were yesterday. Possession of those stocks gave Wizards control of TSR. The company that began the role-playing game industry was now owned by the company that began the collectible card game industry. The next decades of *D&D*'s history turned on this one deal.

HEALING THE WOUNDS

If others had not been foolish, we should be so.

—WILLIAM BLAKE, *PROVERBS OF HELL*

ON TUESDAY MORNING, June 3, 1997, Lorraine Williams met Peter Adkison in the driveway of the old Q-tip factory on Sheridan Springs Road to give him the keys to TSR.

For Williams, it was the end to her twelve years at the company. The last CEO of TSR left Lake Geneva that day, never to return to the city bearing that title ever again. For her, it was an ending, and perhaps it felt like a defeat. Or was it a relief?

Peter Adkison held the keys to the company in his hands, but did not enter the building. The refurbished Q-tip factory shone in the morning, corporate and bright. It was all too much. The keys. The building. TSR. *D&D.* In his hands.

He returned to his car, sat down, and began to cry. He said, "It was a moment of surreality. A moment of ecstasy. A moment of fear." Waves of emotion rolled over him. Adkison, who spent summers growing up on the farm with horses and cattle, who went to Walla Walla College, had just bought a company. It sounded so elitist. He didn't envision himself as the kind of man who bought businesses. He was Peter. And he was only thirty-five years old. The people inside the building were the brilliant minds who had created, run, and grown *D&D* for decades. They were his idols. Now, he was in charge of them. He was intimidated, unsure.

But at the same time, he was excited. He held *D&D* in his hands like he held the keys to the building. It was unbelievably cool. *Man,* he thought, *I'd better not fuck this up.*

Lisa Stevens was also there that morning. She said her emotions were much less complicated. She described walking into TSR on June 3, 1997, as "triumphant. It was like buying your childhood."

Adkison collected his nerves in the car and went inside. There the receptionist stood as he entered, a ball of nerves herself meeting the new boss. She asked him, "What do you want to do first?"

He replied, "Let's have an all-hands meeting."

She responded, "What's that?"

He said, "You know, a meeting with all the employees."

She said, "We've never had one of those before."

Adkison was stunned. All-hands meetings were held monthly at Wizards. He said, "To me, it was an integral part of creating a unified spirit and mission."

The receptionist asked him, "Where shall we have it?"

He replied, "You know the building better than I do. Pick a place."

The remnants of the TSR staff gathered before him, the people who had not been driven away from the company or fired in cost-cutting efforts. Steve Winter, Dale Donovan, Sue Weinlein, Monte Cook, Bruce Cordell, Skip Williams, and Bill Connors were all there.

Peter Adkison felt nervous standing before the assembled staff. He said, "And I have no idea what I said, really, other than welcome and some encouraging words."

The staff had a plethora of reactions to and recollections of the meeting. Some were worried. Some thought his comments were nebulous but that a purchase by Wizards was a positive path forward. Some remembered him sticking up for Lorraine Williams, saying he didn't want to hear anyone bad-mouthing her. Sue Weinlein remembered worrying about the company moving to Seattle, because she and Monte Cook had bought a house in Lake Geneva.

But the one thing everyone I interviewed about this meeting recalled with clarity was the song that Adkison made them sing.

Since fear and uncertainty pervaded the room and he himself was nervous, Adkison decided to have the staff sing the Wizards of the Coast company song. He hoped it would loosen up everyone. The song is a jolly number about a father's advice to his son for the care and feeding of a severed human head.

Now the staff raised their voices in song, warbling out the tune about the severed human head. By the end of the song, Adkison's face was red, and the room giggled. The message of the moment, according to Lisa Stevens, was, "We may be executives from Wizards of the Coast, but we're gamers and we're geeks and we're a little bit goofy at times."

For his new employees, the song landed differently. Peter Adkison was sure enthusiastic about it, and he was the new boss, so everybody piped it out as best they could. Who would want to send the message that they weren't a team player in the first meeting with the new boss who could be looking to let people go? But it was about a human head and tied into ancient Wizards lore. It was a strange start, one that Weinlein would see as a prophecy for much to come in the future of TSR alumni at Wizards of the Coast. She said, "It was the first sign that this might be a challenging integration."

Lisa Stevens spent the summer of 1997 in Lake Geneva, but when she'd left Seattle, she'd only packed for a weekend. Short on clothes, and an hour from a proper mall, she ended up raiding TSR for attire. Gen Con and old Planescape T-shirts became her uniform for the summer.

And in a turn worthy of a novel, she ended up working out of Jim Ward's old office. Stevens and Ward had a bit of history.

In 1988, Stevens's first company, Lion Rampant, had a booth at Gen Con. The company's first RPG, *Ars Magica*, had just won an award. Ward stopped by the booth to say that if Lion Rampant ever became a threat, TSR would utterly annihilate it. I want to note that Jim Ward does not recall this, but every person I spoke to from Lion Rampant does. Nine years later, Lisa Stevens was sitting in his office on Sheridan Springs Road, using Ward's very desk. It was still full of his things! She said, "It was like he'd walked up and left one day."

It was as though the threat Ward had issued that day in 1988 was a curse that had rebounded on himself. He was gone, and Stevens was literally in his place. It was the most unlikely of turnabouts. She said, "It felt like things had come full circle."

THE RELEASE OF THE PRISONERS AND THE RETURN OF THE EXILES

When Zeb Cook found out about the purchase of TSR by Wizards of the Coast in 1997, he wasn't surprised. "I knew they were having trouble," he said. In his mind, the purchase provoked the question of "What is Wizards going to do" with the company? He worried that Wizards would chop it up into pieces and sell it off to the highest bidder. But his biggest greatest fear was, "What would happen to all my friends?"

He need not have worried. One of the most immediately palpable differences between management under Lorraine Williams and under Peter Adkison was their approach to staff. Under the former, brand came first, and staff was replaceable, no matter the creativity or brilliance of those involved.

As a fan who held *D&D* in his hands, creators to Adkison were not replaceable cogs in some corporate creativity contraption. Rather, these were the holy orders, the massed brothers and sisters who had imagined strange new worlds, then heaved them out of the black depths and into the light. Staff retention was one of the reasons he had advocated for buying TSR now instead of waiting for it to go into bankruptcy. Likely the company would have been cheaper then, but the staff would have scattered.

That said, while the bulk of the company would make the transition to Wizards, not everyone would. Now, Adkison had decisions to make. He met all the company's employees and even received counsel from Williams. Since Wizards wanted to make *D&D*, it made sense to retain everyone involved in the game's creation. Therefore, the closer an employee was to producing a product, the likelier they would be offered a position. The vast majority of the company's artists, writers, editors, and game designers would find a new home in Renton, the Seattle suburb where Wizards' offices were located. Some would even continue to live in Wisconsin while working for Wizards.

Then, there was the thing nearly no one wanted to go on the record about, but would hint at or talk around. That was the fact that some, perhaps only one person, but certainly no more than two people, did not make the transition to Wizards due to credible claims of sexual harassment. Lisa Stevens said that TSR was run like an aristocracy, with the nobles in their offices lording over serfs toiling away in their cubicles. She heard rumors about how one or two of those elites took advantage of their position. Wizards HR had to deal with the situation. She said, "We wanted to send a strong signal that whatever happened under the old rules was not going to be accepted in Seattle." Stevens said that "this was the dark side" of the company's purchase by Wizards.

What of those who had been exiled during the old regime? Bob Salvatore, John Rateliff, David Wise, the list went on and on. Adkison began calling former workers and, according to him, "talking to them, and treating them with respect." His message was, "We'd love for you to come back and work with us." He also emphasized the importance of listening to these former TSR staff. It helped him make things right where he could. For example, John Rateliff got his old job back as a games editor and went on to edit the third edition of *D&D*.

What about David Wise? He had moved on. After making list after list of people to be fired by Williams and then getting fired himself, he thought his career in gaming was over. Yes, he was starting a new company with Jim Ward, but who knew if that would pay the bills? He looked for work outside the industry.

Then Peter Adkison called him and asked him to lunch at the Next Door Pub. When he sat down with Adkison, the first thing Wise said was, "I'm not here to ask for a job. I'm here because I love my staff." He believed Williams "had limited insight into the staff's day-to-day performance and suspected her opinions could be misleading to Adkison."

Wise wanted to set the record straight. He knew the staff's strengths and weaknesses, and the conversation would help Adkison make better hiring decisions.

Unbeknownst to Wise, a number of people had already told Adkison he needed to hire Wise back with all possible speed. After Wise said he wasn't here to ask for a job, Adkison asked, "Does that mean you won't accept a job if I offer it to you?"

Wise said, "That threw me for a minute." He'd already given up on gaming.

He needed to digest this and asked Adkison to tell him about himself. A two-hour conversation ensued during which Adkison unfurled the entire history of Wizards, *Magic,* and his personal ethos of leadership. When finished, Adkison invited Wise to come back and visit his friends at TSR. Wise said of the moment, "I immediately accepted, noting the incredible change in protocol." Under Williams, such a trip would have required an appointment, a check-in at reception, and a guide to accompany him at all times.

While hanging out in the halls of the old Q-tip factory, Adkison's assistant found Wise and asked him to come to a conference room. There he assumed he would be offered his old job again. Instead, he found himself attending a department managers meeting headed by Adkison, at the end of which the new boss added simply, "Welcome back, David. We're glad you're with us again."

Leaving the meeting, another one of those things happened that, if written in a movie or novel, you'd think, *That's an impossible coincidence. Life doesn't work like that.* Because when Wise left that meeting, who should he see across the way, standing at the doorway of Brian Thomsen's office, but Lorraine Williams. Who knows why she was there or what she was doing, but there she was.

Williams saw Wise. She waved.

Wise responded by laughing. It wasn't a cruel laugh, and it wasn't a rude laugh. Rather, the laugh was one of euphoria. He said, "The weight and pain of having been unceremoniously thrown out of the company by her had suddenly and unexpectedly lifted from my shoulders. I was staying. *She* was going."

Wise did feel guilty about leaving the company he was starting with Jim Ward. He said Ward "had always been like a brother and a father to me." But when told of the situation, Ward insisted he go. "Is he a hero or what?" Wise said of the moment.

Wise went on to work for Wizards in Washington, where he attended business school. The company paid for his tuition and even reduced his workload, but not his salary, while in school. He said, "The contrast in working environments couldn't have been more stark."

One day in 1997, Jim Lowder's phone rang.

It was Peter Adkison. He'd called to ask him why he was no longer working for TSR. He unfolded his tale about the machinations surrounding *The Screaming Tower* and how the company would neither relinquish the rights to the book nor pay him for it. He also mentioned the royalty payments he and other freelancers had failed to receive from the company.

Lowder recalled, "Peter listened to my concerns and solved the legal problems then and there in ways that made it very clear to me he valued what I had done for TSR."

First, all rights to *The Screaming Tower* were returned to Lowder, and it fell to Brian Thomsen to announce it. (What a moment that must have been!) Second, all late royalties would be paid. Third, Wizards of the Coast reimbursed Lowder for his legal fees. Fourth, Adkison invited him to return to write for Wizards. There, he would produce stories, essays, and a novel, *Spectre of the Black Rose.* Lowder said, "That was all Peter Adkison." He is adamant that the tale of Adkison redeeming creatives injured by TSR is not told nearly enough.

Today, Jim Lowder is the executive editor for Chaosium, publishers of *Call of Cthulhu* and *RuneQuest.* He said that in that position, he tries to show authors the same respect that Adkison showed him.

Forgotten Realms cocreator Ed Greenwood first knew something was wrong at TSR when his freelance checks stopped showing up. Soon, the TSR magazine he subscribed to failed to appear as well. When Greenwood heard how dire things were in Lake Geneva, he offered to write products for free to get the company back on its feet, but as those products could not be printed, the offer went nowhere.

Of course, Adkison wanted him back.

A librarian by trade, Greenwood was working at the North York Central Library the day that Adkison called him. It was a Sunday, the only day of the week he worked at that particular branch. "He had to chase me down," Greenwood said of the call. He wanted to know if Greenwood would come back and work on *D&D.*

He told Adkison, "I was eager to go on doing Realms releases until I fell into my grave, hopefully decades in the future." Greenwood said the conversation was "great," but he kept it short because he was on the clock.

But there were alumni with far more acrimonious partings. Could Adkison get them back? What about Bob Salvatore?

Adkison called Salvatore to tell him he wanted to pay him the royalties he was owed, but he couldn't because Salvatore was still suing TSR, which was now Wizards. Salvatore stopped the suit, and Adkison then asked him to come back and write novels again.

Salvatore was hesitant. He had already signed an exclusive contract with Del Rey. He'd need their permission to do any work for Wizards. And if he returned to writing in the Forgotten Realms, they'd ask him to write Drizzt, and he'd already said the character was dead to him. Even if he wrote something else, he'd have to work with Brian Thomsen, and there was enough bad blood between them to drown in.

Then, events transpired.

Brian Thomsen, whom Adkison described as "poisonous," was fired. Mary Kirchoff returned to the Book Department. And Mark Anthony's Drizzt novel was canceled, even though it was completed and so near publication that advertisements for it had already appeared in *Dragon*.

After all of that, Salvatore agreed to return. In my interviews with him, he did want to be clear he did not demand Adkison do any of those things. For example, regarding the cancellation of the Anthony book, he said, "I didn't really give a damn about that book getting burned. But I never asked for it to be burned." Nor did he ask for Thomsen to be fired. But once those events transpired, he was willing to come back. He asked Del Rey for permission due to his exclusive contract with them, it was granted, and he was back writing Drizzt again.

But perhaps the ultimate exiles were Dave Arneson and Gary Gygax. Could Adkison win them over as well?

There was a complicated legal labyrinth surrounding the IP of *D&D,* its two creators, and even an ex-wife that had accrued over decades. Adkison was determined to solve it. He said, "We wanted to get a clean title on everything and take care of those guys. We wanted to heal wounds and put us in a position to go forward without controversy." He already knew Dave Arneson, so he called him and said that he wanted to clean up the *D&D* IP. To do this, he was willing to write Arneson a check, in exchange for which he would give up all claims on the intellectual property. He said Arneson was "excited to do the deal." He then moved on to Gary Gygax. There, he had to write checks to both Gary and his ex-wife, Mary, in exchange for which all rights to the property were waived. He said, "They were all low-six-figure checks." Given all the time, energy, and money that had been spent in litigation between TSR, Gygax, and Arneson, it is surprising to think how easily Adkison resolved all these issues with respect and a willingness to pay the parents of *D&D* what they were due.

But maybe the most dramatic example of Adkison making things right concerned the art that TSR had acquired over its decades of existence. Reflecting on it decades later, Ryan Dancey said the company was home to some of "the most talented artists of their generation." Later, a friend in art told him that based on the historical and cultural value of the company's art, many of the color cover originals could have brought a million dollars apiece at auction. The art TSR had in its possession at the time of sale may have been worth more than the rest of the company combined, Dancey speculated.

Despite the value of the art, Dancey said that during the negotiation of the purchase, "I don't think anybody from TSR or Wizards of the Coast ever sat down and thought of that as an asset. What is this art worth? One day you will go to the Met and there will be a Larry Elmore exhibit, and that art was essentially valued at zero in the sale of TSR."

And after years of the company's changing policies about freelancing and whether or not the company could retain the originals of an artist's work, Adkison was about to make it all right in a moment.

A small group of artists and other staff gathered around Adkison. He led them to a room on the second floor of the old Q-tip factory that held the company's art. He opened the locked door, turned on the lights, and then turned back to the crowd behind him, eyes agog as if to convey how impressed he was at what he had just seen. Inside was a treasury of art. He told the assembled artists that they were welcome to take whatever they had done, because it was theirs. No questions, no negotiations, no back-and-forth. Simply take what you made.

I heard about Adkison giving work back to artists dozens and dozens of times during interviews for this book, but when I asked the man himself about it, he simply said, "I just approved giving back the art. Wizards policy was always that artists keep the originals." Why did the company give originals back? "What were we going to do with it?" he asked in reply.

Is the above story myth? Is he just being humble?

He was the new boss in Lake Geneva. He held people's careers in his hands. It makes sense that others would remember his actions more sharply than he did. It is also possible that these tales have grown in the telling, creating a Peter Adkison who is more folk hero than man. However, there is another tale that may explain this discrepancy. Apparently at gaming conventions, if encountering gamers who did not know that he was CEO of Wizards of the Coast, he would introduce himself to fans as the company's janitor. The story goes that this was his way of getting to hear honest fan reactions. I can't help but notice that claiming to be the janitor also shifts the spotlight off him, and I can't help but remember that upon finally getting the keys to TSR, one of his reactions was to think that the purchase was elitist and not him. And in the hours of interviews and countless dozens of emails I've traded with him, he comes off as humble, modest, and self-effacing. It brings to mind the words of Saint Matthew the Evangelist, who wrote, "Be careful not to perform your righteous acts before men to be seen by them."

In sum, one of Adkison's first goals as new management was to reverse the long-standing company attitude toward creatives. Writers, artists, and game designers were each unique and brought something irreplaceably special to the company and the brand. They were to be wooed and cherished.

Next, the new management would reverse another long-standing company policy: the fish-bait strategy.

EXAMINING THE CORPSE

In 1997, everyone knew what had happened to TSR, but perhaps no one really knew why. It fell to Ryan Dancey and Lisa Stevens to perform the autopsy on the company. They discovered that the fish-bait strategy was not just a debacle but arguably the foundational mistake undergirding the entire collapse of the company.

Dancey and Stevens have gone on to prove that they are some of the best businesspeople in the geek field, true giants of the twenty-first century. Dancey, in addition to midwifing the sale of Five Rings and TSR, was a fierce advocate of the Open Gaming License. He convinced Wizards to adopt it and convinced other companies to produce material under it. Lisa Stevens, as CEO and founder of Paizo Publishing, as previously mentioned, is today the most powerful woman in role-playing games.

But we are not here to discuss this pair in their roles as creators or innovators but rather as financial coroners. Dancey set Stevens to the task of discovering why TSR died. She said he supplied her with "a shit ton of data and spreadsheets from the financial files of TSR. It was a mountain of numbers. Thank God I was getting my MBA at the time." Given that amount of access, it is worth pointing out that Lisa Stevens may be the person most familiar with the finances of the company who is currently willing to talk about it.

She found that the company's sales numbers told the story we already know. Nearly every setting sold worse than the one before it, supplements always sold worse than initial releases, and revised settings always sold worse than originals.

Then Dancey and Stevens went a step further and analyzed the profitability of those products. How many copies would a release have to sell to make money?

What they learned was shocking.

After adding up the costs of design, art, editing, printing, and shipping, then comparing that to the sale price of the product . . . Well . . . It's so hard to write the words, I'll let Dancey say them; the capitalization is his.

> An enormous number of TSR setting products would NEVER BE PROFITABLE. The price the company sold them for meant they'd never recoup the sunk costs. Then we realized that there were entire campaign settings that had never been profitable.

What about Planescape, the greatest setting ever produced at the company?

"Essentially," he said, "none of it ever made a profit."

Danovich and Fallone, of course, knew this. They spoke of unprofitable products, maybe even a lot of them. But the scale of the unprofitability outlined here was much larger. Entire lines? Planescape made the company no money? It was flabbergasting.

Stevens then asked the follow-up question: "Why is that happening?" She found that "I could correlate the drop in profitability per product with the proliferation of campaign settings." She said that the company "wasn't making *D&D* customers, they were making campaign setting customers, and that was killing them." People were identifying as fans of the settings, not fans of the game. A Dark Sun fan would not purchase a Planescape product. Al-Qadim fans would not purchase adventures for Birthright.

Stevens had already seen this phenomenon in the wild. She was a passionate devotee of Gary Gygax's first *D&D* setting, Greyhawk. She said, "If there was a cool Forgotten Realms product, Greyhawk fans would say, 'I can't use that. Unclean!' And Forgotten Realms fans would do the same thing for Greyhawk."

The end result of this was cannibalism.

Each new setting release went into competition with TSR products that already existed. A Forgotten Realms fan might fall head over heels for Ravenloft and cease buying Forgotten Realms releases. Literally, the company was stealing customers from itself, forcing it to make two products to keep the same number of customers. And because sales were down, the company's solution was to make another new setting, which only exacerbated all the existing problems. Stevens said, "I don't think TSR ever grokked that this was the death spiral they were going into." Which is somewhat ironic, actually. TSR creatives were broken up into teams by setting. There was the Dragonlance team headed by Harold Johnson, the Planescape team headed by Steve Winter, and so on. If employees were compartmentalized by setting, why wouldn't fans be organized in like fashion?

Arguing against this finding were TSR alumni now employed at Wizards. They said that fans of the settings were loyal completists and that the very logo over the title generated sales. Dancey was uncertain. Despite Stevens having incredible access to that mountain of data, the idea that settings helped kill TSR was just a hypothesis.

So an experiment would be run.

There were two upcoming adventures slated for release on the schedule. Wizards would release one with the Forgotten Realms logo, and the other would be released under the *AD&D* second edition banner. Which would sell better, the generic title or the one explicitly set in the Realms?

The adventure for *AD&D* second edition sold three times as many copies.

The lesson was now plain as the glasses on Gary Gygax's face. The multitudinous settings, no matter how ineffable and luminescent and masterly, were a direct cause of the company's downfall.

At that time, when evaluating how many of TSR's more than one dozen settings it would continue to create products for, Wizards of the Coast decided to support a mere two—*two!*—of the already existing *D&D* game worlds.

Wizards tossed the fish-bait strategy into a dumpster and never looked back.

IN DEATH A NEW BIRTH

The purchase of TSR represented a number of seismic shifts. First, the mecca of role-playing moved from the Midwest to the West Coast, a move that I found humiliating in the 1990s, but that now doesn't really bother me at all, possibly because the purchase also represented a generational change. For the first time, *D&D* was controlled by fans, people who had grown up playing the game. Love for it lived in their hearts. In an additional blessing, the *D&D* fans at Wizards also had business degrees. With great dispatch, the company went about fixing the mistakes that had driven TSR into a ditch.

Prior management valued brand over people? Wizards went out of its way to retain and bring back vital personnel.

Prior management didn't listen to their customers? Wizards did market research and based production decisions on what they learned.

The fish-bait strategy was cannibalizing the company's own customers? Wizards shuttered over a dozen settings.

Unprofitable releases and decreasing sales forced the company to overship to Random House to generate loans? Wizards of the Coast was making so much money off *Magic: The Gathering* that it could afford to let *D&D* lose money for a while as the company figured out where to go with the game.

The result of all these fixes would be a renaissance. In the Renton, Washington, offices of Wizards, *Dungeons & Dragons* would undergo a true rebirth with a third edition and the Open Gaming License. The work the company did in revitalizing the brand speaks for itself. In the spring of 2021, Wizards announced that after seven consecutive years of growth, *D&D* had its best year ever, and said that over fifty million people have played the game. A *D&D* movie and TV show are in production. Let's hope at least one of them is good.

With the vantage point of decades, there are significant legacies of the Williams era at TSR. One was the production of those rich and varied settings that fueled the company's demise. They can be purchased in PDF form online and are still dazzling. We gamers who lived through that time will get misty-eyed with yearning when we remember all of those outlandishly amazing boxed sets that revealed to us new worlds.

Another legacy is that TSR attempted to use transmedia strategies to sell its intellectual property. A transmedia narrative is a story told across multiple media platforms. For example, within years of its creation, the story and setting of Dragonlance were used in role-playing games, novels, comic books, and video games. The expansion of the company's fiction lines produced many bestsellers, and the company's efforts in that field outlasted it. The fans that Bob Salvatore established with his fiction at TSR have followed him through an impressive career as a fantasy author. In the twenty-first century, gaming companies have continued to publish tie-in fiction for their games, though with less regularity.

TSR was a forerunner of companies that employed similar strategies to greater success. Jim Fallone said the company was "the foundation of what today's pop culture is built on. It was trying to operate more like a studio than an actual publisher. The way Disney manages the Marvel Cinematic Universe can be directly traced to the influence of [TSR's] sourcebooks and internal world bibles. Each and every character created is a part of this giant universe."

There is another possible legacy of the Williams era—namely, that the collapse of the company in 1997 is the single most high-profile failure of any role-playing game company in the history of the industry. It seems every gamer geek who decided to start an RPG company since that disaster has looked at TSR to learn what not to do. For example, despite the genius and wonder of those setting boxed sets, most game companies since then have studied the commandments laid down like scripture by Lisa Stevens and Ryan Dancey: *Thou shalt not create an excess of game worlds.* In the seven years that have passed between the release of the newest edition of *D&D* and the writing of this book, Wizards of the Coast has released six setting books for the game. In the six years between 1989 and 1995, TSR released literally dozens of setting products. One could argue that Wizards is leaving money on the table. Fans of Dark Sun and Planescape will beg, plead, and cajole all over the internet in the hopes that the company will finally release new material for those settings.

Yet they do not.

Finally, fans and alumni look back on the Williams era as a time of marvels and miracles. It might not have been *D&D*'s golden age, but it certainly was its silver age. Nearly everyone I interviewed who worked at the company would at some point wax on about the wonders of the TSR community. Bob Salvatore said that the people he worked with at the company were "kick-ass." Brom agreed, saying that he got to work with true creatives there. People praised the company for launching their careers. People found best friends, life-mates, and family. And those lucky enough to work at the company got to do something no one anywhere else on the planet got to do: create *Dungeons & Dragons* for a living. TSR was, without a doubt, a dream factory.

Then the factory moved.

Jim Ward still dreams of TSR more than two decades after he walked out the door of the office on Sheridan Springs Road. He said, "Those dreams always put me in a bad mood as the nightmare spins out something I would hate." He dreams of management trying to raise money. He dreams of "clearing out design and editing cubicles to have garage sales." He dreams of selling "old furniture and computers" in a desperate attempt to raise a much-needed influx of cash. And he dreams it was his fault because "my editors and designers couldn't get their work done on time." Twenty-five years later, Ward's subconscious is still busily concerned with trying to make money for the company. He said, "I did love working there, but years and years later, it is time to get over it."

Dale Donovan recalled, "In rural Wisconsin, TSR was a world unto itself. Everyone had so much in common; we worked together, we socialized together, and more. Seeing that world crumble was difficult, and many of us still carry emotions from that time. How could things have been different, and how could that wonderful world have been saved? Why aren't we all still working at TSR today?"

Given that Lisa Stevens has gone on to found what may be the second-most successful RPG company of all time, and given the incredible access she had to TSR's financial records, I asked her what was the number one lesson she learned from it.

She replied, "Don't do stupid shit."

First Wizard
Last Dragon

ACKNOWLEDGMENTS

SO MANY HELPED so much to make this book what it is. I owe all of you more than I can say. But to give some specifics . . .

Thanks to Susan Velazquez of the JABberwocky Literary Agency and Peter Wolverton of St. Martin's Press for believing in this book.

To Jim Ward, who is a strong voice for TSR decades after he left the company.

Jim Fallone set the ball of this book rolling by telling me about "El Banco de Random House," and for that, I will be forever grateful.

Jon Peterson is the Thucydides of role-playing games history. I owe him a debt that cannot be repaid for the time and care he took in reading and suggesting changes to the first chapters of this volume.

Ernie Gygax was generous with his time, memory, and honesty in speaking with me, and I appreciate it very much.

Jim Lowder and Dale Donovan were less like sources and more like mentors during the years it took me to write this book. I have no doubt that without their patience and help, this volume would not exist.

Bruce Nesmith not only wrote some of the most important games of my youth but was generous enough with his time to spend hours talking to me about it decades later.

Bill Connors was my game hero growing up, and he vastly improved this book with his honesty and comedy decades later.

John Rateliff is as kind as he is brilliant. His generosity in taking time to speak with me and sharing with me his resources can never be repaid.

Thanks to Sue Weinlein for all her insights and sharing images from the 1990s with me. She also makes a mean cup of tea.

Thanks to Monte Cook, who provided what may be the climax of this book.

I can't thank Flint Dille enough for his honesty, time, and being the man that he is. Also, I can't thank him enough for putting me in touch with his sister.

Thanks to Gerald Brom and Jeff Easley for taking the time to speak with me. Brom was especially helpful with his fact-checking and use of images for this book! Jeff Easley also provided me with beautiful images.

To Ryan Dancey, without whom this book would not have been even half of what it is. Many thanks for his contributions.

To Lisa Stevens for her candor. She was my first and last interview for this book!

To Peter Adkison. He may be the busiest man in gaming, but he was always shockingly prompt in getting back to me when I had a question about what he ate in 1997.

To Bob Salvatore, for his candor, memory, and patience in answering my incessant questions.

To John Danovich, for finishing the job that Jim Fallone started, of giving me a complete painting of the problems at TSR.

Thanks to Michael Calleia, for helping a brother out.

Thanks to Shannon Appelcline, for his ambitious and clear-cutting work in RPG history.

Thanks to Margaret Weis, for patiently answering all my questions about events twenty to thirty years ago.

To Kevin Kulp, whose product histories on DriveThruRPG have been of immense help, and who is a genius game designer in his own right. Check out *TimeWatch*. It's *Loki* the RPG.

I want to thank Steve Winter, for giving so many details about wild times at TSR.

To David Wise, for his perspective on that terrible day in 1996 when so many were fired at TSR.

Thanks to Bill Slavicsek, with the hope that everything he told me about third edition ends up in a sequel.

To Rob Wieland and Teri Litorco, without whom this book would not exist.

Thanks to Bob Abramowitz, who filled in important gaps in the story of the purchase of TSR.

Thanks to Rags Morales, Brad Munson, Steven Grant, Elliot S! Maggin, and Scott Haring for giving me everything they could on TSR West.

To Chris Koehnke, for taking the time to talk.

To Rich Baker, Skaff Elias, and Jonathan Tweet for help in what will hopefully be a sequel to this volume.

To Skip Williams, for remembering the early days in Lake Geneva.

To Jon Pickens, who answered about a million of my questions on Facebook.

To Harold Johnson, who was hard to get ahold of, but very willing to talk.

To Tim Kask, for giving me the straight shit about the early days in Gary's basement.

To Lawrence Schick, for his attention to detail and thoughts about the early days of TSR.

Thanks to David M. Ewalt for hooking me up with his connections.

To Zeb Cook, for his clear recollections of all his times at TSR.

To Ed Greenwood, for taking the time to look at this book and answer pesky questions about selling IP to TSR.

To Jeff Grubb, for all his memories about Canadian cellophane and his brilliance as a storyteller.

Thanks to my beta readers, Michael O'Brian, Mike Mason, Shari Wied, Rick Meints, Shane Skinner, Callahan Klatt, Nidhi Kashyap, Rachel Rohr, Mike Moser, Ryan Smith, Aaron Andries, Michelle Andries, and Mike Mearls.

Thanks to Kate Novak for taking the time to talk.

To Jean Rabe, for her time in answering my pesky questions.

To Lorraine Williams, for keeping TSR going as long as she did.

Penultimately, to everyone whose help I may have forgotten here, my sincerest apologies and sincerest thanks.

Finally, to my sun and moon, my wife, Tara Monnink, and my son, Simon Tyler Riggs.

SELECTED BIBLIOGRAPHY

Appelcline, Shannon. *Designers & Dragons: The 70s.* Silver Spring, MD: Evil Hat Productions, 2014.

Dille, Flint. *The Gamesmaster.* Los Angeles: Rare Bird Books, 2020.

Ewalt, David M. *Of Dice and Men.* New York: Scribner, 2013.

Laycock, Joseph P. *Dangerous Games.* Oakland: University of California Press, 2015.

Newman, Kyle, Jon Peterson, Michael Witwer, and Sam Witwer. *Dungeons & Dragons Art & Arcana: A Visual History.* New York: Ten Speed Press, 2018.

Peterson, Jon. *The Elusive Shift.* Cambridge, MA: MIT Press, 2020.

———. *Playing at the World.* San Diego: Unreason Press, 2014.

Witwer, Michael. *Empire of Imagination.* New York: Bloomsbury USA, 2015.

INDEX

INDEX

INDEX

INDEX

INDEX

INDEX

Tara Monnink

BEN RIGGS is a writer, teacher, and podcaster. He traveled the world teaching in his twenties. During his journeys, he tutored a princess, saw both the Sahara and Mt. Fuji at dawn, and discovered his wife and fellow traveler, Tara. He has settled down in his hometown of Milwaukee, Wisconsin, where he teaches English and history, and he and Tara have a son, Simon. Ben's RPG podcast, *Plot Points*, has been running for a decade, and his work has appeared on NPR and Geek & Sundry. *Slaying the Dragon* is his first book.